BARCELONA ALBERTVILLE 1992

(ALLSPORT / VANDYSTADT)

**the official
publication
of the
U.S. Olympic
Committee**

A torch-lit slope touched off
the medals' presentation for
the men's downhill, *the first
of the five men's alpine
skiing events held.*
(ALLSPORT / COLE)

publisher Mikko Laitinen
Commemorative Publications
Salt Lake City, Utah

corporate manager Judd L. Parr

managing editor Lisa H. Albertson

USOC editor Frank Zang

USOC associate editors Gayle Plant
Jeff Cravens
Barbara Gresham

printing Banta ISG-Bushman Press, Inc.
Provo, Utah

binding Prizma Industries, Inc.
Denver

color separations Color Image, Inc.
Salt Lake City

typesetting Linda Vrieze
Salt Lake City

computer input Teresa Jones
Salt Lake City

linotronic output Ultra Type, Inc.
Salt Lake City

production thanks to ALDUS PageMaker
FreeHand
PhotoStyler

Adobe Systems Incorporated

USOC contributors John Halpin, Greg Harney,
Kathy Harper, Barry King,
Patricia Olkiewicz

publisher's thanks Sue Baldus, Michael J. Bray,
Steve Bushman, Len
Corbosiero, Francisco J.
Fernandez, Florence Griffith-
Joyner, Marian Haws,
Barry King, Paul Klug, Tarja
Laitinen, Bill McCormick,
Stephanie Mullen, Sharon
Parr, Allan Woods

photographers

Allsport / Los Angeles
Koji Aoki
Nathan Bilow
Shaun Botterill
Simon Bruty
David Cannon
Chris Cole
Tony Duffy
Lee Farrant
Mike Hewitt
David Leah
Bob Martin
Gray Mortimore
Gary Newkirk
Mike Powell
Steve Powell
Pascal Rondeau
Rick Stewart

Vandystadt Agence de Presse / Paris
Bernard Asset
Didier Givois
Yann Guichaoua
Jean-Pierre L'Enfant
Richard Martin
Gerard Vandystadt

DUOMO / New York
Mitchell Layton
David Madison
Rick Rickman
Paul Sutton
Steve Sutton

Dave Black / Colorado Springs

Long Photography / Los Angeles

profile writers Lee Benson / *Deseret News*
Christine Brennan /
The Washington Post
Sharon Robb /
Fort Lauderdale Sun-Sentinel
Mike Spence /
*Colorado Springs Gazette
Telegraph*

Published under license from
the U.S. Olympic Committee
by Commemorative Publications
P.O. Box 21038
Salt Lake City, Utah 84121

BACKGROUND / *A newcomer to the Olympic program, mogul skiing was an immediate crowd-pleaser as skiers bumped and grinded their way down the gnarly course.* (ALLSPORT / STEWART)

OPPOSITE / *Once believed to be a ritual for peasants to climb closer to God, human castles entice modern-day Catalonians for the communal fun of it. At Barcelona's Opening Ceremonies, up to five or six tiers high of men and women supported each other while a pint-size child scrambled to the top to become the crowning glory.* (ALLSPORT / BOTTERILL)

CONTENTS

(ALLSPORT / BRUTY)

Red, White And Blue Visit White House

Nearly 650 athletes from the 1992 U.S. Olympic Teams that competed in Albertville and Barcelona paid a red, white and blue visit to the White House as the guests of President George Bush and his wife Barbara.

"Whether you took home a gold, silver, bronze, or simply just gave it your best, in my book, in the book of your countrymen, you are all winners, indeed heroes," said Bush to the winter Olympians.

President and Mrs. Bush both received USA warmups during the ceremony from U.S. gold medalists Kristi Yamaguchi, Cathy Turner, Bonnie Blair and Donna Weinbrecht.

Bush called Yamaguchi, who graced the front of cereal boxes, "the real Special K." He then turned to Turner, who had retired from sport for a singing career before coming back to win a gold and silver medal, as a story that "even Ripley would disbelieve."

Fresh off their outstanding 108-medal performance in Barcelona, members of the summer Olympic Team didn't let the rainy weather dampen their spirits as they were entertained with a tour of the White House, an indoor cookout, music by the U.S. Marine Band and individual photos with President and Mrs. Bush.

Freestyle wrestler Chris Campbell, who made a comeback at the age of 37 to win a bronze medal, made a presentation to Bush, giving him the American flag that was carried at Opening Ceremonies.

"You really paved the way magnificently for a knockout punch in Atlanta," Bush said. "I just can't wait until 1996. A proverb says, 'On the day of victory, no one is tired.' And today we celebrate Olympians, like America, who are victorious, refreshed and free."

(PHOTOS: ALLSPORT / BILOW)

All Dressed Up

The U.S. athletes always take a special pride in their parade outfits worn at the Opening Ceremonies. In both Albertville and Barcelona, the American contingent proved to be a stylish group in its debuts for audiences around the world.

The USA parade outfits were the design of Henry Grethel, who put a twist on the traditional colors of red, white and blue by selecting neighboring vibrant hues to dress up Team USA.

"I consider it a privilege and a great responsibility to be chosen to design the clothing for the U.S. Olympic Team," Grethel said. "My goal is to create clothing of which the athletes and the country can be proud."

In Albertville, the men's outfit consisted of a cobalt blue wool overcoat, plaid pants and a hand-knit turtleneck sweater with a patchwork star motif. The women wore a berry wool overcoat, cobalt blue gabardine pants and a hand-knit texturized sweater with an abstract Olympic design. Both the men's and women's ensembles were topped off with fedoras and stadium scarves.

In Barcelona, the men wore royal blue blazers with white shirts and khaki pants along with colorful print tie of stars and stripes. The women wore magenta jackets with patterned skorts. Both the men and women wore white hats with blue bands.

The trick came in accommodating the various shapes and sizes of the Olympic Team members. Ranging from bobsledder Herschel Walker to figure skater Kristi Yamaguchi and weightlifter Mark Henry to gymnast Shannon Miller, Grethel designed the clothes to fit all sizes.

(ALLSPORT)

A changing world

BY KEYVAN ANTONIO HEYDARI

Perhaps nowhere was the changing world of the '90s reflected more poignantly than at the 1992 Olympic Games. Henceforth, the Games will also change dramatically. For the last time, the Games were held in the same calendar year. They will now be staggered. Next winter stop? Lillehammer, Norway, in 1994, and then Atlanta in the summer of 1996.

Albertville's futuristic Opening Ceremonies were a preview that the Olympic Games were to break with tradition. There were a record 64 countries in the procession of nations. Estonia, Latvia, Lithuania, Slovenia and Croatia marched, as did Yugoslavia, a right that would be restricted five months later in Barcelona. Severine du Peloux, an 11-year-old girl from the Savoie region, sang a stirring rendition of *La Marseillaise* and the Olympic year began.

The U.S. women held their own (and more) in Albertville, winning nine of the 11 medals and all five American golds. Renaissance woman and short-track speed skater Cathy Turner based her race strategy on raw speed, not form, and came out in winning style in the 500 meters, an event that resembled a track meet on ice. The songwriter-singer-computer programmer-water skier extraordinaire draped an American flag around her shoulders and added another title to her resume: Olympic gold medalist.

Bonnie Blair glided home with America's first gold medal in speed skating's 500 meters — and became the most highly decorated American at the Games when she captured her second gold in the 1,000 meters, while a hometown cheering section from Champaign, Ill., watched at the Olympic oval.

The grace and elegance of Kristi Yamaguchi won out over the power jumping of Japan's Midori Ito as Yamaguchi became the first U.S. woman to win a figure skating Olympic gold medal since Dorothy Hamill in 1976.

New Jersey skier Donna Weinbrecht's legs pumped like pistons as she was "Born to (mogul) Run." The result? Gold for the women's Boss of the bosses (French for moguls).

Elsewhere in the Alps, the USA's Kristin Krone — whose nickname is "Crash" — took a spill on the fearsome downhill course and experienced a chilling testimonial of the danger of La Face de Bellevarde. And the Italian Stallion Alberto Tomba was back to defend his double alpine golds. Never one to take himself too seriously, Tomba grabbed a gold, narrowly missed the other, then skied off the slopes, out on the town and into the disco, without missing a beat. Meanwhile, on the track at Les Saisies, the Norwegians had a heyday, winning all five gold medals in the nordic events, and giving the competition a taste of what to expect on their home turf in 1994.

While Albertville gave us the first draft of the new European map, the ink was still not dry by the start of the Summer Games. The athletes from ravaged Bosnia arrived in Barcelona hours before the Opening Ceremonies. Nobody boycotted and there was only one absentee on the guest list: Yugoslavia. The IOC adhered to a United Nations resolution and barred Yugoslavia from competing in team sports, but allowed its

BACKGROUND / *Against the midnight blue sky, the Olympic flame eclipses the silhouetted skyline of Barcelona.* (ALLSPORT / BOTTERILL)

athletes from Serbia and Montenegro to participate in individual events. Still, South Africa was back, and Germany was unified. The Unified Team, however, was a splintering collection of athletes together in one last hurrah for the Soviet sports machine.

In Estadi Olimpic on Montjuic, it was not just any Opening Ceremonies. It was theater — grand and spectacular. History, allegory, pageantry and an unprecedented, if risky, lighting of the Olympic flame. Archer Antonio Rebollo's one shot lit the basin high above the stadium in a parabola of Olympic fire.

Barcelona, for years turned inward to the mountains, was reconfigured by the Olympic architects to open to the sea and welcome its visitors from around the world. Its *Jocs Olimpicos*, which showcased Catalonia's fiercely proud identity, will be remembered for some great individual performances and one titanic Team of Dreams.

While the changing Olympic world witnessed the doors of professionalism opening wider, it also experienced the closing of another door. The Russian gymnasts bemoaned the breakup of their sports machine and their farewell as a team. The changing world opened doors for Vitaly Scherbo, who won more golds than any other athlete in Barcelona. Now he will take his six golds and move from Minsk "to where I get the most money. We all will."

During the Barcelona Games, Lillehammer, the host of the '94 Olympic Winter Games, started an effort to give refuge to citizens of Sarajevo, an Olympic sister city of 1984. So, while Olympic tradition breaks after this year, Olympic brotherhood fostered, from aid to the war-torn to gifts of uniforms to athletes from proud, but penniless, new nations.

Swimmer Nelson Diebel, a self-described former "rebel without a clue," won the first gold for the Red, White and Blue. Pablo Morales had hung up his trunks, enrolled in law school but, at 27, gave it one last shot in the 200 butterfly and made his case in the pool.

On the basketball court, it was *no lo contendere* as opponents awarded custody of the gold to the "Dream Team," whose 12 members were "Supreme on the Court."

On the track, old man Linford Christie (32 years old) earned the Olympic title of "World's Fastest Human." Fellow Brit Derek Redmond's father showed what parental support means, charging out of the stands to come to the aid of his injured son on the track.

American Gail Devers, a hurdler stricken with Graves' Disease, a thyroid condition which almost caused her foot to be amputated in 1991, was the winner in the 100 meters. "I always considered myself a sprinter first," she said after her victory.

Bob Kersee, Devers' coach, had another prize pupil, his wife. Jackie Joyner-Kersee, seeking to defend her gold in the long jump, was overtaken by Heike Dreschler of Germany. But Joyner-Kersee successfully captured her second straight Olympic gold medal in the heptathlon, advancing the argument that Jackie — not Dan nor Dave, or anyone else — is the world's greatest athlete.

Also at the Olympic Stadium, a valiant effort from Dave Johnson was not enough for the gold, only bronze. The answer to Reebok's marketing riddle? It was Robert ... Zmelik of Czechoslovakia in the men's decathlon.

The USA's Kevin Young shattered the long-standing 400-meter hurdles record of Edwin Moses, and Quincy Watts, who was converted to a 400-meter sprinter after a brief tryout of college football, delivered a gold and showed great promise for the future.

King Carl Lewis, 31 years old and never truly appreciated by American fans, finally had *the* Olympic moment to crown his achievements. Gold medals he had (seven), his records were numerous, excellence was his standard for more than a decade, but the one moment of unmitigated and untarnished triumph to be engraved in the mind forever was the world record-setting 4x100-meter relay. "It's about timing," Lewis said simply.

Nicole Haislett, Melvin Stewart, Summer Sanders and Mike Barrowman added to the USA's underwater haul of gold. The men's and women's 4x100-meter relays both set world records, as did the women's 4x100 medley relay. Hungarians Tamas Darnyi (200 and 400 IM) and Krisztina Egerszegi (100 and 200 backstroke, 400 IM) and Russians Aleksandr Popov (50 and 100 freestyle) and Evgeny Sadovyi (200 and 400 freestyle) also earned multiple medals.

In men's diving, Mark Lenzi showed there was life after Louganis as he delivered a gold-medal performance from the three-meter springboard. In the women's platform competition, China intro-

duced an new weapon: 13-year-old Fu Mingxia, so young and so talented.

Gymnast Trent Dimas of Albuquerque, N.M., who had taken a break from his competitive career to sort out his life, spun thrice on the dismount from the bar, stuck the landing and his spirits soared. He mobbed his coach with joy after seeing his gold-medal score: 9.975.

Boxing's controversial computer scoring system required judges' fingers to be as fast as the boxers' hands. Oscar de la Hoya of Los Angeles won the gold for his deceased mother, who at one time skipped radiation treatment to watch him compete.

For the host country, the Games were especially sweet. Spain, which had accumulated four gold medals in the previous 96 years,

found a treasure in Catalonia: 13 golds. The most-awaited gold medal in Spain: Jacksonville, Fla., native (but Spanish citizen) Martin Lopez-Zubero's in the 200 backstroke. Maybe the most unexpected of Spain's golden haul, Fermin Cacho gored the favorites in the 1,500 and fanned the excitement in the city. And the grand finale was the soccer team's gold, which, for once, galvanized the whole country in support.

It was the passion for life, nightlife and *calor* of Barcelona that was the thread that gave the Games of the XXVth Olympiad its spirit and reinforced the notion that bringing together the world works — whatever its boundaries. To Barcelona, *adios* and *gracias*. ◆

OPPOSITE (TOP) / *"Go Donna!" A favorite to win and, obviously, a favorite of this colorful crowd, Donna Weinbrecht bumped her way to the gold on the moguls course at Tignes.* (ALLSPORT / RONDEAU)

OPPOSITE (BOTTOM) / *The best, bar none. A teammate gives Trent Dimas the high five and the judges' score of 9.975 on the horizontal bar gave the USA gymnast the gold.* (ALLSPORT / MARTIN)

ABOVE / *A moment to savor. Anchor Carl Lewis brings home the gold in the 4x100-meter relay in a world-record time of 37.40 seconds.* (ALLSPORT / VANDYSTADT)

First impressions made lasting impressions on the colorful slopes of Les Trois Vallees. (ALLSPORT / M. POWELL)

A bird's-eye view of Kim Zmeskal soaring high above the vault.
(ALLSPORT / MORTIMORE)

The United States Olympic Committee, a streamlined organization of 41-member organizations, is the moving force for support of sports in the United States that are on the program of the Olympic and/or Pan American Games, or those wishing to be included.

The USOC is recognized by the International Olympic Committee as the sole agency in the U.S. whose mission involves providing opportunities for all American athletes at all age and skill levels to prepare for their challenges that range from domestic competitions to the Olympic Games.

America is unique in the Olympic world to the extent that the nation's Olympic effort is propelled by its individual citizens, and by major support from the corporate community. The USOC is one of only a few National Olympic Committees in the world that does not receive continuous support from the federal government.

Therefore the USA's Olympic teams are truly representative of the free enterprise system, and the USOC is proud to say, "America doesn't send its athletes to the Olympic Games, Americans do." During the 1989-92 quadrennial period, the USOC had a budget of $300 million dollars, of which more than 80 percent was spent for support of the athletes and National Governing Bodies (NGBs).

Athletes may receive direct benefits in many ways through grant programs that offer several levels of direct financial assistance, a job opportunities program, a tuition assistance program, and an elite athlete health insurance plan. More than $26 million was designated for athlete subsistence from 1989-92.

The athletes also have an important voice in the U.S. Olympic Movement through the Athletes' Advisory Council. All governance councils of the USOC and the NGBs have at least 20 percent membership and voting power held by recent or active athletes representing each sport.

The USOC currently maintains and operates Olympic Training Centers in Colorado Springs, Colo., and Lake Placid, N.Y., with a third complex being built in San

(ALLSPORT / HEWITT)

U.S. OLYMPIC COMMITTEE

Guardian of the Olympic Movement

Diego. In all, the OTCs serve more than 15,000 athletes each year. For athletes selected by their respective NGBs, the USOC offers the athletes free room and board, training facilities, sports medicine care, sports science testing and analysis, local transportation and recreational facilities.

The Colorado Springs complex, which originally opened in 1977, is the headquarters for all the Olympic Training Center programs, as well as the USOC's adminis-

trative offices and home of several sports NGBs. Some of the facilities include a swimming flume, the world's third largest Olympic Shooting Center, the Olympic Sports Center, which can meet the training requirements of 13 different sports, and the nearby world-class, 7-Eleven velodrome.

The Lake Placid OTC opened in November, 1982, and primarily serves athletes who participate in the Olympic winter sports. The Olympic Training Center in San Diego will be the USOC's first year-round, warm weather, multisport facility. The USOC also supports the U.S. Olympic Education Center at Northern Michigan University in Marquette.

Through these facilities, the USOC's sports medicine division offers a clinical services program which is charged with providing a total health care package for all athletes in residence at the Olympic Training Centers, as well as those athletes at the U.S. Olympic Festivals and USOC-sponsored international competitions. The USOC also has a s a sports science division to help aid the athletes' performances through sports biomechanics, sports physiology, sport psychology, computer science and engineering technology.

In addition to entering and underwriting the full expenses of U.S. teams at the Olympic and Pan American Games, the USOC also operates the U.S. Olympic Festival, which has become the nation's premier multisport event, involving more than 3,000 athletes in 37 sports. Dating back to 1978, the Festival is held during non-Olympic summers in cities throughout the U.S.

Another annual event is the gathering of the U.S. Olympic Committee's "family" for the Olympic Congress of the USA, which is a convention that focuses directly on the Olympic Movement and culminates with the induction ceremony for the U.S. Olympic Hall of Fame.

With a wide-range of responsibilities and duties, the USOC, which has existed in varying forms since the first Modern Olympic Games in 1896, has maintained its critical role as the guardian of the Olympic Movement in the United States. ❖

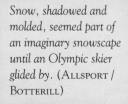

Snow, shadowed and molded, seemed part of an imaginary snowscape until an Olympic skier glided by. (Allsport / Botterill)

Suspended momentarily high above the hills of Courcheval, a ski jumper has an unparalleled view of the valley below — but at 60 miles per hour, who has time to notice? (ALLSPORT / VANDYSTADT)

The 50-meter freestyle event is a flat-out speed race where a swimmer may take two or three breaths the entire length of the pool. A mere 21.91 seconds later with the water still churning, a 20-year-old Russian, Aleksandr Popov, won the gold. But, at 28, American bronze medalist Tom Jager (PICTURED) still owns the world record at 21.81. (ALLSPORT / BRUTY)

Carl Lewis may not have been there to challenge Linford Christie — who won the silver in Seoul behind King Carl — for the title of the world's fastest man, but the 31-year-old Brit was still a step ahead of the field. (ALLSPORT / BRUTY)

BARCELONA

the city that never sleeps

BY CHRISTINE BRENNAN

The Olympic Games have been held in more famous cities. They've been held in bigger places. They've been held in towns with more money and more hands-on potential.

But they've never been held in a more fitting place, in a more hospitable, inviting and festive city, than Barcelona.

With its dancing fountains, magical Montjuic, refurbished Estadi Olimpic and dramatic diving pool, Barcelona played the perfect host to the rejuvenated Olympic Games of 1992. Only a city that never sleeps fully understands the breadth of the Summer Games; in Barcelona, no one wanted to miss a thing.

An ancient city full of new-world charm, Barcelona became a grand place to find the reunified Germany, the newly-welcomed South Africans, the returning Cubans, the soon-to-be-divided Unified Team.

Yet, the city itself reminded us that politics can never be fully removed from the Games. Barcelona is the capital of Catalonia, one of Spain's 17 autonomous regions. With a language (Catalan) and culture of their own, the people of Catalonia are pushing for independence from Spain by the year 2000. That effort was revealed to the world during the Olympics in various ways, from the striped Catalonian flags draped from balconies around town to the use of the Catalan language by everyone from King Juan Carlos on down.

To prepare for the 16 days of the Olympics, the three million citizens of Barcelona endured six years of renovation and construction — with an $8 billion price tag — in various locations around the city. There was Parc De Mar, the Mediterranean seaside site of the acclaimed Olympic Village, which rose from a dilapidated coastline of old factories and warehouses. There was the Diagonal area, featuring two grand, old soccer stadiums. There was Vall d'Hebron, with its vast tennis courts and sparkling velodrome. There were out-of-town sites for rowing, canoeing and some soccer games.

BACKGROUND / *On a clear day, you can see the infamous spires of the Familia Sagrada from the Piscina de Montjuic, venue of the diving well.* (Allsport / Bruty)

But, most of all, there was Montjuic, arguably the most beautiful Olympic setting in history. For a look at the sporting history of Barcelona, one only needed to take a peak at the facilities of Montjuic.

If you build it, they will come

THE CITY BID for the 1924 Olympic Games, the 1936 Games and the 1972 Games. It lost all three times. But, with each effort came a new stadium, a new athletic push, a new hope for a future Games.

Estadi Olimpic, the 65,000-seat structure that hosted the track and field events and the Opening and Closing Ceremonies, was built in 1929 as part of Barcelona's bid for the 1936 Olympic Games. Planners believed a brand-new stadium would bring the Games to the city after the disappointment of 1924. But when Berlin won the Olympics, the stadium went from monument to monstrosity, and fell into such disrepair that some wanted to tear it down in the early 1980s.

After a massive facelift, it was unveiled and reintroduced at the World Athletics Cup in 1989. Although it sprung some leaks on rainy nights, it was ready to go.

But stadiums are only part of the story of Barcelona and its Games. This is the land of Picasso and Miro and Gaudi. It is the home of the trendy Rambla, the tree-lined pedestrian mall that snakes through the old city to the Christopher Columbus statue at the Mediterranean shore.

As artist and mascot Cobi creator Javier Mariscal said, "Every night in restaurants, you hear loud and crazy arguments about sculptures, fountains and plazas."

Nearly 100 floodlit fountains line the street below Montjuic. The scene attracted hundreds of thousands over the two weeks of the Games, many of whom had no intention of going to a sporting event. They rode the escalators to the top of the mountain; they watched the fireworks from the Opening and Closing Ceremonies; they created human traffic jams that lasted until 3 a.m. The Olympic Games were their excuse to celebrate.

For those who were interested in the Games themselves, Montjuic was a delight. Swimming, gymnastics and track and field were next-door neighbors. Fans could stay on the mountain all day, choosing to take in sports or the view from a shaded cafe. The Olympics never had it so good.

Then again, nearly 70 years ago, Baron Pierre de Coubertin, father of the modern Olympic Games, realized the potential that existed on Barcelona's majestic hill.

"Before I came to Barcelona, I thought I knew what a sporting city was," he wrote on his 1926 visit.

Now, the world has discovered exactly what he meant. ◆

CLOCKWISE (FROM TOP) / *From the setting sun on the spires of the old city (ALLSPORT / HEWITT) to the grand fireworks of the Opening Ceremonies (ALLSPORT / M. POWELL), Barcelona staged the "world's greatest show" for 16 days. Barcelona flaunted its beauty (ALLSPORT / BILOW) and showered the people with cool, colorful fountains (ALLSPORT /HEWITT), not to mention a political statement from the separatist cause of the Catalonians. (ALLSPORT /MORTIMORE) And when it all began on July 25, spectators were treated to a feast of colors — of fire (ALLSPORT / MORTIMORE) and sea* (**BACKGROUND** - ALLSPORT / BRUTY) — *and an archer whose shot was cheered around the world. (ALLSPORT / BRUTY)* **SUCCEEDING PAGES** / *From opera stars to flamenco dancers, the fanfare never stopped until the last firework exploded over Estadi Olimpic. (ALLSPORT / VANDYSTADT)*

FREEDOM FOR CATALONIA

ARCHERY
Drama builds in new format

The 1992 Olympic Games marked the beginning of a revolution for the sport of archery as dramatic changes were made to make this sport more exciting for spectators and television alike.

The new format featured a 32-athlete, 12-arrow, direct elimination tournament for both the men's and women's individual competition and a 16-team, 27-arrow, direct elimination tournament for both men and women.

It turned out to be a format that introduced a pressure not known in past archery competition and — for beginners, anyway — favored the steel nerves of gold medal-winning teams from Spain and South Korea and individual gold medalists from France and South Korea.

For the U.S., the change in format was not as kind. For the first time since archery was reintroduced to the Games in 1972, the U.S. failed to win a medal.

"It was dramatic — real dramatic for me," said Jay Barrs of Mesa, Ariz. "The crowd was really into it and that's what the sport needs. You had people cheering for their favorite archer. From an archer's standpoint, that's great.

"We finally got some people into the sport. People are out there yelling and screaming. It used to be that archery tournaments were no fun to watch. Nobody wants to go watch a chess match. It's kind of like the popularity in tennis now. Instead of the little clap that they used to do, people can go out and really yell for their favorite player and that's helped that sport."

Perhaps no U.S. archer saw how much importance one arrow can bring in the elimination round than Barrs. After qualifying 12th in the individual competition, Barrs won two matches to reach the quarterfinals against Simon Terry of Great Britain.

Barrs needed a nine or 10 on his last arrow to clinch a victory, but shot an eight. Terry answered with a 10 to tie, then scored a 10 in the one-arrow, sudden-death overtime while Barrs hit an eight to be eliminated. Terry eventually captured the bronze while France's

Sebastian Flute was crowned the gold medalist and South Korea's Chung Jae-Hun won the silver medal.

The U.S. men's team — consisting of Barrs, Rick McKinney and Richard "Butch" Johnson — also reached the quarterfinals, where it faced Finland. Barrs, battling a tough wind, shot a six on his last arrow and Finland pulled out a 239-237 win. Spain, the 10th-seeded team, shocked the field by winning the team title ahead of Finland and Great Britain.

The quarterfinals proved no better for the U.S. women. Denise Parker of South Jordan, Utah, qualified fifth for the elimination round, then faced Natalia Valeeva of the Unified Team, who had already eliminated U.S. archers Sherry Block of Colorado Springs, Colo., and Jennifer O'Donnell of Farmington, Mich.

Parker got off to a hot start and led throughout the quarterfinal match. However, shooting last in the last end of three arrows, Parker managed only a six on her final arrow and Valeeva advanced with a 107-105 victory.

"This is what you work for and it's hard when it comes down to one arrow, but that's the way the elimination round works and that's why I had a shot at a medal," Parker said. "I've shot last-second free throws before, but that's not like the Olympics. It's hard to compare a regional high school final or something like that. This is completely different."

South Korean Cho Youn-Jeong dominated the women's qualification and elimination rounds

ABOVE / *Cho Youn-Jeong of South Korea, the 1984 gold medalist, beat out her compatriot and defending 1988 gold medalist Kim Soo-Nyung with a world record for the gold.* (ALLSPORT / BOTTERILL)

OPPOSITE / *Denise Parker, the 1988 bronze medalist, went home empty-handed after being eliminated in the quarterfinals. Parker's performance mirrored the rest of the Americans, who failed to medal in archery for the first time — the 1980 boycott year excepted — since the sport's reintroduction to the Olympic program in 1972.* (DUOMO / RICK RICKMAN)

to win the gold medal. Cho set three world records and helped the Koreans obliterate the field in the team qualification round.

Parker came back in the team quarterfinals and gave the USA a shot to advance against France. In her last three arrows, Parker scored three 10s to put the pressure on France. France was able to hold its lead, however, and gain a 232-225 victory, eliminating the U.S. in the quarterfinals once again. The Koreans — including Cho, defending individual gold medalist Kim Soo-Nyung and Lee Eun-Kyung — won the gold medal followed by China and the Unified Team.

"Obviously we had a rough Olympics," said McKinney, who failed to qualify for the elimination round. "We just couldn't get it

In Barcelona, archers competed head-to-head, alternating shots and turning what was a rather drab spectator sport into an intense competition that engaged the crowds.

together. There was just something missing. The funny thing was that I thought this was the strongest team we had ever fielded for the Olympics. The last Games, everybody went home with a medal, and this time, nobody did."

The 1992 Games, which marked the first time that an Americans had not won the men's individual gold medal in a Games in which the U.S. had participated, marked a changing of the guard of sorts. While South Korea continued to be a major factor, winning four medals, the Unified Team and Great Britain, each with two medals, and France, Spain, Finland and China — all with one medal each — indicated the sport's worldwide appeal. ❖   **JEFF CRAVENS**

ATHLETICS
House of legends

The climb up Montjuic to Barcelona's Estadi Olimpic took athletics fans past a series of terraced gardens and spectacular fountains. It was described by one American writer as "a heavenly ascent to a paradise of earthly excellence, crowned by the Olympic flame." By the close of the 1992 Olympic Games, it could also be called a climb to glory for the United States track and field teams.

These Games marked the beginning of a new era of Olympic competition. With several former Soviet states competing independently for the first time and South Africa rejoining the International Olympic family, it truly was a gathering of historic proportions.

The U.S. impresses

AMERICAN NEWCOMERS ARRIVED on the Olympic scene with a bang, time-tested veterans performed with flair, and the end result was one of the greatest performances ever by a U.S. team. In fact, track and field aficionados were hard-pressed to recount a more impressive U.S. showing.

Not since the 1956 Games in Melbourne had the U.S. won as many track and field medals. In those Olympic Games, which were contested before all but two members of the current team were born, the Americans won 31 medals (16 gold, 10 silver, five bronze). In Barcelona, they earned 30 medals (12 gold, eight silver and 10 bronze).

The Americans not only brought home medals, they also produced three world records, six Olympic marks and five American standards.

Event after event, day after day, capacity crowds of 65,000 wondered how anything could top what they had just witnessed. The answer came in the final event fully contested on the track, as the U.S. men shattered the oldest record in track and field.

Since the U.S. had set the world record in the 4x400-meter relay in Mexico City, the record had stood at 2:56.16. The U.S. squad in Seoul tied it, but, still, the 24-year-old mark remained as the sport's most venerable.

RIGHT / *Linford Christie, at 31, is no new kid off the blocks, but in Barcelona he was in fine form, powering past a disbelieving Dennis Mitchell (#1738) of the U.S.* (ALLSPORT / M. POWELL)

SUCCEEDING PAGES / *After being disqualified in Seoul for passing the baton out of the exchange zone, the U.S. men's 4x100-meter relay team had to swallow a bitter pill. This time, the taste was sweet victory. Amid the watchful eyes of the judges, Dennis Mitchell passes the baton to anchor Carl Lewis whose blistering leg brought home the gold in a world-record time of 37.40 seconds.* (ALLSPORT / DUFFY)

So it seemed entirely appropriate that in this most electrifying of competitions, the U.S. team of Andrew Valmon, Quincy Watts, Michael Johnson and Steve Lewis put an exclamation point on the Barcelona Olympic Games with a world record of 2:55.74.

Lewis, the anchor, churned down the homestretch like a 100-meter runner. "When I came around the curve and saw how far we were ahead on the television screen, I thought, 'This could be the record.' It was a thrill," he said.

400 Watts electrifies

THE RELAY PRODUCED Watts' second gold medal of the Games. Earlier he won the open 400 in the second-fastest time in history at 43.50. Watts' performance answered the question about who America's next great 400-meter man would be.

Two years ago, Watts had given up track, frustrated by repeated hamstring injuries suffered as a 100- and 200-meter sprinter. Instead, he gave football a try. A year on the gridiron, however, convinced him that track was his sport. At the urging of University of Southern California head coach Jim Bush, he decided to try the 400, even though in Watts' mind it was just strength training for the 200. But after running 46 flat in his first race and then lowering his best to 45.54 in just a few weeks, Watts decided to commit to the 400.

"I loved track so much I wanted to give it another try, this time in the 400," Watts said. "I've come a long way real fast." Only 22 years

old, Watts seems poised to become the greatest 400-meter performer the world has ever seen. If that happens, Barcelona will be remembered as his coming out party.

The U.S. men's 4x100-meter relay team played a part in the U.S. world record parade as well. Mike Marsh, Leroy Burrell, Dennis Mitchell and Carl Lewis blistered the Olympic oval in 37.40, taking .10 seconds off the mark set by the American entry at the 1991 World Championships in Tokyo. Mitchell, Burrell and Lewis were members of the Tokyo team as well.

"We wanted to put a time out where, if the four of us never ran

*OPPOSITE / After giving Southern Cal football a try, Quincy Watts returned to his first love: track. Watts was talked into running the 400 meters, a decision he's not likely to regret. Watts beat fellow American Steve Lewis for the gold in an Olympic record 43.50 seconds. (*ALLSPORT / M. POWELL)

*TOP / At a towering 6-4, Kevin Young has the stride of a world-class hurdler and on race day he proved it. Young smashed the 47-second barrier in the 400-meter hurdles, chopping off .24 seconds from Edwin Moses' long-standing world record. (*ALLSPORT / BRUTY)

*ABOVE / Joe Greene joined gold medalist Carl Lewis and silver medalist Mike Powell to make it an American sweep in the long jump. (*ALLSPORT / M. POWELL)

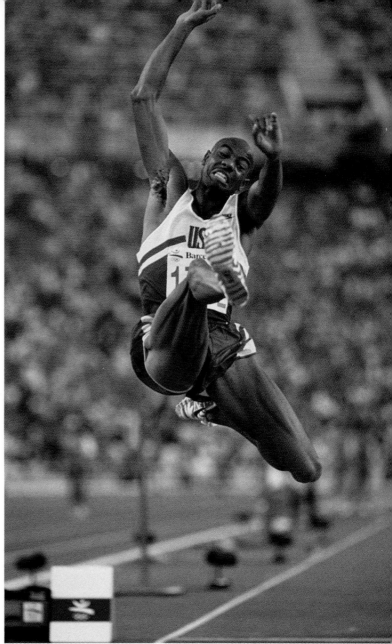

"I will take it one year at a time. But I'd love to be back in Atlanta in '96.

—Carl Lewis
triple gold-medalist
in long jump

"In my gut, I knew it was a centimeter or two short when I landed."

—Mike Powell
world record-holder
in long jump

ABOVE / *In the unfamiliar underdog role, the ever-so-cool Carl Lewis collected his third Olympic gold with his first jump of 28-5 1/2.* (ALLSPORT / M. POWELL)

CENTER / *Competitors to the bone, Carl Lewis and Mike Powell are nonetheless true sportsmen.* (ALLSPORT / M. POWELL)

ABOVE / *World record-holder Mike Powell nurtured a tight hamstring and talked a good game, but, at the end of the evening, he came up short —* 1 1/4 inches too short. (ALLSPORT / M. POWELL)

OPPOSITE / *A slow start in the 200 meters meant catch up time for Mike Marsh, who powered past Frank Fredericks (left) of Namibia to take the gold in 20.01 seconds.* (ALLSPORT / MARTIN)

again, it would be tough for generations to beat that record, and I think we did that today," said Mitchell shortly after the race.

By the evening of August 8, 1992, it was clear that the reports of Lewis' demise were greatly exaggerated. These Games gave him an

King Carl reigns in Spain

LEWIS, WHO MANY believe ran one of the fastest 4x100 anchor legs ever, and Marsh, brilliant out of the blocks, claimed their second Barcelona golds with the slick baton work.

Earlier, Lewis outdueled fellow countryman Mike Powell for the long jump gold medal. Lewis jumped 8.67 meters (28-5 1/2) to top Powell's 8.64 meters (28-4 1/2), proving that, at the age of 31, his unmatched skills remain intact.

LEFT / Hwang Young-Cho of South Korea collapsed in exhaustion after he crossed the finish line. Hwang broke away from Japan's Koichi Morishita with 1 1/4 miles left in the marathon. It was a symbolic day for South Korea. In the stands Sohn Kee-Chung, who won the gold at the 1936 Berlin Games, cheered. But the Korean flag never flew in 1936. Sohn was forced to run under a Japanese name, uniform and flag since his country was occupied by the Japanese. (ALLSPORT / BOTTERILL)

Entering the meet, Lewis was scheduled to compete in only one event, the long jump. At the U.S. Trials in June, a then-undiagnosed virus brought Lewis to his knees. He was a badly-beaten sixth in the 100-meter final and later was outleaned at the tape in a bid to make the 200-meter squad. He arrived in Barcelona to find a hoard of reporters pronouncing his track career finished and questioning whether he could compete with Powell in the long jump.

arguable claim to the title of America's greatest Olympian ever. He entered the long jump as an underdog and began the meet as a relay alternate. Yet, in beating the world record-holder (Powell) in the long jump, and making the most of his relay opportunity, Lewis upped his career haul to eight Olympic gold medals.

"I had a rough time earlier this summer and I was so down; to come back and win is so exciting," Lewis said. "I was ill at our Trials and at that point I really didn't know what to expect."

ABOVE / Mike Conley was long overdue for Olympic gold, but he'll have to wait for the world record. His jump of 59-7 1/2 inches, which exceeded Willie Bank's mark of 58-11 1/2, was disallowed because of a 4.5 mph tailwind. (ALLSPORT / GRAY MORTIMORE)

ABOVE / Mark McKoy of Canada got the lean on everyone in the 110-meter hurdles, including a frustrated Florian Schwarthoff (#849) of Germany, who finished fifth. (ALLSPORT / VANDYSTADT)

With world champion and miler favorite Noureddine Morceli of Algeria boxed in the pack of this tactical, slow-trotting race, Fermin Cacho took a gamble of a lifetime and won. Bolstered by a roaring partisan crowd, the Spaniard broke from the pack and ran away with the gold in the 1,500 meters. (ALLSPORT / POWELL)

TOP LEFT / *Perhaps no one was more surprised than Sergei Bubka himself when he no-heighted the pole vault at 18-10 1/2 — the Ukrainian owns the outdoor world record of 20-1. Bubka packed it up (ALLSPORT / HEWITT), leaving the field and the gold up for grabs. It was teammate Maxim Tarassov of the Unified Team (**ABOVE**) who nabbed top honors with a height of 19-0 1/4. (ALLSPORT / MARTIN)*

LEFT / *Elsewhere on the field, American Mike Stulce captured the shot put with a throw of 71- 2 1/2. (ALLSPORT / DUFFY)*

LEFT / *A medal of honor goes to Derek Redmond of Great Britain, who went down with a torn right hamstring in his 400-meter heat. Eluding security men, Derek's father jumped the barricade and embraced his injured son, who had gamely fought to his feet. The two finished the race together.* (ALLSPORT / MORTIMORE)

ABOVE / *The 3,000-meter steeplechase race was a Kenyan sweep with Matthew Birer taking the gold in 8:08.84. Patrick Sang and William Mutwol collected the silver and bronze medals, respectively.* (ALLSPORT / M. POWELL)

BACKGROUND / *The 10,000-meter final was a barrel of controversy with the gold medal being stripped from Morocco's Khalid Skah and awarded to Kenyan Richard Chelimo. Skah was accused of being in cahoots with teammate Hammou Boutayeh for impeding the Kenyan's progress. The next day, the disqualified Skah was reinstated and, to the crowd's jeers and whistles (Spain's equivalent of boos), the gold hung around his neck.* (ALLSPORT / VANDYSTADT)

"Of all the medals I've won, this long jump medal was the toughest," Lewis said. "Mike Powell is the world record-holder and today I won a great battle. We had a tough wind out there. The conditions and the competition made it really the toughest medal. My first gold medal (in 1984) was the most special, but this was the toughest."

While Lewis and Powell drew most of the attention, American Joe Greene jumped 8.34 meters (27-4 1/2) to take the bronze. It marked the second consecutive long jump sweep for the U.S. and the fourth overall.

WORLD RECORDS
...on the horizon

MARSH EARLIER WON the 200 meters in 20.01, but not before blistering a 19.73, the No. 2 time in history, in the semifinal round. Since Marsh's race plan was to merely advance to the finals, he slowed noticeably at the finish, losing a sure world record.

"I am a little regretful there was no world record, but the gold medal is more important. It's in my pocket and you can't take that away," he said. "World records come and go, but you have a gold medal forever."

For Marsh, the gold medal was the realization of tremendous potential after years of lofty, but largely unmet expectations. Ever since he ran 20.35 back in 1988, people looked for Marsh to break into the world's elite. But his highest national ranking was sixth and his only prior world ranking was No. 8.

This year, however, Marsh began to turn in the type of performances expected of him. Entering the Olympics he had posted the year's top legal 100-meter time (9.93) and the second-fastest 200-meter clocking (19.86). While the Santa Monica Track Club member had previously participated in three world record relays, he was itching to make a name for himself in open races as well. In his

Barcelona exploits, Marsh found the salve to cure that itch.

...in the bag

YET ANOTHER LEGEND fell from the record books when Kevin Young amazed the world with a 46.78 clocking in the 400-meter hurdles, breaking Edwin Moses' mark of 47.02 which had stood since 1983.

"I came here with the goal of winning the gold medal, but the world record was in the back of my mind," Young said. "My other goal was to run 46.89, I have that time on the wall of my room at home. Now I can say I'm the first man to go under 47 seconds in the 400 hurdles."

...gone with the wind

VETERAN TRIPLE JUMPER Mike Conley came within a breath of yet another world standard. He soared 17.63 meters (57-10 1/4) to claim the Olympic record, but because an aiding wind of 2.1 meters per second blew down the runway, the performance could not be entered in the world record book. The allowable wind is 2.0 meters per second.

When asked if he was disappointed by missing the world mark by less wind that an average fan creates, Conley grinned and said, "That would be greedy. I've got a gold medal."

TOP / *American Gail Devers' smile tells the story best: In a textbook case of Olympian feats, Devers overcame Graves' disease to celebrate her gold medal in the 100 meters as the world's fastest woman.* (ALLSPORT / M. POWELL)

ABOVE / *No use crying over spilt milk must have been on the mind of pre-race favorite Gwen Torrence after coming in sixth in the 100 meters. The 27-year-old American beat the 200-meter field in 21.86 seconds. This time, as the national anthem rang out, the tears rolled.* (ALLSPORT / HEWITT)

TOP / *Evelyn Ashford, Esther Jones, Gwen Torrence and Carlette Guidry-White (from left) celebrated their gold-medal victory in the 4x100-meter relay, where the 35-year-old Ashford wrapped up her Olympic career with her fourth gold.* (ALLSPORT /DUFFY) *The sprinters* (**ABOVE**) *then turned their attention to the cameras to share their golden moment with the world.* (ALLSPORT / VANDYSTADT)

LEFT / *Elena Romanova held off another Unified Team challenger Tatiana Dorovskikh to win the 3,000 meters in 8:46.04.* (ALLSPORT / BRUTY)

Heike Henkel leaped to victory with her jump of 6-7 1/2 in the high jump. Galina Astafei of Romania and Joanat Quintero of Cuba took second and third, respectively. (ALLSPORT / VANDYSTADT)

The top American female high jumper was American Tanya Hughes who jumped 6-2. (ALLSPORT / DUFFY)

Barcelona bits

THE U.S. SQUAD took a gold and silver in the shot put with Mike Stulce's toss of 21.70 meters (71-2 1/2) and Jim Doehring's throw of 20.94 meters (68-9 1/4.) Stulce so dominated the competition, that all four of his fair throws would have won the title. He became the first American shot putter to win an Olympic gold since Randy Matson turned the trick in 1968.

Stulce and Matson are both Texas A&M alumni. "He [Matson] called me before I left and wished me good luck," Stulce said. "I figured I'd better medal or not come back to town."

Other Olympic highlights included Great Britain's Linford Christie, who won the 100 meters in 9.96 while the USA's Mitchell claimed third in 10.04; hometown hero Fermin Cacho of Spain, who thrilled the crowd by winning the 1,500 meters; a victory by Canada's Mark McKoy in the 110-meter hurdles; a medal sweep by Kenya in the 3000-meter steeplechase; an Olympic record by Czechoslavakia's Jan Zelezny in the javelin; South Korea's Hwang Young-Cho winning the marathon in the final event of the '92 Games; five athletes clearing 7-8 in the high jump with medals determined on misses as American Hollis Conway was one of three bronze medalists; and the crowning of Czechoslavakia's Robert Zmelik as the "world's greatest athlete" with U.S. decathlete Dave Johnson winning the bronze.

Two shocking non-results from the Games were the failure of the Unified Team's Sergei Bubka to clear a height in the pole vault and the absence of American Michael Johnson in the finals of the 200 meters, an event in which he holds the world record.

Meanwhile, the American women refused to let their male counterparts completely steal the show. The U.S. sprinters were dominating and Jackie Joyner-Kersee made a bid to be considered the greatest athlete of all-time, male or female.

Hail Gail

GAIL DEVERS LAID claim to the title of the world's fastest woman with her gold-medal performance of 10.82 in the 100 meters. A few days later, it appeared Devers was going to become just the second woman in history to win the 100 meters and sprint hurdles in the same Olympics, as she held a commanding lead heading into the 10th and final barrier in the 100-meter hurdles. Her pace was so fast, in fact, that she clobbered the last hurdle and tumbled to the track. Rather than give up, Devers crawled across the finish line, finishing fifth.

More inspiring than her 100-meter race and more compelling than her hurdles drama was the story of how she arrived at the Olympic Games in the first place. Just two years before, Devers was suffering with Grave's Disease, a thyroid condition causing multiple symptoms.

At one point a doctor told Devers she was within 48 hours of having both feet amputated, had not a new program of medication taken effect. Healthy in Barcelona, she came within 10 meters of sweeping one of the toughest doubles in all of track.

The U.S. women won the 4x100-meter relay for the third consecutive time as Gwen Torrence anchored the relay brilliantly, coming from two meters behind to overtake the Unified Team's Irina Privalova. The U.S. ran 42.11 to the Unified Team's 42.16. "I had no doubt Gwen could catch up and win," said Evelyn Ashford, the leadoff runner.

ABOVE / *Long-legged Marie-Jose Perec of France crossed the finish line in 48.83 seconds in the 400 meters, well ahead of second-place finisher and 1988 Olympic champion Olga Bryzgina of the Unified Team.* (ALLSPORT / HEWITT)

GAIL DEVERS

Greatness Becomes Her

BY LEE BENSON

Gail Devers wasn't just a one-woman Olympic high-light film in Barcelona — the thrill of victory and the agony of defeat all rolled into one — she was a full-length movie. It isn't every athlete who, in a single Olympic Games, is able to: A) establish herself as the fastest woman in the world; B) experience the most heart-breaking crash-landing of the Games; and C) leave the world spellbound with her personal story of overcoming adversity.

After winning the gold medal in the women's 100-meter dash, Devers' dramatic story unfolded. How she contracted Graves' Disease — a hyperthyroid condition that has also afflicted George and Barbara Bush — in 1988 just as she was climbing onto the international track and field scene. How it was two years before doctors correctly diagnosed her condition. How subsequent radiation treat-ments corrected the Graves' Disease but caused her body to swell. How her feet became so inflamed that she could not walk. How she came within 48 hours of having her feet amputated before her radiation therapy was regulated.

Devers told her story frankly in front of the world press. The daughter of a Baptist minister, she spoke with fervor, in the hope that she could be an inspiration for others with their own hurdles to overcome.

All eyes were on her by the time of her second Olympic event — the 100-meter hurdles — when the 25-year-old American shot out of the blocks and flew down the track to what appeared to be a sure second gold medal.

But she generated so much momentum that she got to the last hurdle earlier than expected and hit it with her front foot. Devers crashed to the track as the gold medal van-ished. But she finished the race, crawling across the line in fifth place.

The 65,000 spectators in the Olympic Stadium groaned in empathy for Devers, who quickly composed herself and stood up wearing a smile. She said not to feel sorry for her. After all she'd been through, she knew there were worse things than crawling across an Olympic finish line with one gold medal already draped around your neck. ◆

Fast out of the block and leading the field, Gail Devers' legs simply got ahead of her on the last hurdle and physics took over. Devers crawled to the finish line in fifth. (ALLSPORT / M. POWELL)

What goes up, must come down ... but not usually like this. Devers takes a painful fall after hitting the hurdle at full stride.
(ALLSPORT / M. POWELL)

After two days of competition and seven events, Jackie Joyner-Kersee outstrided the entire heptathlon field to take the gold. For the record, Joyner-Kersee accumulated her 7,044 point total with a 12.85 in the 100-meter hurdles, 6-3 1/4 in the high jump, 46-4 1/4 in the shotput, 23.12 in the 200-meters, 23-3 1/2 in the long jump, 147-6 3/4 in the javelin and 2:11.78 in the 800 meters. (ALLSPORT / MARTIN)

Jackie Joyner-Kersee is an American portrait of strength and beauty, of prowess and composure in a seven-event discipline that requires just that: discipline. Joyner-Kersee proved herself to be the greatest female athlete winning back-to-back Olympic golds in the heptathlon. (ALLSPORT / DUFFY)

Tears of joy

EARLIER IN THE COMPETITION Torrence won the 200-meter gold medal in 21.81, controlling the race from start to finish. Her semifinal time of 21.72 made her the fifth-fastest woman in history. On the all-time U.S. list, Torrence is second only to Florence Griffith-Joyner. Torrence then came back to run the fastest leg on the U.S. silver medal-winning 4x400 relay which battled the heavily-favored Unified Team stride for stride until the final 50 meters. The two golds and the silver medal helped Torrence deal with the disappointment of her fourth-place finish in the 100 meters.

Ashford's grand finale

IT WAS ALSO an emotional Olympics for Ashford, the "queen of American sprinters." The 36-year-old Ashford was competing in her fourth and final Olympic Games in the open 100 and as a member of the U.S. 4x100-meter relay squad.

In the 100, a sub-par start in her semifinal race prevented Ashford from advancing to the final. "It just wasn't a good race for me today," she said shortly after the semi. "This is my last Olympics and I feel sad for that. But it's been a long career and I've still got the relay to go."

Several days later, Ashford demonstrated that her competitive fires still burned brightly. Running a brilliant opening leg, she teamed with Esther Jones, Carlette Guidry-White and Torrence to win the fourth gold medal of

her storied career. "I wanted to leave Barcelona with a gold medal and I am," Ashford exclaimed. "I feel great."

After the race, Torrence said the foursome wanted the gold for Ashford: "She's been around so long and has done so much for the sport. We're really happy she can go out this way."

Another chapter in another brilliant career was written by Joyner-Kersee, a woman called by 1976 gold-medal decathlete Bruce Jenner "the greatest multiple-event athlete ever, male or female."

JJK back for gold

JOYNER-KERSEE TOOK her second consecutive Olympic heptathlon gold, scoring 7,044 points to easily outdistance the field. Her point total was the sixth highest of Joyner-Kersee's career and her 2,908 second-day point total was her fourth best ever.

After taking a bronze in the long jump, jumping 7.07 meters (23-2 1/2), Joyner-Kersee left Barcelona with a career medal haul of three gold, one silver and a bronze. She is now tied for second on the all-time Olympic women's medal list with Shirley Strickland De la Hunta of Australia.

If she couldn't defend her long jump title from Seoul, Joyner-Kersee was

TOP / *Gail Devers' disaster was Paraskevi Patoulidou's fortune. The 100-meter hurdler gave Greece its first track medal since 1896.* (ALLSPORT / MARTIN).

MIDDLE / *The Africans have long held court in the long-distance races, but not in the sprints. Count Nigeria among the up-and-coming. The Nigerian women won the bronze in the 4x100-meter relay, finishing in 42.81.* (ALLSPORT / MARTIN)

LEFT / *When the modest Hassiba Boulmerka won the 1991 World Championships in Tokyo, she unleashed a series of healthy primal screams, uncharacteristic for a woman of Muslim upbringing, which frowns on public display of emotion or bare legs for that matter. But the 24-year-old was back at it again, yelling 'Algeria, Algeria' for her homeland after winning the 1,500-meter gold in Barcelona.* (ALLSPORT / MARTIN)

OPPOSITE / *Heike Dreschler of Germany reaches for the gold. In a friendly contest of the long jump, Dreschler defeated her friend Jackie Joyner-Kersee with a leap of 23-5 1/4. Joyner-Kersee, the 1988 gold medalist, took the bronze behind Inessa Kravets of the Unified Team.* (ALLSPORT / M. POWELL)

He competed under the glare of the media; the hoopla of Dan (O'Brien) and Dave, then Dave and no Dan; he was befelled by controversy in the shot put and plagued by a stress fracture in his right ankle. And he slid from gold-medal favorite to long-shot as the second day progressed. In all, it was not smooth sailing for the 29-year-old decathlete Dave Johnson, who managed the bronze in a Herculean effort and on a foot that had a 20 percent chance of a bone snapping in two when he hurdled. (ALLSPORT / BRUTY)

It was the longest-standing track and field record: Vincent Matthews, Ronald Freeman, Larry James and Lee Evans ran a 2:56.16 in the 4x400-meter relay in the 7,347-foot elevation Olympic stadium of Mexico City in 1968. On the 15th day of the Barcelona Games, the record fell as Andrew Valmon, Quincy Watts, Michael Johnson and Steve Lewis ran a 2:55.74. Afterward, the foursome (from left: Johnson, Valmon, Watts and Lewis) took the standard jog around the track to celebrate what will be now a new standard to conquer. (ALLSPORT / DUFFY)

happy that the gold medal could be won by her friend, Heike Dreschler of Germany. "Today was Heike's day," Joyner-Kersee said. "You want to win all the time, but today she was fortunate enough to come out on top and I'm happy for her."

In the spotlight

THE OLYMPIC SPOTLIGHT also shone on Marie-Jose Perec of France, the winner of the 400 meters; Hassiba Boulmerka, who ran around the track shouting "Algeria, Algeria" after capturing the 1,500 meters for her homeland; German high jump champion Heike Henkel; marathon winner Valentina Yegorova of the Unified Team; and Maritz Marten of Cuba, who dominated in the discus throw. In the 100-meter hurdles race that ended in a crash for Devers, the winner was Paraskevi Patoulidou of Greece, the first woman track and field medal win-

ner in her nation's history.

There are other scenes which will remain for years to come as well. The vision of PattiSue Plumer, battling lower back and resulting nerve problems to finish fifth in the 3,000-meter final and then just days later collapsing at the finish line from sheer exhaustion in the 1,500-meter final, will undoubtedly linger. And there was 10,000-meter star Lynn Jennings breaking away from pre-meet favorite Liz McColgan on the final lap to gain the bronze medal, set an American record and become the first U.S. woman to medal in an event longer than 800 meters. Derartu Tulu of Ethiopia was the winner.

Atop Montjuic, the Olympic Stadium became a house of legends. From Carl Lewis to Jackie Joyner-Kersee, the world held its collective breath at the world's greatest track meet in the world's greatest show. ❖ **STEVE HURLBUT MAXEY PARRISH DOUG VANCE**

TOP / With a look past her shoulder, South African Elana Meyer takes it all in — Derartu Tutu looking fresh, focused and coming up strong on the inside. The Ethiopian blasted past Meyer to take the gold in the 10,000 meters in 31:06.02 to Meyer's 31:11.75. (ALLSPORT / M. POWELL)

OPPOSITE / Sally Gunnell of Great Britain is a stride ahead of American Sandra Farmer-Patrick. Gunnell won the 400-meter hurdles in 53.23. Farmer-Patrick's time of 53.69 was good for the silver medal. (ALLSPORT / MARTIN)

TOP / The heat and humidity of Barcelona took its toll on many athletes, including this Polish 10-kilometer walker who gets a helping hand from her teammate. (ALLSPORT / B. MARTIN)

CENTER / They battled the ascent of Montjuic together and ran the last lap around the track in a race still up for grabs. But Valentina Yegorova of the Unified Team gained a slight edge on Yuko Arimori of Japan to win the marathon in 2:32.41. Arimori crossed the line just .08 seconds behind. (ALLSPORT / M. POWELL)

BADMINTON
Not just a backyard game

Respect. Simply put, that was the goal not only of the U.S. men's and women's teams, but of all 177 athletes who competed in badminton as it made its debut as a full medal sport at the 1992 Olympic Games.

Badminton came to the Olympic Games not as a rising wonder of recent decades, but as an established sport that has spread quietly and progressively through the world. The first rules of the game were written before those for tennis and table tennis, and the organized game of badminton will celebrate its centennial in 1993. Badminton was a demonstration sport during the 1972 Olympic Games in Munich, and an exhibition sport in 1988 at the Seoul Games.

Fundamentally, the game demands the execution of such skills as running, jumping, twisting, striking, throwing and various combinations of these skills executed in rapid hand-eye coordination. Considerably different from the backyard game that most Americans know, it's the second-fastest racket sport with the shuttle-cock propelled at speeds up to 200 miles per hour.

Greeted by an enthusiastic public in Barcelona, badminton found an ideal setting for the beginning of its Olympic venture. The 4,000-seat newly constructed Pavello de la Mar Bella was among the best situated of all venues nestled beside the Olympic Village.

As expected, the Asian countries of China and Indonesia dominated by each winning five medals. Indonesia swept the men's singles with sixth-seeded Alan Kusum upsetting third-seeded Ardy Wirananta, 15-12, 18-13, in the championship. In men's doubles, top-seeded Kim Moon-Soo and Park Joo-Bong of South Korea beat No. 2 seeded Eddy Hartono and Rudy Gunawan of Indonesia, 15-11, 15-7.

Susi Susanti of Indonesia, ranked No. 1 in the world, won the gold medal in women's singles after beating Bang Soo Hyun of Korea, 5-11, 11-5, 11-3.

Korea also captured the gold medal in women's doubles as top-seeded Chung So-Yung and Hwang Hye Young rallied to beat No. 2 seeded Guan Weizhen and Nong Qunhua from China, 15-12, 2-15, 15-8.

Not only will these medalists be remembered for their inaugural triumphs in Barcelona, but years from now, Chris Jogis will be the answer to a trivia question — Who was the first U.S. athlete ever to play badminton in the Olympic Games?

Jogis not only fulfilled a dream, but did so in a convincing manner. It took only 26 minutes for the 27-year-old U.S. southpaw to whip Dean Galt of New Zealand, 15-1, 15-3, in a first-round match.

"My goal has always been to be the first American to play in the Olympics and by the luck of the draw I was the first one here to compete," said Jogis, a six-time U.S. men's singles national champion who, at the time of the Games, was ranked No. 63 in the world. "Anything else I do here is a bonus."

The U.S. men's doubles team of Tom Reidy and Ben Lee also survived a first-round test with a 15-1, 15-5 romp past Ricardo Fernandes and Fernando Silva of Portugal. The challenge was stiffer in the second round when the duo fell to Rudy Gunawan and Eddy Hartono of Indonesia, ranked second in the world.

Other members of the U.S. badminton contingent who competed in Spain were

ABOVE / *Susi Susanti of Indonesia, ranked No. 1 in the world, proved her claim to the title in Barcelona. Susanti beat Bang Soo-Hyun of South Korea for the singles gold in badminton.* (ALLSPORT / BOTTERILL)

Joy Kitzmiller, Erika Von Heiland and Linda French in women's singles; Reidy and Lee in men's singles; and Kitzmiller and French in women's doubles.

The Americans entered the Olympic Games knowing that medals were only a distant glimmer, but they were all grateful for the opportunity to compete.

French was eliminated by Hau Huang of China, ranked third in the world, in the second round.

"I have such a passion for badminton that I'm glad to share it and educate other American athletes about the sport here in the (Olympic) Village," Von Heiland said.

But Jogis doesn't want to be remembered for just participating in the Olympic Games. Jogis also would like to be one of the ambassadors in having badminton gain more exposure in the United States.

> **Badminton requires the agility of an acrobat, the killer instinct of a panther, the accuracy of a marksman, the power of a racehorse, the speed of a sprinter and the stamina of a marathon runner.**

"Every sport hopes for the U.S. market to accept it because this is such a big sports marketing country," Jogis said. "Badminton is dominated by the Asian countries. But we hope our experience in the Olympics has educated people back in the U.S."

Watching a Jogis 140-mile-per-hour smash should convince the American public that the world's most demanding racket sport has a bright future in the U.S. Especially with the Centennial Olympic Games in Atlanta in 1996.

"If people can see it, I think there is a bright future for badminton. At this point, misconception in the United States is a hard thing to overcome because it is so misunderstood. It's going to take a lot of exposure and a lot of effort to be accepted as a true sport in America more than it just being perceived as a backyard game," Jogis said. ❖   **MIKE MAHON**

ABOVE/ *American Chris Jogis got what he wanted: to be the first American to play badminton in the Olympics. Jogis, who has a 140-mile-per-hour smash, considers himself an ambassador of the sport.* (DAVE BLACK)

BASEBALL
Cubans in league of their own

After 80 years, baseball was finally part of the Olympic Games, and the team from the United States, the birthplace of this growing international sport, was poised, in the name of poetic justice, to make a mad dash for the gold.

As it turned out, however, older and more experienced teams from baseball's best-established colonies — namely Cuba, Taiwan and Japan — turned a cold shoulder to sentimentality and birthrights and laid claim, respectively, to the gold, silver and bronze medals. The U.S. team finished just behind, in fourth place.

It was smooth sailing early for Team USA as it opened the Barcelona Olympics with three straight wins. Then came a matchup with old nemesis Cuba that started like a dream for the red, white and blue — five first-inning runs. The Cubans — loaded with a lineup to make major league scouts drool — clawed and slugged back and scored a 9-6 decision.

"It's very unusual for anyone to jump on Cuba for five runs in the first," said USA Head Coach Ron Fraser. "Give them credit, they didn't quit and were able to come back."

After two relatively easy victories over Puerto Rico and the Dominican Republic in its next two outings, the USA was set for a showdown with Japan in its final pool game. A win meant a second-place finish and a rematch with the Japanese in the semis. A loss meant fourth place and Cuba in the semis.

Back-to-back Japanese homers in the sixth broke a 1-1 tie and three innings later the verdict was in, 8-3 for Japan. Fourth place and Cuba. But that didn't seem to matter to the players.

"We knew that we would have to beat Cuba to win the gold medal, it just so happens that it now has to be in the semis," said outfielder Jeffrey Hammonds. "We'll be ready when we take the field."

Cuba was more ready. Victor Mesa's two-run homer off Rick Helling in the sixth broke open a tight 2-1 Cuban lead, and Omar Ajete stymied the USA bats as Cuba advanced to the finals with a

ABOVE / *Obviously something is amiss here as catcher Charles Johnson, U.S. coach Ron Fraser, pitcher Willie Adams (#25) and Jason Giambi (#21) look ready to do battle.* (ALLSPORT / M. POWELL)

LEFT / *Pitcher Rick Helling faced some major competition against Cuba in the semifinals.* (ALLSPORT / M. POWELL)

ABOVE / *Cuba fielded a "Dream Team" of its own with major-league talent like left-handed pitcher Omar Ajete, who has a 95-mile-per-hour fastball.* (ALLSPORT / M. POWELL)

6-1 win. The Cubans proceeded to extend their amazing winning streak in international competition by winning the gold medal in a 11-1 rout over Taiwan.

"I thought our ballclub played real well," Fraser said. "Any time Cuba plays a perfect game, you usually lose about 16-1 or 20-1. The only way to beat Cuba is to get them on an off day and play the best you can."

The best the USA could play against the Japanese, a surprise 5-2 loser to Taiwan in the semifinals, in the bronze-medal game wasn't good enough. Final score: Japan 8, USA 3. No medal.

"It's difficult not coming out of here with a medal," said USA pitcher Jeff Alkire. "We had a dream and it was to come out a winner. Our goal definitely was to win the gold medal and that just didn't work out."

> **Baseball may be America's favorite pastime, but it's the national sport of Cuba, which fielded its own "Dream Team."**

The loss also sent Fraser, the head coach at the University of Miami for the past 32 years, into retirement.

"It hasn't really settled in yet that this will be the last game," Fraser noted at the conclusion of the Olympics. "I've been with amateur and international baseball for 30-35 years and the most exciting time for me was when they announced baseball would be a full-medal Olympic sport. Looking down the road I think it's going to be an exciting time for amateur baseball in the USA in the coming years."

Excitement that will culminate in Atlanta in 1996 with Cuba looking to defend its gold. And a USA Team that will see if a home country advantage will yield a first-ever Olympic baseball medal. ❖ **BOB BENSCH**

BASKETBALL
A majestic team

From the start they were penciled in as the 1992 Olympic gold medalist team. The media, the opponents, and fans of basketball all agreed that this team would be unbeatable.

And it was.

Cruising through the Olympic qualifying tournament with an unblemished 6-0 record, the USA Olympic men's basketball team later strolled almost as easily past its Olympic opponents en route to an 8-0 record and the Olympic gold medal.

Featuring basketball's best of the best, the U.S. men were never challenged as a new era of international basketball made its debut. International rules, which had previously prevented NBA players from being eligible for the Olympic Games and other major international basketball competitions, were changed by the FIBA (International Basketball Federation) membership on April 7, 1989, by virtue of a 56-13 vote in favor of "open competition." With the rule change, USA Basketball set forth on its mission of assembling the best possible team.

And what a team USA Basketball assembled!

First, then-Detroit Pistons head coach Chuck Daly, who had led the Pistons to back-to-back NBA world championships in 1989 and 1990, was selected to coach this historic team. Later, Seton Hall University head hoop mentor P.J. Carlesimo, Duke University head coach Mike Krzyzewski and NBA Cleveland Cavaliers head coach Lenny Wilkens were named as Daly's assistant coaches.

On September 21, 1991, the first 10 members of the "Dream Team" were announced. They included some of basketball's greatest legends. Larry Bird, Earvin "Magic" Johnson and Michael Jordan were among the 10, so were Charles Barkley, Patrick Ewing, Karl Malone, Chris Mullin, Scottie Pippen, David Robinson, and John Stockton. Portland's Clyde "the Glide" Drexler and Duke University's Christian Laettner, the 1992 college player of the year, were later named to fill the team's final two roster positions.

Beginning its training and gold-medal quest on June 22 in La Jolla, Calif., the USA's first challenge came seven days later in Portland, Ore., when the "Dream Team" played its first game in the Basketball Tournament of the Americas. The United States and nine other teams from North, South and Central America partici-

pated in the June 27-July 5 tournament knowing that only the top four finishers would qualify for Barcelona and the Olympic Games.

The USA team hit the Portland Memorial Coliseum court in high gear and never looked back as it breezed past the competition, posting a 6-0 record. How dominating was the U.S. team? The smallest USA margin of victory was 38 points (119-81 versus Puerto Rico), the U.S. club averaged 121.2 points a game, and the USA's average margin of victory for the tournament was an eye-popping 51.5 points.

After a two-week break following the Tournament of the Americas, the U.S. team resumed its training, this time in Monaco (July 19-24). While in Monte Carlo, the U.S. romped past the French National Team, 111-71, in a July 21 exhibition game and tuneup for the Olympics.

At the Olympic Games, the U.S. dominance continued. Opening against Angola, the U.S. squad stomped to a dominating 116-46 victory, sending a crystal-clear message that they were taking no team lightly.

Facing a talented Croatia team a day later, a team expected to battle for a medal, the U.S. dominance was again underscored as the "Dream Team" managed a 33-point win, 103-70. Jordan led the U.S. team with 21 points, while Pippen and teammates limited European and Croatia superstar Toni Kukoc to just four points. But it was not all good news for the USA team. Magic Johnson suffered an injury early in the game that was later diagnosed as a strained muscle in his right knee -- leaving his playing status as day-to-day.

The U.S. team had an easy time with a solid Germany team, next, as the USA rolled to a 111-68 victory. Bird, who had been bothered by a nagging back injury, returned to his All-Star form. Connecting on seven of 11 field goal attempts, Bird score 19 points while Malone chipped in 18 in the win.

While seven "Dream Team" members scored in double digits, Barkley, who dropped 12 of 14 attempts from the field, set a USA

> "When will there be another Olympic team as good as this one? Well, you guys won't be around, and neither will I."
>
> —Magic Johnson

ABOVE / *An attempted block nets results of a different kind.* (ALLSPORT / M. POWELL)

OPPOSITE / *Leading U.S. scorer Charles Barkley, who averaged 18 points a game, puts the freeze on the Angolan defense with a slam dunk. Final score: 116-48.* (ALLSPORT / M. POWELL)

Olympic gold medal-winning team, the American team jumped out to 11-0 and 34-8 leads to quickly put this contest out of reach. The U.S. went on to record an impressive 127-76 win as nine U.S. players scored in double figures. Lithuania would later win the bronze medal.

Facing Croatia in the gold-medal contest, the U.S. again prevailed in the rematch, this time winning by 32 points, 117-85. Jordan led the U.S. in the gold-medal contest with 22 points, while Barkley and Ewing accounted for 17 and 15 points, respectively.

In compiling an unblemished 8-0 record and capturing the Olympic gold medal, the USA team left little doubt that it was one for the record books. Averaging an Olympic record 117.3 points a game in Barcelona, the USA squad won by an average of 43.8 points and the closest any opponent could come was 32 points (117-85 versus Croatia in the gold-medal game). The "Dream Team" shot 57.8 percent from the field as a team and 40.0 percent from three-point distance, while its opponents managed to make just 36.5 percent of their field goal tries and just 30.5 percent of the three-point attempts. The U.S. also recorded a record 239 assists.

Claiming its 10th gold medal in 12 Olympic appearances, the USA Olympic men's basketball overall record is now 93-2 in Olympic competition.

"You will see a team of professionals in the Olympics again," said USA coach Chuck Daly. "But I don't think you'll see another team quite like this. This was a majestic team." ❖ **CRAIG MILLER**

Fond Farewell

JOURNEYING TO BARCELONA with high hopes of earning the United States' third straight Olympic gold medal, the U.S. women fell short of their goal despite an impressive showing but still managed to capture the bronze medal while posting a 4-1 record.

The 1992 USA Olympic women's basketball team was an experienced lot. Vicky Bullett, Cynthia Cooper, Teresa Edwards, Katrina McClain, Suzie McConnell and Teresa Weatherspoon were all repeat Olympians who had been members of the USA's 1988 Olympic squad which earned the gold. Olympic newcomers, but still internationally-seasoned veterans, who rounded out the '92 USA team included Daedra Charles, Clarissa Davis, Medina Dixon, Tammy Jackson, Carolyn Jones, and Vickie Orr. The 1992 squad was coached by Theresa Grentz, who had directed the USA women to gold-medal finishes at the 1990 World Championship and 1990 Goodwill Games, and rounding out the coaching staff were assistants Lin Dunn, Jim Foster and Linda Hargrove.

"Our goal was to try and win the gold medal. We fell a little short, but I am very pleased and very proud of the way our players regrouped and came back. They showed an awful lot of class and an awful lot of pride," USA head coach Theresa Grentz said.

ABOVE / *Legend Larry Bird, who at 35, announced his retirement from basketball a week after the close of the Olympic Games, wrapped up his career in a dream fashion.* (ALLSPORT / M. POWELL)

Olympic single-game scoring record with 30 points as the USA crushed Brazil, 127-83. Closing out its pool play against host Spain, the U.S. scored a convincing 122-81 victory. But more significant to the USA team than its win was the return to action of Johnson, who had missed the two prior games because of his knee injury, and the return of Stockton, who had not played since breaking his right fibula in the second game of the Tournament of the Americas.

Advancing to the quarterfinals, Mullin enhanced his outside shooting reputation by nailing three of five three-point tries and accounting for a team-high 21 points as the USA again won easily against Puerto Rico, 115-77.

Meeting Lithuania in the semifinals, a talent-filled team that featured four of the top six scorers from the Soviet Union's 1988

OPPOSITE / *Plenty of Germans in the vicinity, but none seem too bent on stopping a driving Karl Malone. The "Mailman" delivered as the team's third-leading scorer while sharing the top rebounding honors with Patrick Ewing.* (ALLSPORT / M. POWELL)

Opening the 1992 Olympic basketball competition against Czechoslovakia, the U.S. women's performance was nothing short of totally dominating as the Americans stormed to a 111-55 victory. Cooper led the U.S. charge with 18 points as seven U.S. players scored in double digits. The USA's 111 points were the most ever by a USA team in Olympic competition.

Facing China, a team expected to contend for a medal, two days later, the U.S. exploded in the second half and behind scoring spurts of 18-0 and 22-2 went on to a 93-67 victory. Dixon led the U.S. attack with 19 points and Orr and Davis each added 14.

Rounding out its pool play against host Spain, again the USA's pressure defense and fast-paced offensive attack rolled as the USA scored an impressive 114-59 win. Dixon tallied a USA Olympic team single-game scoring record with 28 points in the win which saw six U.S. players hit for double figures. The USA's 114 points reset the U.S. Olympic scoring record, breaking the mark the '92 team had just set four days earlier.

Advancing to the semifinals, a match with a strong and very experienced Unified Team was ahead for the U.S. women, and a trip to the gold-medal game was the reward for the victor.

Almost from the start the USA team found the game's pace slowed as the former

Soviet squad ran its deliberate offense while sitting back defensively in a zone.

At halftime the U.S. trailed 47-41, and early in the second half the U.S. lagged behind by 11 points at 54-43. Rallying, the U.S. outscored the Unified Team 13-2 over 3:36 to take a narrow 57-55 lead with 12:39 to play. The game continued to seesaw back and forth and was tied 67-67 with 5:25 remaining, but a 6-0 scoring spurt earned the Unified Team a 73-67 advantage and eventually the 79-73 victory. Cold shooting doomed the U.S. as the Americans shot just 35.8 percent (29-81 FGs) from the field and just 52.6 percent (10-19 FTs) from the foul stripe. Dixon finished the contest with 12 points and Edwards contributed 11.

With China's surprising 109-70 upset of previously unbeaten Cuba in the other semifinal contest, the USA women had the unenviable task of facing Cuba in the bronze-medal game.

Remaining true to the two teams' track record, the USA-Cuba matchup was a tight affair. Tied 44-44 at halftime, Cuba edged out to a 59-54 lead in the second half and led 63-60 with 11:07 remaining. However, the USA's pressure defense began to pay dividends and its running game came to life and the result was a 12-4 U.S. run that lifted the Americans to a 72-67 lead with 6:26 to play. Leading 75-71 with 5:31 to go, the U.S. closed out the game with

TOP / *An injured John Stockon got little time to show the driving force he is on the court.* (ALLSPORT / CANNON)

MIDDLE / *Magic moment. Gold medalist and captain of the Dream Team Magic Johnson congratulates a member of the Lithuanian team. Lithuania beat the Unified Team for the bronze.* (ALLSPORT / M. POWELL)

BOTTOM / *Christian Laettner, the sole collegian on the team, got a taste of NBA-style basketball.* (ALLSPORT / M. POWELL)

OPPOSITE: *Snapshots of the Dream Team…David Robinson shoots* **(TOP LEFT)**, *Clyde "the Glide" Drexler* **(TOP RIGHT)** *makes a slick pass, Patrick Ewing* **(BOTTOM LEFT)** *provides a towering defense* (ALLSPORT / GRAY MORTIMORE) *and Michael Jordan* **(BOTTOM RIGHT)**, *well Jordan, is certainly not about to turn the ball over to Drazen Petrovic of Croatia. Then there's the bench* **(CENTER)** *where there was no end in talent as the Americans put together the greatest team ever.* (ALLSPORT / M. POWELL)

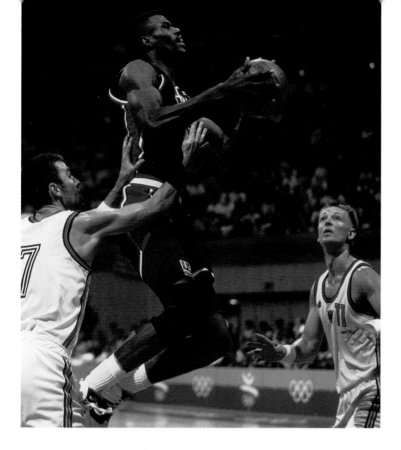

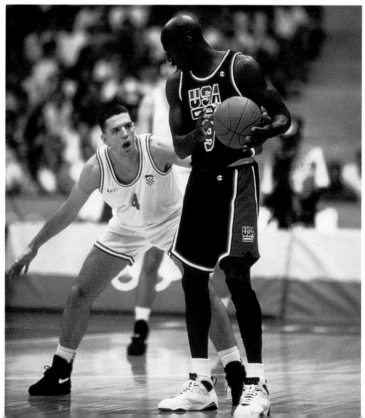

a 13-3 spurt to earn an 88-74 victory and the Olympic bronze medal. Edwards, the USA's first male or female to play in three Olympic basketball competitions, possibly finished her storied Olympic career as the USA's high scorer with 18 points, Davis added 14 points and McClain recorded 13 points and 12 rebounds. In the gold-medal game, the Unified Team edged China 77-66.

"I'm happy to be going home with what we're going home with (the bronze medal)," Edwards said. "It's a closeout (of my Olympic career). I looked at the whole game as the last one. I took all the cheers as my last cheers for the USA, and I tried to enjoy it as much as I possibly could." ❖ **BILL HANCOCK**

ABOVE / *Before the game, USA coach Theresa Grentz said speed and quickness would be the key in the game against the Czechs. Cynthia Cooper, a six-year veteran of international play and returning Olympian, put her coach's words into action.* (ALLSPORT / M. POWELL)

LEFT / *Early in her career, Katrina McClain, 26, took some hard knocks on the court before she learned to stand up for herself. But the hardest knock of all had to be the loss against the Unified Team, 79-73, which knocked the Americans out of the gold-medal game.* (ALLSPORT / DUFFY)

ABOVE / *Tammy Jackson (in blue) is a seasoned player of international basketball, having played in Sweden, Spain, Italy and Japan. But for the 6-3 Florida native, it was her first trip to the Olympic Games.* (ALLSPORT / DUFFY)

ABOVE / *Three-time Olympian Teresa Edwards drives in for the basket. Reminiscent of their counterpart, the Dream Team, the American women beat Czechoslovakia by a healthy margin of 56 points.* (ALLSPORT / M. POWELL)

BOXING
Facing up to tough times

The confused expressions on the faces of U.S. boxers Oscar de la Hoya and Eric Griffin minutes after their final bouts were remarkably similar in light of the starkly different situations.

Both faces, however, were equally telling of the 1992 U.S. Olympic Boxing Team's experiences in Barcelona that yielded three medals — one gold, one silver and one bronze.

It was a considerably more modest medal haul than had been anticipated for the country that dominated the previous Olympics in Seoul, when the U.S. won a total of eight medals. But there was one major difference between Seoul and Barcelona: Cuba. Boxers from a Cuban team that had been noticeably absent in Seoul when Cuba boycotted the Games, won a total of nine medals, seven golds and two silvers — far in front of Germany's four medals, two of them gold, and the U.S.'s medal cache of three.

For De La Hoya, the youngest of the 12 U.S. boxers at 19 years old, the look of confusion followed his 12-7 win over world champion Marco Rudolph of Germany in the finals of the lightweight division.

With the win, De La Hoya avenged his only international defeat — a first-round loss to Rudolph at the 1991 World Championships — and captured the United States' lone gold medal in Barcelona. More importantly, he finally fulfilled a two-year personal promise to his deceased mother, Cecelia.

Since his mother's death from breast cancer in 1990, De La Hoya had pledged to win the Olympic gold medal and return it to her gravesite in an East Los Angeles cemetery.

As the pressures mounted on him to fulfill the promise, De La Hoya's training regimen and competitive desire to win became even more focused. Following each of his four wins en route to the gold-medal match, De La Hoya dropped to one knee and blew his customary kiss to the heavens in memory of his mother.

But all of the dreaming and training could not prepare De La Hoya for that unfamiliar and somewhat confusing moment when the decision in the gold-medal match was announced. In an instant, De La Hoya was overcome by "a feeling that the weight of the world had suddenly lifted from my shoulders."

For four-time world champion and U.S. team co-captain Eric Griffin of Broussard, La., the U.S. team's smallest member (5-3, 106 pounds) and biggest inspiration, the look of confusion followed the announcement of a stunning and controversial 6-5 decision for Spain's Rafael Lozano in the second round of competition.

The decision not only cast a look of confusion on Griffin's face,

RIGHT / *"Watching for the left": Chris Byrd's slick slipping-and-counterpunching style couldn't escape the hard-punching Ariel Hernandez of Cuba, who won the gold in the middleweight division.* (ALLSPORT / M. POWELL)

RIGHT / *Mission accomplished. Oscar de la Hoya kept a promise to his mother when he outboxed world amateur lightweight champion Marco Rudolph of Germany, 12-7, to win the gold.* (ALLSPORT / M. POWELL)

OPPOSITE / *Wayne McCullough lands a solid punch in the face of Joel Casamayor of Cuba. In the end, the fighting Irishman suffered the biggest blow: he lost the gold to the Cuban bantamweight. Still, Ireland went home with two boxing medals, one of them gold.* (ALLSPORT / M. POWELL)

OSCAR DE LA HOYA

FOR HIS MOTHER

BY SHARON ROBB

Oscar de la Hoya buried his mother two years ago with a promise.

The highly-touted 19-year-old boxer from East Los Angeles dedicated the winning of the gold medal at 132 pounds to his mother Cecelia, who died of breast cancer in 1990 at the age of 39.

Near her death, she made her son promise that he would fulfill his Olympic dream for her.

Leading up to the Olympic Games, De La Hoya did most of his roadwork around Resurrection Cemetary where his mother was buried.

The first place he visited when he got home was his mother's grave. He bought armfuls of flowers and arranged them around her grave. He put the gold medal on her headstone as if hanging it around her neck. He stayed there for hours praying.

She helped him out by looking over him, the soft-spoken De La Hoya said.

Known as a bruising puncher with power in both hands, De La Hoya jabbed his way to victories at the U. S. Olympic Trials, boxoffs and finally the Olympic Games. Cecelia de la Hoya's dream came alive when he knocked off Germany's world champion Marco Rudolph, 12-7, with a decisive third round that included a knockdown 50 seconds into it.

The judges scored the bout a tie after one round and had De La Hoya ahead, 3-2, after two rounds. But there was little doubt about the third round as De La Hoya showed why he had been considered perhaps the most promising American fighter among the 12 who entered this Olympic tournament.

"Mission accomplished," De La Hoya said after winning, waving a U.S. flag and the flag of Mexico, the birthplace of his parents. De La Hoya said he didn't cry on the victory stand because he was so happy and he knew his mother would have wanted him to be happy. "But, later on, it hit me that she wasn't here to hug me and that was sad," he said.

Fighting primarily with his left hand, the gold medal victory avenged the only international blemish on his record in five years — a 17-13 loss to Rudolph at the 1991 World Championships. De La Hoya explained his reliance on the left to an injured right thumb suffered during an early round fight.

He said the combination of his mission for his mother and an eagerness to fight quality opponents had him primed for the Olympic Games. ◆

but also on the faces of U.S. boxing officials, who immediately lodged an official protest with the International Amateur Boxing Association (AIBA).

The protest centered around, among other points, the fact that Griffin had won on all five judges' individual scorecards, but had failed to receive the decision under the combined score calculated by the electronic scoring system.

The electronic scoring system, which registers only those scoring blows recorded by a majority of five judges within a one-second interval, was making its Olympic debut and had been the subject of much scrutiny for the surprisingly low scores reported.

The U.S. protest, which marked the first official protest of a decision rendered under electronic scoring, was rejected by two AIBA deliberative bodies.

The emotional shockwaves of the Griffin decision could be felt in two subsequent U.S. losses by bantamweight Sergio Reyes of the U.S. Marines, stationed at Camp Lejeune, N.C., and welterweight Pepe Reilly of Glendale, Calif., in second-round action later that day.

But, with U.S. ring confidence waning, middleweight Chris Byrd of Flint, Mich., the son of U.S. team head coach Joe Byrd,

Boxing, by nature, seems to attract controversy. In Seoul, the flap revolved around judges playing favorites. In Barcelona, computerized scoring was supposed to eliminate biased judging. But questionable results only spelled more scrutiny for the system.

became a spark for U.S. optimism.

Not a heavy medal favorite entering the Olympics, Byrd dazzled the crowd and baffled opponents with a slick slipping-and-counterpunching style that landed him in the finals with Cuba's Ariel Hernandez. In the finals, the hard-punching Hernandez bested the elusive Byrd, who earned the silver medal.

Flyweight Timothy Austin, a hard-throwing southpaw from the rough-and-tumble Over-the-Rhine section of East Cincinnati, Ohio, had seen the strong U.S. start in the Olympic competition fade to disappointment before he had the opportunity to take to the ring for the first time. The beneficiary of a first-round bye, Austin was forced to wait until the competition's eighth day before making his Olympic debut.

Austin answered the belated call with two wins to advance to a semifinal matchup with Cuba's Raul Gonzales. In the bout with Gonzales, Austin sustained an injury to his left eye early in the first round that prompted the referee to stop the match. Austin settled for the bronze medal.

The U.S. entries in the two heaviest weight classes — heavyweight (201 pounds) and super heavyweight (+201 pounds) —

advanced to the quarterfinals, where they were bested by Cuban opponents that went on to win gold medals in their respective divisions.

U.S. super heavyweight Larry Donald of Cincinnati, Ohio, a poetic, self-proclaimed protege of Muhammad Ali, fell short in his quest for Olympic gold by losing a 10-4 quarterfinal decision to two-time world champion and eventual gold medalist Roberto Balado of Cuba. In addition to the Olympic title, Balado was named the recipient of the Val Barker Cup, an award given to the tournament's outstanding boxer.

U.S. heavyweight Danell Nicholson of Chicago, Ill., came within one round of pulling off one of the greatest upsets in Olympic boxing history in his quarterfinal matchup with five-time world champion Felix Savon of Cuba. While Savon won the final round of the bout to avert the upset, the 13-11 decision would be his narrowest margin of victory in his march to the gold medal.

Another American, Montell Griffin of Chicago, Ill., proved to be undaunted by a world champion when he faced Torsten May of Germany in the quarterfinals of the light heavyweight division.

Griffin, battling an eight-inch height disadvantage, led the bout until the final seconds of the third round, when he was administered a controversial three-point penalty for ducking his head. The infraction cost Griffin the 6-4 decision, and May went on to win the gold medal.

The only other American to advance to the quarterfinal round, light middleweight Raul Marquez of Houston, Texas, appeared poised to fulfill many observers' pre-Olympic medal predictions before being upset by Orhan Delibas of The Netherlands, 16-12.

Featherweight Julian Wheeler of the U.S. Navy, stationed at Little Creek, Va., and light welterweight Vernon Forrest of Augusta, Ga., attending Northern Michigan University, saw their Olympic dreams dashed through decision losses in the preliminary rounds of the competition.

Cuba's domination was thorough. In 12 gold medal bouts, nine Cubans were involved. In those bouts, only Su Choi-Choi of North Korea at 112 pounds and Michael Currath of Ireland at 148 pounds were able to stop their Cuban opponents. In addition to Su, Currath and De La Hoya, other non-Cuban gold medalists were a pair of Germans, May at 179 pounds and Andreas Tews at 126 pounds.   ❖   **JAY MILLER**

RIGHT / *Nineteen-year-old Oscar de la Hoya brought home the only gold for the U.S. It was the poorest Olympic showing for U.S. boxers in 26 years, who came home with a total of three medals.*
(ALLSPORT / M. POWELL)

CANOE • KAYAK
Chasing the impossible dream

In practice each day, the double canoe combination of Joe Jacobi and Scott Strausbaugh stole a page from Don Quixote de la Mancha, the fabled knight errant of Cervantes' writings. Instead of tilting at windmills, though, they pursued a more ephemeral foe: an imaginary boat.

The imaginary boat was a device used by Olympic assistant coach Fritz Haller as the impossible standard, one which they could chase but never catch. That all ended on the boiling whitewater of the 1992 Olympic Games course in La Seu d'Urgell.

"We caught the imaginary boat," Haller told the newly-crowned Olympic champions, gold medals gleaming on their chests, after Jacobi and

Strausbaugh had, indeed, reached the unreachable star.

"We definitely weren't the favorites," Strausbaugh said. "We came into this race feeling there were five to eight boats we knew could win. We knew if we went out there and had the best race we knew we were capable of, if we achieved that goal, we would be in the medals. We never dreamed of a gold."

The duo blistered the 25-gate course for the fastest raw time and no penalty points on their first run. However, they were concerned while waiting for their second and final stab at Olympic greatness.

"Fritz came into the tent and said 'That's a great first run, now let's get to business,'" Jacobi said. "Look at how

ABOVE / *A stunning sunset bathes this lone canoeist at the end of a practice day on the Castelldefels Olympic Canal where the flatwater sprint races were held.* (ALLSPORT / RONDEAU)

INSET / *Practice makes perfect: stroking in sync.* (ALLSPORT / HEWITT)

OPPOSITE / *It was a long wait for Jon Lugbill and a disappointing one for the man who is a five-time whitewater canoe world champion. Whitewater slalom vanished from the Olympic program after a one-time appearance in 1972. Lugbill was a favorite coming into the reinstated competition but finished a disheartening fourth.* (ALLSPORT / VANDYSTADT)

They came in as the underdogs and left with the gold. Joe Jacobi and Scott Strausbaugh produced a clean, fast second run of 2:02.41 to snatch the gold in front of Czechoslovakia and France. (ALLSPORT / VANDYSTADT)

ABOVE / *Flatwater kayaker Greg Barton, a double gold medalist in Seoul, proved he still has what it takes to medal — he added a bronze to his collection.* (DUOMO / RICK RICKMAN)

ABOVE / *The whitewater course at La Seu d'Urgell provided an adventure-packed venue for spectators as Czech Lukas Pollert negotiates the course to win the gold in the singles canoe slalom event.* (ALLSPORT / RONDEAU)

our guys were sitting after the first run yesterday. He said 'I'm determined to not let that happen again today.'"

What Haller alluded to was the first-run results of the men's single canoe and women's single kayak races. Favorite Jon Lugbill stood in second after one run, only to be knocked out of the medals by faster paddlers on the second go-around. Dana Chladek was first in the women's race, but slipped to the bronze medal after two paddlers passed her in the final.

"The first thing Fritz said was 'We've got a lot of work to do,'" Strausbaugh said. "He didn't let us sit on that one run in the bank. He made it clear that that was a good first run, now let's go out and improve it."

And improve it they did, shaving two more seconds off their previous time. Then came the greatest challenge of all: keeping their emotions under a tight rein as challenger after challenger flew down the course. When the final boat became caught in the swirling waters near the end of the run and lost precious seconds, the celebration began. The Americans had the gold, relegating Miroslav Simek and Jiri Rohan of Czechoslovakia to second place and Franck Addison and Wilfrid Forgues of France to third place.

It was the high point in a canoeing competition which left

> **"We definitely weren't the favorites," Scott Strausbaugh said. "We knew if we went out there and had the best race we knew we were capable of, if we achieved that goal, we would be in the medals. We never dreamed of a gold."**

Americans with mixed emotions. The gold of Jacobi and Strausbaugh and the bronzes won by Chladek and by Greg Barton in flatwater sprint gave the U.S. three medals in canoeing, its best showing since the 1948 London Olympic Games. However, fractions of a second separated U.S. paddlers from an even greater haul as experienced paddlers from Germany, France, Hungary, Bulgaria, Sweden and France continually mounted the medals podiums.

In whitewater, a feather-light gate touch committed by Lugbill cost him five precious seconds in penalties on his first run. The ever-so-slight rub of the gate pole against fabric moved the 12-time world champion from first to sitting maddeningly close but out of the medals.

"My first run was seven one-hundredths of a second faster than (gold medalist Lukas) Pollert," Lugbill said. "If I hadn't touched that gate, it might have been a different game."

In men's single kayak, Rich Weiss was called for a gate touch which cost him the bronze medal. For Weiss, it was the worst kind of deja vu. At the 1989 World Championships, he was called for a gate touch which also knocked him out of the bronze medal.

The flatwater sprint team also suffered from tantalizingly close-but-no-cigar races. The most snakebitten of the team was Norman

Bellingham. A Seoul gold medalist in the men's double kayak 1,000-meter event with Barton, Bellingham was hoping to establish himself as the fastest paddler in the world by winning the single 500-meter event. All signs pointed in that direction, as he dominated his preliminary heats. When it came to the final, though, an unfortunate lane draw left him struggling to assess the field during the race.

"It was a bit of a disadvantage," said Bellingham of his lane one starting position, "because I didn't know where the competition was. I had to gauge my whole race off (Norway's Knut) Holmann for the most part because I couldn't look past him. I had to gauge my race on how he was going, assuming he was going to take the lead. I didn't realize I was going after third place, but that's sport."

Bellingham's heartache was compounded just 25 hours later in the doubles 1,000, as he and Barton, who announced his retirement from Olympic competition, attempted to become the only team to successfully defend an Olympic gold in the event. That dream was not to be, though, as again the result was a fourth-place finish, again maddeningly close but not quite. Teams from Germany, Sweden and Poland claimed the medals.

"I just put everything I had, just cranking behind Greg," Bellingham said. "I thought we'd be in the race more than we were. I felt strong out there. I pretty much blacked out at the end. I'm surprised we weren't in there."

Although the medal return wasn't what the U.S. had hoped for out of the flatwater competition, the signs of how far America has come in Olympic canoeing were evident. The United States was the only country to place all five of its men's kayak boats in the finals, including the four-man kayak, which made its first trip to the start line in an Olympic final. All told, the United States put six boats in the final — the five men's kayaks and the four-woman kayak — and every U.S. boat advanced to the semifinals before being eliminated. ❖ **CRAIG BOHNERT**

ABOVE / *In the doubles kayak flatwater 500-meter final, it was the German duo of Ramona Portwich and Anke Von Seck who turned in the best time of 1:40.29.* (ALLSPORT / HEWITT)

CYCLING
Waiting game pays off for Twigg, Hartwell

Perhaps nowhere in the 1992 Olympic Games was the breakup of the former Soviet Union and East Germany sports machines more evident than in cycling. In the past, USSR- and GDR-produced cyclists tended to dominate the world. The most recent example prior to Barcelona being the 1988 Games in Seoul, when, of 27 medals awarded, 13 were awarded to Soviet or East German riders.

Not this time. With 30 medals on the line in the velodrome and on the road, no less than 14 nations lined up to claim them. Germany — now combined — led with six, followed by Australia with five, the Netherlands with four, Italy with three and — to round out the multiple winners — the United States and France with two each.

Kathryn Watt of Australia, with a gold in the individual road race and a silver in the 3,000-meter individual pursuit, and Jens Lehmann of Germany, with a team pursuit gold and a silver in the individual pursuit, were the only individual multiple-medal winners. As the competition unfolded, the Unified Team of former Soviet states failed to medal while the now independent, ex-USSR republics of Latvia and Estonia claimed one medal apiece.

For the U.S. medalists — Erin Hartwell and Rebecca Twigg each with a bronze — the Games of Barcelona were as nerve-wracking as they were rewarding. In the case of each, they posted their times early and then had to be patient and watch as subsequent racers tried to take them out of the medal standings.

Hartwell had dreamed of being an Olympian his entire life. Originally, he thought his path would be through track and field, specifically the pole vault, until he suffered an injury in high school. Cycling was a form of rehabilitation, but he quickly excelled, winning his first national title in 1989. A year later, he moved to the Colorado Springs Olympic Training Center to train exclusively for the 1992 Games.

Twigg, one of cycling's most recognized names as a four-time world champion and 1984 Olympic bronze medalist in the road race, was coming back from retirement. A training accident in 1987 and her failure to make the 1988 Olympic Team resulted in her leaving the competitive sports world to become a computer programmer. But the addition of the women's individual pursuit event to the 1992 Olympic program made her change her mind.

For Hartwell, the kilometer time trial is a grueling event. It is man against the clock. Hartwell posted his fastest time ever at sea-level, clocking a 1:04.753. Australia's Shane Kelly was the only cyclist in front of him, but Hartwell had to wait for seven other riders

to complete their four-lap attempts.

The 1988 Olympic gold medalist, Aleksandr Kirichenko of the Unified Team, did not surpass him. The 1991 Pan American Games champion, Gene Samuel of Trinidad, did not beat him. And two-time world champion, Jens Gluecklich of Germany, fell .04 seconds short, assuring Hartwell of a medal.

INSET / *A blur of color races through the Spanish countryside.* (ALLSPORT / COLE)

ABOVE / *Bronze medalist Erin Hartwell openly admits he does not like training for his event — the one-kilometer time trial — a grueling, one-minute race that exhausts the body and saps the mind.* (ALLSPORT / MORTIMORE)

OPPOSITE / *The Germans came out like gangbusters and stole the team 100-kilometer competition in 4:08.791, 1.427 seconds ahead of the Aussies.* (ALLSPORT / VANDYSTADT)

TOP / A little encouragement always pays off: Rebecca Twigg grabs the bronze in the women's 3,000-meter individual pursuit. When the event was officially added to the Olympic program in 1991, Twigg came out of a three-year retirement to compete in her favorite event. (ALLSPORT / BRUTY)

ABOVE / A rider falls in the women's individual match sprint. The race was won by Erika Salumae of Estonia. (ALLSPORT / VANDYSTADT)

TOP / Jose Moreno's one minute of glory on the track gave Spain its first gold medal of the Games and Moreno a place in his country's history. Moreno won the one-kilometer time trial in 1:03.342. (ALLSPORT / MORTIMORE)

ABOVE / Jeannie Longo-Ciprelli has the lead in the women's road race but loses it and the gold to Kathryn Watt of Australia. (ALLSPORT / VANDYSTADT)

OPPOSITE (ABOVE) / Fabio Casartelli of Italy holds onto the lead in the men's road race. (ALLSPORT / VANDYSTADT)

(INSET) / The velodrome track action in fast motion. (ALLSPORT / VANDYSTADT)

Of the remaining riders, only Spain's Jose Moreno could break into the top three. He did so with style, winning Spain's first gold medal of the 1992 Games and dropping Hartwell back to third place. "Still, I couldn't have felt better," Hartwell said. "Everything went really as I would have liked. I got third and I've never been happier in my life."

Twigg faced a star-studded field in the individual pursuit with eight-time world champion Jeannie Longo-Ciprelli of France, 1991 world pursuit champion Petra Rossner of Germany, and Australia's Watt.

Twigg met Longo in the quarterfinals, a matchup that might have been better suited for the finals. The duo had been rivals many years, each being four-time world champions in the individual pursuit. Twigg led for most of the race and then held off Longo's last lap charge by .39 seconds.

The semifinals would be the most important — and fateful — race for Twigg where she faced Watt, who beat Twigg and advanced to the finals with a 3:49.790 clocking. But Twigg's time of 3:52.429 was good enough for the bronze medal when compared against the time of the other semifinal loser, Hanne Malmberg of the Netherlands at 3:53.516. Rossner went on to defeat Watt for the gold medal and Twigg was third.

"I just took it one step at a time," Twigg said. "When I got to the Olympics, I saw how fast everyone was going and I had to change my goals a little bit and hope for any kind of a medal, especially knowing I did not have the last four years of training to help my recovery from ride to ride."

The two bronze medals by the U.S. cycling team were an improvement over 1988 when Connie Paraskevin-Young brought the team its only medal, a bronze in the women's match sprint.

But the U.S. had another highlight performance in the match sprints by Ken Carpenter. He finished fifth in the event that was won by Germany's Jens Fiedler. Carpenter's counterpart in the women's match sprint, Paraskevin-Young, was eliminated in the quarterfinals. But one of her training partners, Erika Salumae of Estonia, won the gold medal.

Fabio Casartelli of Italy won the men's individual road race while Watt took the women's crown. Jeanne Golay and Lance Armstrong were the top finishers for the Americans as Golay was sixth and Armstrong took 14th. Gold medals went to Germany which won the team 100-kilometer time trial while the U.S. team took 16th. The Germans also took top honors in the 4,000-meter team pursuit while the Americans claimed ninth. Great Britain's Chris Boardman won the 4,000-meter individual pursuit. The top U.S. performer was Carl Sundquist in 12th. The United States did not qualify for the final in the men's point race which was won by Italy's Giovanni Lombardi. ❖   **STEVE PENNY**

DIVING
Taking a golden plunge

Overlooking Barcelona, the beautiful Piscina de Montjuic diving arena may have qualified as the most scenic venue in Olympic history. And the competition was as spectacular as the view as divers from the United States, China and the Unified Team jostled for world supremacy.

In the end, the United States managed to come up with an heir to Greg Louganis in Mark Lenzi, who took the gold medal in men's springboard ahead of Tan Liangde of China, a silver medalist two Games in a

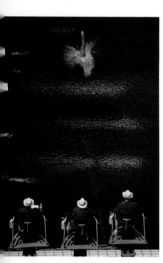

China, with five medals, surpassed both the U.S. and the Unified Team, with three medals each in diving.

row. But in the overall medal standings, the Chinese, with five medals, surpassed both the U.S. and the Unified Team, with three medals each.

Chinese divers won three of the four gold medals, while Lenzi of the U.S. broke through on the springboard to prevent a Chinese sweep. In overall depth, the Americans were the winners, qualifying two divers into the finals in every event.

The USA got off to a strong start with a bronze medal in women's platform. Mary Ellen Clark, 29, of Fort Lauderdale, Fla., put together a solid list of dives to fulfill a long-time dream of winning an Olympic medal. China's 13-year-old Fu Mingxia won the gold, and the Unified Team's Elena Mirochina claimed the silver.

"I have a lot of experience after diving for 22 years," said Clark after the final. "I always set so many goals for myself, but I did not come here saying I wanted a medal. I just wanted to dive well."

Dive well she did. With the exception of her seventh dive, Clark consistently received 7's, 8's and 9's. She was among the leaders the entire way in a close contest and finished just 1.35 points ahead of China's Zhu Jinghong. Less than 20 points separated second through

ABOVE / *The judges, with the best seats in the house, most likely had to block out their own distractions — namely the highly-touted view from the Montjuic pool — and keep their focus on the divers.* (ALLSPORT / VANDYSTADT)

seventh place.

In seventh was the USA's other entrant, Ellen Owen, 29, of Belleuve, Wash. Owen was in the medal hunt through five rounds as she stood seven points out of second place. She hung tough throughout, but could not move up in the standings. Her performance was highlighted by an inward 1 1/2 pike that drew five 9's and two 8.5's.

Lenzi prevents a Chinese sweep of golds

AMERICAN MEDAL HOPES were high in men's springboard with 1991 World Cup champion Lenzi and 1991 World Championships and Pan American Games gold medalist Kent Ferguson. China's Tan Liangde, a two-time Olympic silver medalist, was viewed as the biggest obstacle to a U.S. gold medal.

Lenzi, of Fredericksburg, Va., qualified second for the finals, and Ferguson, battling a case of nerves, qualified 12th. In the finals, Lenzi took the lead from Tan in the seventh round and never relinquished. He received straight 9's on his forward 3 1/2 somersault pike in the

ABOVE / *Thirteen-year-old diving sensation Fu Mingxia of China easily grabbed the gold, and then grabbed Cobi, the Games' cuddly mascot, to make the victory rounds. Elena Mirochina of the Unified Team and American Mary Ellen Clark (left) won the silver and the bronze, respectively.* (ALLSPORT / AOKI)

OPPOSITE / *Battling a shoulder injury, a meditative Gao Min temporarily lets go of the pain to garner the gold in women's springboard. Gao, who has not lost an international competition since 1986, helped China lay claim to three of the four diving golds in Barcelona.* (ALLSPORT / MARTIN)

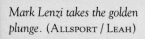

Mark Lenzi takes the golden
plunge. (ALLSPORT / LEAH)

MARK LENZI

Star-Spangled Diver

BY SHARON ROBB

Six years after going against his father's wishes by telling him he was giving up wrestling to become a diver like Greg Louganis, Mark Lenzi followed in his idol's footsteps by winning the Olympic gold medal in the three-meter springboard.

Born on the Fourth of July, the 24-year-old Lenzi, the star-spangled son of a physicist from Fredericksburg, Va., got the gold and proved there is life for American divers after Louganis.

Lenzi said that he dreamed about his gold-medal moment even before he started to dive. "I wanted to win the Olympics no matter what," Lenzi said.

So begins a new era while continuing the U.S. domination in men's springboard that dates back to 1908. Not counting 1980 when the U.S. did not participate in the Games, the U.S. has won 15 of the last 16 Olympic springboard titles.

Lenzi had to move out of the house for a few weeks after he turned down a college wrestling scholarship and told his father he wanted to be a diver. That was two years after Lenzi watched Louganis win a gold medal at the 1984 Olympic Games in Los Angeles.

After a two-week stay with a neighbor, Lenzi returned home more determined than ever. And somehow, in a city without a pool, Lenzi commuted to Washington, D.C., and improved enough to earn a scholarship to Indiana University.

Lenzi had his share of hard times before his first Olympic Games. Less than two years ago, Lenzi was competing and called his father for $200 when the hotel wouldn't accept his American Express credit card. To help underwrite his son's training expenses, Bill Lenzi wrote to 13 millionaires in Virginia asking for help. None replied. The Lenzis managed to get by.

Dad and mom beamed with pride at the pool in Barcelona where their son's dives drew loud cheers. Both Bill and Ellie Lenzi wore shirts bearing his name. And Bill rushed to his son's post-victory news conference to give his son a bearhug.

"Sometimes parents don't always know what's best for their kids. He proved me wrong," his father said. ◆

ninth round, then went on to win the gold by nearly 31 points over Tan. The Unified Team's Dmitry Sautin won the bronze.

After the medal ceremony, Lenzi, who had turned 24 on the Fourth of July said: "I'm very patriotic...I love my country. I dreamed of this moment even before I started diving. I always wondered what this moment would be like, now I know."

Ferguson, 29, of Fort Lauderdale, Fla., rebounded in the finals to be in contention for the bronze. He trailed Sautin by five points with two dives remaining after getting 7's and 8's on his inward 2 1/2 somersault pike. Mostly 8's on the final two dives by Sautin and Australia's Michael Murphy, however, left Ferguson in fifth place.

Golden Gao

AFTER TWO OFF DAYS, diving resumed with women's springboard. Americans Julie Ovenhouse, 23, of Howell, Mich., and Karen LaFace, 26, of Fort Lauderdale, Fla., were up against stiff competition. China's Gao Min, the defending Olympic champion, had won every major international event she entered since 1986.

Ovenhouse started off slow and was 11th after the first five required dives. She began working her way up on her optional dives, and found herself in second place at the end of eight rounds after receiving six 8's and one 7.5 on her reverse 1 1/2 with 2 1/2 twists. A missed back 2 1/2 somersault tuck in the final round ended her medal hopes as she finished fifth.

"I'm proud I went for it on the final dive," Ovenhouse said. "I missed it going for it. If I had missed it not going for it, I would have regretted it. I knew what I needed and I went for it...it just didn't happen."

Gao broke out of a tight contest in the seventh round and never looked back. Mostly 8's and 9's on her final three dives sealed a commanding 54-point victory over Irina Lashko of the Unified Team. Germany's Brita Baldus won the bronze.

LaFace was diving well through six rounds until missing two

consecutive dives and dropping into 12th place. She fought back in the last two rounds with 6's and 7's on her back 1 1/2 with 2 1/2 twists and on her inward 2 1/2 somersault tuck to move up into ninth place.

Donie joins Chinese platform divers

U.S. DIVERS SCOTT DONIE, 23, of Fort Lauderdale, Fla., and Matt Scoggin, 28, of Austin, Texas, entered the men's platform final knowing they had the potential to win medals. It would be no easy task with world champion Sun Shuwei, 1988 Olympic silver medalist Xiong Ni of China, and 1990 Goodwill Games champion Jan Hempel of Germany heading the list of favorites.

Donie scored mostly 8's and 9's on his first six dives, but was fourth behind the two Chinese divers and Hempel. His reverse 3 1/2 tuck in the seventh round propelled him into second place with one 9.5, one 9, three 8.5's and two 8's. He solidified second place on his next two dives and wrapped up the silver medal with 8's on his back 1 1/2 with 3 1/2 twists in the final round. Sun won the gold and Xiong captured the bronze.

"I said I would be pleased with a great performance," Donie said. "This was probably my best performance...it's all I can ask for. The only thing I can think of is that it was meant to be."

Scoggin was also in medal contention before a mishap during his back 3 1/2 somersault tuck in the seventh round. Scoggin's left hand slipped off his left leg while somersaulting in the tuck position, causing him to spin out of control and land flat on his back. The failed dive dropped him to 11th place. Scoggin gallantly completed his final three dives and finished 10th.

In all, the USA proved it was still a force to be reckoned with. Lenzi's gold medal gave the USA 14 of 18 Olympic gold medals in men's springboard, and the number of medal-winning events is now at 64. ❖   **DAVE SHATKOWSKI**

PRECEDING PAGE / *To keep errant and distracting thoughts from popping into his head, Scott Donie popped on his headphones and listened to the Grateful Dead's Bird Song as he climbed the ladder to the 10-meter platform. Then, as graceful as a bird in flight, the 23-year-old American drove a wedge between China's diving powerhouses Sun Shuwei and Xiong Ni to capture the silver.* (ALLSPORT / LEAH)

ABOVE / *Arguably the most picturesque venue in Olympic history, the Piscina de Montjuic scored a perfect 10 with the diving well on the left, the pool for water polo matches on the right and Barcelona in the background.* (ALLSPORT / VANDYSTADT)

American Julie Ovenhouse
is a picture of concen-
tration. In a difficult dive
that is over within seconds,
concentration can make or
break the dive. Ovenhouse
was poised to take a medal
in women's springboard
when, in her final dive, she
thought she felt her hair
graze the board. A mo-
ment of hesitation, a split-
second of confusion added
up to a costly mistake and
a fifth-place finish.
(ALLSPORT / MARTIN)

Mary Ellen Clark turned her back on the odds to grab the bronze in the 10-meter platform final. (Allsport / Duffy)

EQUESTRIAN
The wait is over

Though horses and riders from Germany continued to rule the equestrian world at the Barcelona Games, a pair of bronze medals for the U.S. team represented not only the end of a long wait for the winners, but an indication that European supremacy could be on the decline.

Germany came to the Olympic Games with its version of the "Dream Team," winning two of the three individual medals and winning the team gold as it has at every Olympic Games and World Championships since 1972. The excellence of the German squad though did not diminish the joy of the Americans' bronze-medal effort.

The U.S. equestrian team won two bronze medals at the 1992 Olympic Games in Barcelona, and both medal performances ended long waits for the winners.

The U.S. dressage squad ended a 16-year medal drought when Carol Lavell, Charlotte Bredahl, Robert Dover and Michael Poulin proved to the world that not only can the U.S. develop world-class

> **"We may never be the equal of Germany," conceded American Carol Lavell, "but we're closing the gap." Lavell helped clinch the bronze medal for the U.S. squad and end the 16-year medal drought in dressage.**

dressage horses, but that Americans can also ride them with the skill needed to win an Olympic medal.

"Our medal here in Barcelona is a significant step for dressage in the United States," U.S. Chef d'Equipe Jessica Ransehausen said. "Each of our four riders worked their way to the top, and they've now proven that the U.S. dressage community is capable of succeeding at the highest level."

All of the riders took pride that the bronze-medal team was truly made in America.

"When we won our last medal in Montreal in 1976, we bought three of the horses from Germany and three of the riders had trained extensively in Europe," Poulin said. "This time all four horses were developed in the U.S. and all four riders stayed home to train."

"We may never be the equal of Germany, but we're closing the gap," Lavell said. "The time may not be far off when we can even beat them once or twice."

Also playing the waiting game had been American show jumper

Norman Dello Joio, who won an individual bronze medal in his first Olympic appearance. The 36-year-old Dello Joio had been selected to the 1980 Olympic Team but did not participate due to the boycott. Twelve years later, the 1983 World Cup champion made the most of his first Olympic experience.

"Riders tend to have longer careers than most Olympic athletes," said Dello Joio, who along with Michael Matz, Lisa Jacquin and Anne Kursinski placed fifth in the team show jumping competition. "But because my horse was so inexperienced, I never expected to win a medal."

Most experts considered Dello Joio's horse, Irish, who came to Barcelona still shy of his eighth birthday, too young to handle the challenges of the Olympic courses. However, Dello Joio showed why he has been regarded as one of the world's top riders by carefully

ABOVE / *The grueling individual three-day event on a difficult course eliminated American Todd Trewin riding Sandscript.* (ALLSPORT / COLE)

OPPOSITE / *In equestrian events, the rider and the horse are a team.* (ALLSPORT / MARTIN)

managing his budding star. He brought Irish along from a 12-fault ride over the Games' first course to a total of only 4.75 faults over the two courses in the individual final.

"Norman rode as well as you'll ever see anywhere," U.S. Chef d'Equipe Frank Chapot said. "He got the maximum out of a horse that really didn't appear ready for this level of competition."

Many observers had felt that the three-day event horses on the 1992 U.S. team also weren't ready for the Olympic level of competition. Although eventer J. Michael Plumb was on his record eighth U.S. Olympic Team, his three teammates and all four horses were shy on international experience. Still, led by Jil Walton and her nine-year-old mare Patrona, the U.S. team placed 10th to improve over the 1988 Games when the U.S. recorded no score for failing to complete the cross country course.

"We came here with four young horses and three inexperienced riders," said U.S. Chef d'Equipe Michael Page, referring to Walton, Stephen Bradley and Todd Trewin. "We gained valuable experience in Barcelona which will help our team in the upcoming years."

Although he will be 56 years old when the 1996 Olympic Games are held in Atlanta, Plumb said he expects to be there. "Sure I intend to take part in the next Olympics," said Plumb, who has won six Olympic medals. "We have some talented young horses and riders, and I want to be there when we return to the medal stand."

The next Olympic Games, in Atlanta, will move the Europeans off their continent, which may further help the rest of the world. Of 18 medals awarded in Spain, only four went to non-Europeans — two each for the U.S. and New Zealand — and none were gold medals. ❖ **MARTY BAUMAN**

OPPOSITE / *Who's the last laugh on? A costly fall in three-day event.* (ALLSPORT / VANDYSTADT)

ABOVE / *Jil Walton riding Patrona had the best U.S. showing in the three-day event, helping the U.S. team place 10th in the team competition.* (ALLSPORT / CANNON)

FENCING
Cuba and China foil a European medal sweep

In an Olympic fencing competition dominated as usual by the always-strong Europeans, Michael Lofton of the U.S. team still felt his prayers must have been heard. The 28-year-old New Yorker came home from Barcelona with the best finish among U.S. individual fencers, 21st in men's sabre. The finish was reflective that the last year has been nothing but positive for him.

He finished 12th at one of the World Cup events and then went on to win his first National Championship in 1991. At the 1991 Pan American Games in Havana, Cuba, he won the bronze medal. Lofton kicked off his Olympic Trials season with wins at the first two events, then won his second straight National Championship in 1992.

In Barcelona, Lofton advanced automatically to the direct elimination of 32 with repechage with a record of 3-3 from the qualifying round in a difficult pool. He breezed by eighth-seed Vilmos Szabo of Romania in straight bouts, 5-2, 5-2, then lost 2-5, 5-6 to ninth-seed Ferdinando Meglio of Italy.

In repechage, Lofton then battled Robert Koscielniakowski of Poland, losing 1-5, 6-4, 5-6.

Bence Szabo of Hungary wound up winning the gold medal in men's sabre, followed by Marco Marin of Italy and two-time defending gold medalist Jean-Francois Lamour of France. It would be one of three Hungarian fencing medals and one of two for Szabo, who added a silver medal as part of Hungary's sabre team.

France, with five total medals and two golds, was the most successful fencing nation. The Unified Team also collected five medals, with one gold, while Italy and Germany tied Hungary with three medals each. Only Cuba, with a bronze and a silver, and China, with a silver, took medals home to non-European addresses.

In addition to Lofton, two other U.S. fencers advanced to the top 24 — Robert Cottingham and Robert Marx.

Cottingham, the youngest member of the 1988 Olympic Team who came back in 1992 with valuable experience, finished 24th in the individual sabre event. He lost in repechage to Alexandre Chirchov of the Unified Team, 5-2, 1-5, 3-5.

"As the rounds went on I got better and better," the 26-year-old

Rutgers law student said. "If I had run into somebody not at Chirchov's level, I might have won. Since I had a poor seeding, I had to deal with guns the whole way. I felt confident, I felt good. He (Chirchov) did some unbelievable stuff."

In the men's sabre team competition, the U.S. team of Lofton, Cottingham, Steve Mormando, John Friedberg and five-time Olympian Peter Westbrook finished ninth.

In the men's epee competition, Robert Marx finished better than expected in 24th.

"I lived up to my potential. I didn't die and I didn't get destroyed," Marx said.

Eric Srecki of France won the gold, followed by Pavel Kolobkov of the Unified Team with the silver and France's Jean-Michel Henry with the bronze. The team title went to Germany with Hungary in second and the Unified Team in third.

Caitlin Bilodeaux-Banos battled and lost to Italy's Francesca Bortolozzi, 1-5, 6-4, 2-5, in the women's foil repechage to finish in 29th place, the highest of all U.S. foil fencers. The loss was still a positive for Bilodeaux-Banos.

Italy's Giovanna Trillini won the gold medal, Huifeng Wang of China took the silver, and Tatiana Sadovskaia of the Unified Team won the bronze. Mary Jane O'Neill finished 36th and Molly Sullivan was 39th.

In the women's team foil, Italy won the gold, Germany the silver and Romania the bronze. The USA team of Bilodeaux-Banos, Sullivan, O'Neill, Ann Marsh and Sharon Monplaisir finished ninth.

Four-time Olympian Michael Marx, brother of Robert, finished 36th in the individual men's foil. Pan Am Games bronze medalist Nick Bravin finished 39th, and Zaddick Longenbach was 45th.

The men's team foil title went to Germany, with surprise 1991 World Championships gold medalist Cuba taking the silver and Poland winning the bronze. ❖ **COLLEEN WALKER**

ABOVE / *Said USA's Michael Lofton of his 21st place in the men's sabre: "This is a step in the right direction for '96."* (DUOMO / RICK RICKMAN)

OPPOSITE / *Giovanna Trillini of Italy foiled Wang Huifeng's attempts to swipe the gold in the women's foil competition.* (ALLSPORT / VANDYSTADT)

FIELD HOCKEY
Field of hockey dreams

Nowhere at the 1992 Olympic Games was the homefield advantage better demonstrated than on the artificial turf hockey pitches of Terrassa where the Spanish women waltzed off with the gold medal in a major upset. The field hockey capital of Spain, Terrassa witnessed two different tournaments. Final results in the 12-team men's field were as predictable as nightfall while surprises abounded and were the only sure thing among the eight women's teams. The U.S. did not participate in either the men's or women's tournaments after failing to qualify a team for the Games.

When Australia and Germany faced each other in the men's gold-medal match, it was a confrontation between the two best teams in the hockey world over the past decade. Each had won five Champions Trophies, a World Cup and assorted other titles. In face-to-face competition, Germany, runner-up in the last two Olympic Games, had a slight edge, an edge that made them the favorites in Spain and was confirmed by a 2-1 victory for the Olympic title. Not since Munich in 1972 had Germany won the gold in field hockey.

As for the lads from Down Under, they were relieved in the beginning not to be the tournament favorites. In the end, they were disappointed not to take it all after a thrilling 3-2 victory over Holland in the semifinals. On the other hand, the silver-medal showing was Australia's best finish in the Games.

The two German goals in the finals told a Cinderella story of sorts as the man who produced them shouldn't have been in Barcelona. Michael Hilgers, a second-stringer who was no longer on the team, was preparing to retire from hockey. Then, at the last minute he was recalled to the team to replace an injured player. The rest became history.

With the Australians scoring a goal only in the waning minutes, the issue was never really in doubt as the Germans projected awesome power and control. The bronze-medal game, however, was a different story.

In this match a Pakistan team, that seemed to have lost its heart and desire after a difficult 2-1 overtime loss to Germany in the

semifinals, had little to show through the first 15 minutes of the second half. The Netherlands, however, showed no mercy for the listless Pakistanis, seizing a 2-0 halftime advantage. Led by tournament high-scorer Floris Bovelander, their powerful corner striker, the Dutch seemed in total control. Continually favored to win an Olympic medal in the past, but always denied, the Netherlands must have thought its time had come.

It was not to be for the Dutch when Pakistan, with little more than 20 minutes left in the game, came to life. Seemingly inspired by an artistic goal off the stick of their slick inside forward Shabaz Ahmed, Pakistan scored four unanswered goals and staved off a desperate Dutch rally to win 4-3.

As for the defending champions, Great Britain garnered no more than a sixth-place finish behind the tenacious Spanish team. It was clear that too many players had been lost from the inspired British team that had won it all in Seoul. Besides, no one was going to stop a Spanish team urged on by such madly-partisan crowds.

If the favorites walked home with all the medals in the men's tournament, it was not so with the women. A more fragile event because eight teams competed, there was no margin for error. But the Spanish women simply won game after game by one goal thanks to the brilliant goaltending of Maribel Martinez.

The favorites, defending Olympic title-holder Australia and World Cup champions Holland, didn't make it to the semifinals, while all those that did had to advance to the Games the hard way through qualifying events.

Spain led throughout the finals against a favored German team thanks to an opening goal by Sonia Barrio, and then simply held on to win, 2-1. Germany was pleased with its young team's performance and its significant improvement from a fourth-place finish in 1988.

Great Britain, led by its redheaded forward Jane Sixsmith, the tournament's high scorer, simply applied a great deal of pressure on Korea from the start. In front of a partisan crowd four years ago, Korea was an upset bronze-medal winner. In Barcelona, however, Great Britain downed the Koreans, 3-2, for the bronze. ❖ **ALLAN WOODS**

OPPOSITE / Germany beat England in the semifinals, 2-1, before falling to a surprising Spanish team, 2-1, in the women's gold-medal match. (ALLSPORT / COLE)

ABOVE / Goal achieved. The Germans, the favorite going into the competition, beat England in this match and went on to win the men's gold, 2-1, over a subdued Australian team. (ALLSPORT / RONDEAU)

G Y M N A S T I C S
Cinderella of the Games

Vitaly Scherbo and Tatiana Goutsou of the Unified Team were crowned the king and queen of world gymnastics at the Barcelona Olympics while their respective teams also ruled the world in a meet, that, despite the Unified Team's domination, held out a few consolation prizes for the rest of the world.

For the U.S., the highlights included the first team medal — a bronze by the women — in a non-boycotted Games since 1948, a five-medal haul by Shannon Miller, and a men's horizontal bar gold medal by Trent Dimas.

Elsewhere in the competition, China made its presence felt, with two individual gold medals and a men's team silver medal, and both Henrietta Onodi of Hungary and Andreas Wecker of Germany proved there is still room for talented individuals without strong teams. Onodi won a silver medal in floor exercise and a gold medal in vault while Wecker won three individual men's medals — bronzes on the pommel horse and rings and a silver on the horizontal bar.

The bronze squad

FOR THE U.S. WOMEN, their bronze medal team performance was punctuated by the excellence of Miller, the fall of world champion Kim Zmeskal and the retirement of Bela Karolyi, gymnastic's most visible coach.

Miller performed almost flawlessly, scoring a 79.311 to finish in first place ahead of veteran Svetlana Boguinskaia of the Unified Team. Miller was the only woman to score 9.9's in all four compulsory events. During optionals, she scored 9.9's on vault and bars and 9.8's on beam and floor. Her consistency qualified her for all four individual event finals, an Olympic first for an American woman.

Zmeskal, considered the most consistent gymnast in the world and the favorite to win the all-around gold medal, took an uncharacteristic fall from the balance beam during the compulsories.

"That is the first major mistake she has made in a major competition. My heart aches for her," said her coach and Olympic head coach Bela Karolyi.

Despite her fall, Zmeskal had a chance, albeit a remote one, to rally. In order to qualify for the all-around competition, a gymnast needed to finish in the top 36 with a limit of three gymnasts per country. Four U.S. gymnasts were ahead of Zmeskal, who stood 32nd individually after compulsories: Miller, Betty Okino, Kerri Strug and Dominique Dawes. Only Wendy Bruce trailed Zmeskal.

In the second night of competition, Zmeskal squeaked into the all-around finals, passing teammate Strug by .014 of one point.

"I've never been under so much pressure," Zmeskal said. "I had to come from behind to make the all-around finals. It was a pretty strong effort."

Karolyi, who coached Nadia Comaneci and Mary Lou Retton to Olympic gold, announced his retirement after Barcelona.

"I am 50 years old," Karolyi said. "I have been coaching non-stop for 30 years except for the six months when I first came to the U.S. in 1981. I'm proud to have penetrated into the highest circles of international achievement. I'm very glad. A solid and sturdy system has been built."

The "Now Boys"

AFTER AN ENCOURAGING fifth-place finish at the 1991 World Championships, the men's program seemed headed in the right direction. The U.S. had improved substantially from its embarrassing 11th-place finish (out of 12) at the 1988 Olympic Games in Seoul.

Led by Chris Waller of Mount Prospect, Ill., and Scott Keswick from Las Vegas, Nev., the 1992 team was talented, healthy and

ABOVE / *Vitaly Scherbo of the Unified Team won six golds — the biggest haul for a gymnast in a single Olympics.* (ALLSPORT / VANDYSTADT)

OPPOSITE / *One step at a time. Trent Dimas flew through the air with the greatest of ease to capture the gold on the horizontal bar, the only medal for the U.S. men's team.* (ALLSPORT / COLE)

confident. The Americans even adopted the moniker, "Now Boys."

"We're tired of being compared to the 1984 team. We are here to compete in the present, the now," said Waller before the competition.

"It seems like everybody always says we're in a rebuilding year, or we're a young team that is developing," said 1988 Olympian Dominick Minicucci. "But we are a great gymnastics team."

But the Now Boys probably wished they could have been beamed into another time and place after their sixth-place finish in Barcelona.

Keswick, a UCLA junior and three-time national still rings champion, fell from three apparatus. Teammate Jair Lynch, from Washington, D.C., also fell, then Minicucci. The gymnasts blamed some of their problems on the hard, thin mats that made landings difficult. Lynch said his hamstrings were sore because he was getting used to the different landing surface.

"The mats were slick and when the mat gets slick, you end up falling," Waller said. "It was very damaging. We lost .5 points on our landings."

Team captain Minicucci said, "I am not pleased, but sixth in the world is still respectable." Keswick added similar sentiments, "The expectations of this team were very high, and I am very disappointed. These are the best bunch of guys I've ever trained with, but the outcome has been disappointing. My dad told me that even the best have bad days, and I guess this was my bad day. It's very frustrating."

Simply super Shannon

SHANNON MILLER, THE SMALLEST U.S. athlete in the Games at 4-feet, 6-inches and 69 pounds, may appear timid and shy but not when she is on the podium.

Miller won the silver medal in the all-around, finishing second to the Ukraine's Tatiana Goutsou. Goutsou's route to the all-around was a bit unusual. A fall from balance beam during the team optionals put her fourth among the Unified Team members, making her ineligible for the all-around. But her teammate Roza Galieva, who finished third, was mysteriously pulled from the competition with rumors of a "sore leg," placing Goutsou in the all-around.

Goutsou and Miller battled all night. On bars, Miller scored a 9.925, Goutsou a 9.950. On beam, Miller's best event, she was awarded a 9.925; Goutsou a 9.912. In floor exercise, Goutsou scored 9.925 to Miller's 9.900. Then, in the final event, the vault, Goutsou hung barely ahead with a 9.950 to Miller's almost-perfect 9.975. The final tabulation showed Goutsou with 39.737 to Miller's 39.725.

"I don't know what the judges were looking for," said Steve Nunno, Miller's coach. "I thought her vault should have been a 10.00. It was a gorgeous vault. I don't know what they wanted. They (the judges) were holding out for a superhuman who doesn't exist. She stuck her bar routine too and only got a 9.9."

Zmeskal, the reigning world champion, finished the night in 10th place, ruining her dreams of Olympic gold. Zmeskal stumbled on the beam, but did not fall, and otherwise turned in a strong performance.

"Obviously, I did not have the meet of my life," Zmeskal said while fighting off tears. "Even when I did hit, the scores weren't high. I had one of the best bar sets of my life. It wasn't all bad. I did the best I could."

Nunno said his protege, Miller, "won the battle that was never fought. Everybody knows she's a winner. The media had her in a battle with Kim. She's never wanted that. The battle is against time and gravity. She's the epitome of a great female athlete. She has beauty, grace and athleticism."

TOP / The U.S. women's team — Betty Okino, Wendy Bruce, Dominque Dawes, Shannon Miller, Kerri Strug and Kim Zmeskal — stands proud and "tall" of their bronze-medal effort. Average age of the budding team was 16; average height 4-9. (ALLSPORT / MORTIMORE)

ABOVE / USA's Jair Lynch sails above the horizontal bar, but got into trouble later with a fall in the team competition. (ALLSPORT / MORTIMORE)

OPPOSITE / With a display of concentration, tiny Li Lu of China dismounts the beam. She collected a silver medal in the balance beam, and a perfect score on the uneven bars netted her the gold. (ALLSPORT / VANDYSTADT)

After the dust settled, Lavinia Milosovici (292) of Romania tied teammate Henrietta Onodi for the gold in the vault with a score of 9.925. (ALLSPORT / VANDYSTADT)

Shannon Miller collected three more medals in the individual event finals, bringing her total medal count to five and a record for a U.S. woman in a non-boycotted Olympics. She was the only gymnast to qualify in all four events. She tied for a silver on the balance beam, won the bronze medal on uneven bars and tied for a bronze on floor.

"I'm really happy with all my medals," Miller said. "I am going to compete at the World Championships next year. I will not retire. Gymnastics is still fun for me."

High flying Dimas

THE UNIFIED TEAM swept the all-around finals just as it did at the 1991 World Championships and the 1988 Olympic Games. Scherbo won the gold, followed by Valeri Belenki and Giorgi Misioutine.

Scott Keswick's 19th-place finish was the best for the U.S. men's team in the all-around. Keswick was in fifth place until the high bar when he fell from his first release move, a Kovacs, which is a backflip over the high bar.

"I was really angry after high bar. I really wanted to hit six routines," Keswick said. Teammate John Roethlisberger and Chris Waller both had rough nights, finishing in 34th and 35th positions, respectively.

"My Olympic experience has been a good one despite tonight," Roethlisberger said. "I haven't had this much fun in my whole life. It's an unbelievable feeling to compete in front of the world."

U.S. head coach Francis Allen was disappointed with the team results but was proud of his squad nonetheless. "I really thought we were going to win a medal," Allen said. "Scott was on fire until he missed his Kovacs on high bar. All the guys have been doing a good job in practice. Maybe I should have trained them harder. We're proud of them no matter how they finished. The Soviets are proof that the system they had worked. Their three gymnasts are the best

I have ever seen from one country."

The best, by far, was Scherbo, who established a record for most medals (six) won in an Olympic competition. Scherbo, with gold in the team and all-around, added four more gold medals to his collection by winning rings, pommel horse, vault and parallel bars.

Trent Dimas, 21, ended the American drought by winning a gold in the high bar, the first U.S. gold medal in a non-boycotted Olympic Games. The Albuquerque native scored a 9.875 on the horizontal bar, beating Misioutine of the Unified Team and Germany's Andreas Wecker. Dimas' routine was highlighted by three release moves, including the difficult Kovacs.

"I can't believe I won," an elated Dimas said. "We've been down for so long. My coach, Ed Burch, peaked me at the right time. Other coaches said it would be impossible to peak me right at the Olympic Games, but this proves Burch knows what he is doing and is a great international coach."

After Dimas completed his routine, he "stuck" his dismount, meaning he landed solidly and took no steps. He remained on the podium several seconds before moving. "I was really scared to move," Dimas said. "I wanted the judges to know I stuck my dismount. I am very proud of what I did tonight. I still can't believe it. I am in awe."

Waller finished fifth in pommel horse. "I did the best I could," Waller said. "The others just had longer routines which were better than mine. I did the best routine I have ever done. We will be stronger in '96."

Lynch competed on the parallel bars with a 102-degree temperature after spending the previous 60 hours in bed. "I was feeling a little queasy in warm-ups, but I could do this routine in my sleep," said Lynch, who finished sixth.

Lynch best summarized Scherbo's golden evening: "If Scherbo were an American, he would be the next Michael Jordan. He flies like Michael with a little cockiness in him. It's great, he can back it up."

Shannon Miller

Smallest Athlete, Biggest Winner

by Lee Benson

Fifteen-year-old Shannon Miller went to Barcelona for her summer vacation and they kept adorning her with jewelry.

The sophomore-to-be from Edmond North Middle High School in Edmond, Okla., couldn't do anything without one Spaniard or another draping a medal around her neck. There was roughly one for every dismount.

Miller, the smallest of all the U.S. Olympians at 4-6 and 69 pounds, cast a huge shadow in the Palau Sant Jordi gymnastics arena. In a week she won five medals. It's impossible to win more than six in the women's competition.

She got a bronze medal for her uneven bars routine, another bronze for her floor exercise, and yet another bronze as a member of the U.S. team that won America's first team medal in a non-boycotted Games in more than 50 years, largely because of Miller's best-in-the-competition scoring.

She won a silver medal on balance beam and celebrated her Spanish holiday with a silver in the all-around competition. At that, she was just .012 away from capturing the all-around goal medal after a "Yurchenko-for-Yurchenko" battle on the vault with the Unified Team's Tatiana Goutsou, who, with a personal four-medal haul, still wasn't as prolific overall as Miller.

It was enough to move Steve Nunno, Miller's coach, to call her "the best gymnast this country has ever produced," and more than enough to move her hometown — where her father is a professor at the University of Oklahoma and her mother works in a bank — to crank up an Oklahoma-style celebration upon her return.

A Lear jet paid for by an Edmond TV station met Miller's America-bound flight in Washington, D.C., and whisked her home to a reception that included a parade through downtown Edmond (watched by 22,000 people even though it was a workday), many speeches, many more speeches, and gifts that included a key to the city and a brand-new car from a local dealership.

The car wasn't better than the medals they kept giving her in Spain, but it came in a close second. Miller eagerly accepted the keys and said she couldn't wait until March — when she'd turn 16 and could drive it. ◆

Juggling Acts

RHYTHMIC GYMNASTICS CROWNED an all-around individual Olympic champion as Alexandra Timoshenko of the Unified Team won the gold medal followed by Spain's Carolina Pascual with the silver and the Unified Team's Iksan Skaldina with the bronze.

A field of 50 rhythmic gymnasts competed for Olympic glory in the events of ball, rope, clubs and hoop. The U.S. had two representatives, but neither of them advanced to the final 12 as Jenifer Lovell of Miami, Fla., claimed 23rd place and Tamara Levinson of Silver Springs, Md., placed 40th. ❖ **SUSAN POLAKOFF**

ABOVE / *Shannon Miller flashes a smile during her beam routine. She lost the all-around gold by .012 but came home with five medals — two silvers and three bronzes.* (ALLSPORT / CANNON)

RIGHT (TOP) / *A composed Tatyana Goutsóu forgot her slip on the beam two nights earlier in the team competition and finished the evening's all-around competition in first place.* (ALLSPORT / MORTIMORE)

(BOTTOM) / *Ashes to ashes, dust to dust. At 19, Svetlana Boguinskaia was the Grande Dame of the Unified Team whose hopes of an all-around were handed down to a younger teammate.* (ALLSPORT / VANDYSTADT)

OPPOSITE / *Alexandra Timoshenko of the Unified Team dares to defy gravity. She won the rhythmic gymnastics competition with a score of 59.037.* (ALLSPORT / MORTIMORE)

JUDO
A silver lining for Morris

An eighth-grade English class in San Francisco lived a lesson through its teacher. Not all stories must conclude in Olympic glory and gold medals to have a happy ending.

"I'm a school teacher back home, and I always tell the kids that whatever you're doing always go 100 percent, full speed and give it your best. That's what I tried to do," said heavyweight judo player Damon Keeve of the U.S. team, who teaches English and physical education classes.

"Winning the Olympic Trials and making the team have been an incredible experience," said the 31-year-old Keeve. "It felt great

to go out and fight in front of all those people."

The worldwide appeal of judo was confirmed in the fact that 19 different nations earned Olympic medals, including Israel which captured a silver and bronze — the countries' first Olympic medals ever. Japan led the medal count with 10 followed by France with seven, Cuba with five and Great Britain, Korea, Hungary and the Unified Team with four each.

ABOVE / *Kate Donahoo seems to have the upperhand, but she dropped the match to her opponent, Driulis Gonzales of Cuba. The American placed fifth in the 123-pound division.* (ALLSPORT / CANNON)

Sellout crowds at the Palau Blaugrana in Barcelona witnessed an Olympic judo tournament where the normal became abnormal. Upsets abounded. World champions were unable to defend. Olympic medalists found a hard road to travel.

The path to the medal stand was taken by one U.S. athlete. Jason Morris captured the silver medal in the half middleweight class while three other Americans placed in the championship bracket as Kate Donahoo claimed fifth in the lightweight division, Grace Jividen took seventh in the middleweight division and Keeve placed seventh.

Morris, of Scotia, N.Y., became the first U.S. judo player ever to win a medal in the half middleweight class and captured only the seventh Olympic judo medal in U.S. history. A two-time Olympian, Morris won the

> **"This was like Douglas beating Tyson," White said. "This guy was way out of my league. He's a special athlete. It's like me beating Magic Johnson in one-on-one. In Europe, these guys are pros."**
>
> **—American Leo White**
> **after upsetting world champion**
> **Stephane Traineau of France**
> **in the preliminary rounds**

silver medal against a tough draw as he compiled a 4-1 record.

Morris dropped the gold-medal bout to Japan's Hidehiko Yoshida by ippon, but he kept his sense of humor in the press conference. "I was flying Air Japan," he said.

"I have had a lot of successes at the world level, and I feel I've actually been a better player at other times, but this has been special," Morris said. "I've been so close, so close, so close. I've trained hard to peak and then had a letdown. There are only so many times you can do that as an athlete. You think, 'Man, I'm never going to win.'"

Part of the upset fever was due in part to the U.S. contingent. U.S. Army captain Leo White of Seaside, Calif., knocked out two-time world champion and half heavyweight favorite Stephane Traineau of France with an ippon only 32 seconds into the match.

"This was like Douglas beating Tyson," White said. "This guy was way out of my league. He's a special athlete. It's like me beating Magic Johnson in one-on-one. In Europe, these guys are pros."

Women's judo had attained full-medal status in Barcelona for the first time. As a demonstration event in Seoul, the Americans won two medals in 1988. This time "real" gold, silver and bronze was on the line, and two U.S. women's judo players made a run.

In the lightweight division, Donahoo of Colorado Springs, Colo., sprung a surprise on two-time world champion Catherine Arnaud of France. The victory advanced her to the bronze-medal match where Donahoo lost to Cuba's Drivilis Gonzalez by a yuko.

"I don't know if I had a career day, but I think I did pretty well," Donahoo said. "I'm not disappointed in my performance at all. I was pretty close to that third place, and I really wanted that bronze medal."

One of her teammates also came close — just two victories shy of winning a bronze medal. Jividen, of Colorado Springs, Colo., advanced to the repechage finals where she lost on one penalty point in a match against a former training partner, Belgium's Heidi Rakels.

"I came in as a darkhorse," Jividen said. "I was fortunate to come here and represent the United States. But in the back of my mind, I knew I did all that work. It's a battle out there. Somebody's got to win and somebody's got to lose."

The Americans themselves fell victims to some surprise losses. Middleweight medal hopeful Joey Wanag, 1988 Olympic silver medalist Lynn Roethke and four-time Olympian Mike Swain were each knocked out after the first round. Others such as Jim Pedro and Jo Anne Quiring were unable to fight their way out of the repechage brackets of the half lightweight division.

"Judo is different from other sports because there are so many variables," Swain said. "You not only have to worry about what you're going to do, but what your opponent is going to do. None of the world champions from last year have won here so far. It's hard to stay on top in judo."

And for the 14-member U.S. judo team, that only leaves the door open for Atlanta in 1996. ❖ **FRANK ZANG**

ABOVE / *Some situations just keep you on your toes.*
(ALLSPORT / CANNON)

OPPOSITE / *Ryoko Tamura of Japan steadies herself against the sly Cecile Nowak of France, who is going for the takedown and the gold. Nowak eventually succeeds, winning the 106-pound extra lightweight division.* (ALLSPORT / VANDYSTADT)

ABOVE / *Hidehiko Yoshida of Japan throws American Jason Morris to the mat — an experience the wry Morris calls "flying Air Japan" — to win the half middleweight title. Morris became only the seventh Olympic medalist in U.S. history with the silver.* (ALLSPORT / BOTTERILL)

MODERN PENTATHLON
World's most diversified athletes

While the U.S. team finished just out of the medals in Barcelona's modern pentathlon competition, Poland's Arkadiusz Skrzypaszek laid claim as the world's best when it comes to running, swimming, fencing, shooting and riding.

Skrzypaszek won the gold medal in the individual competition, finishing more than 100 points in front of Attila Mizser of Hungary and nearly 200 points ahead of Edouard Zenovka of the Unified Team. Then, he teamed with countrymen Maciej Czyzowicz and Dariusz Gozdziak to help Poland win the gold ahead of the Unified Team, Italy and the United States.

The U.S. entry, consisting of Mike Gostigian of Newtown Square, Pa.; Jim Haley of Lake City, Fla.; and Rob Stull of Austin, Texas, came within 111 points of the bronze medal.

In the course of four days, the modern pentathlon put contestants through the paces in a 4,000-meter cross-country run, a 3,000-meter swim, one-on-one fencing combat, equestrian riding, and rifle shooting. The competition in Barcelona was under somewhat of a cloud as the International Olympic Committee announced its intentions for major program restructuring by the 2000 Olympic Games, which could affect modern pentathlon.

The modern pent-athletes reacted with expected disappointment, espousing their sport's virtues. "Running and swimming are man against the elements, fencing is man against man, equestrian is man against horse, and shooting is man against himself," Gostigian said. "Pentathlon is the Edsel of Olympic sports — it will be long gone before anyone appreciates it."

The U.S. team's closest taste of victory came on the fourth and final day of competition at the riding event. Clean through the first 12 gates and on his way to vaulting the U.S. past Italy for the bronze medal, Stull ran into trouble with his mount, Canario, at the 13th obstacle, a triple gate. Two refusals of the second fence in the series cost Stull 80 points in deductions. That, coupled with several knockdowns and a time penalty, resulted in a score of 875, allowing

the Italians off the hook and onto the medal stand.

"I was gritting my teeth every step of the way because in the warm-up ring it was a disaster," said Stull, who ended up 44th in the riding event. "I couldn't get him to the fence. He didn't want to be here.

"What's disappointing," he said, "was that I had this guy's number for 12 jumps, up until the line at 13. Had I gotten him through that line, he could have still shut down on 14, but we would at least have had the bronze, maybe even a silver."

The best U.S. ride of the evening came from Haley, a first-time Olympian, who finished 12th in a time of 1:32 on Soriano.

The four-day team event began with 12 1/2 hours of round-robin fencing in which Stull finished

> "Pentathlon is the Edsel of Olympic sports — it will be long gone before anyone appreciates it."

third with the help of a 17-straight win streak.

"We fenced very good until about 5 p.m.—after that we got tired," Coach Janusz Peczak said. "We lost to Latvia after defeating the Unified Team—we just had a bad moment because everybody was tired."

The team came back strong on day two with a first-place team finish in the 300-meter freestyle swim against the clock. Mike Gostigian posted the fastest U.S. result (3:13.94) and finished second overall.

"The swim was my personal best in the last six years," Gostigian said. "It was physically more demanding because we fenced for so long the day before. A 3:13 time at the Olympic Games is nothing to be disappointed about."

However, Gostigian met with disappointment in the shooting event later that day when the shooter next to him on the line prematurely raised his weapon, breaking Gostigian's concentration

OPPOSITE / *Another casualty of the heat and humidity of Barcelona. Pentathlete winner Arkadiusz Skrzypaszek of Poland crosses the finish line in exhaustion, like every other athlete to follow.* (ALLSPORT / BOTTERILL)

ABOVE / *Ouch! Mike Gostigian (76) makes his point perfectly clear. The 29-year-old pentathlete finished ninth in the four-day event, a remarkable improvement over his 59th-place showing in the Seoul Olympics.* (ALLSPORT / BOTTERILL)

and taking him out of individual medal contention. Gostigian again led the U.S. contingent, shooting a 189.

"I caught it out of the corner of my eye," said Gostigian, comparing the act to a false start that isn't caught in a track race. "I wasn't ready for it, and it threw me out of synch. It changed my role."

With a 10th-place team finish in the cross country race on day three, the U.S. slipped from third to fifth in the overall team standings. Gostigian again posted the highest U.S. finish.

"It was the mother of all runs," Gostigian said. "It was the most terrifying run in the history of modern pentathlon. You had 110-meter elevation changes four times. You had hills, heat, humidity, no shade, direct sunlight, plus no wind."

"After the run I've never been so tired, run down and beat after any event in my life," Haley said. "That's why it comes around every four years and I hope to be around in four more years."

At the end of four days of competition, Gostigian was the top American finisher, in ninth place, while Stull placed 20th and Haley 25th. ❖ **CRAIG BOHNERT AND COLLEEN WALKER**

ROWING
A new world order

En Busca de Ora. In Search of Gold. American coxswain Yasmin Farooq painted the words on the side of the 60-foot shell that would carry her and eight others down Lake Banyoles' mirror-flat 200 meters at the Olympic Games. Little did she realize she was sounding the battle cry for all the crews in Barcelona in a competition that was arguably the closest and fastest in Games history.

Farooq and the rest of the U.S. rowers — 56 in all — played a major part in the drama that unfolded in the rowing venue, with no less than nine American crews qualifying into the finals. Three of those crews — in men's and women's coxless fours and women's coxless pairs — wound up medaling, claiming two silvers and a bronze.

While German rowers claimed the most medals, nine in all, the 14 gold medals available were literally distributed among the Germans and the Canadians, who won four each, and Australia, Great Britain and Romania, with two each. Eight nations would up winning silver medals and 10 won bronze medals. For a sport that had traditionally been dominated by Eastern Europeans, the liberal dispersal of medals reflected a dramatic new world order.

In 1960 there was a gold medal for the United States in men's four. Ted Nash, Olympic coach of the four, was a member of that crew. Throughout the week's competition, Nash listened to talk of the showdown between his four, the 1991 World Championships silver medalists, and their rivals, the defending world champion "Awesome Foursome" from Australia. Each crew made its way through separate heats and semifinals, recording nearly identical times. The U.S. four's semifinal win was 5:58.87; the Australians 5:58.26.

In the finals, the Slovenians — the fastest starting crew in the regatta according to Nash — bolted from the start with an incredible 1:26.06 for the first 500 meters. By the 1,000-meter mark, however, the U.S. team of Patrick Manning, Jeff McLaughlin, Tom Bohrer and Doug Burden had moved into second place — 1 1/2 seconds behind the Australians. That time would also be the difference at the finish.

"The last 200 I kept thinking, 'Pull for Tom, pull for Tom,'" said McLaughlin, "because he already had an Olympic silver medal

(1988), and we all wanted to give him the gold. Afterward you ask yourself a lot of what-ifs, but there are no what-ifs here."

Nash could only shake his head at the blistering pace in the final. "A 5:56 with no help (from the wind)?" he said. "Pretty amazing." Nash's gold medal-winning time in 1960 in Rome was 6:26.26.

The times on Lake Banyoles caused more than a few shaking heads. "We've been training all summer at a gold-medal standard of 7:10," said Stephanie Maxwell-Pierson, the stroke of the bronze-medal women's pair. "And the winning time was 7:06."

The pair's week had mirrored the men's four, although Maxwell-Pierson and Anna Seaton's rivals were not Australians, but the defending world champion from Canada. Drawing the tougher race of the two semifinals, the U.S. pair impressively beat both the French and Germans. In the final, the U.S. pair trailed the Canadians throughout the race, beginning less than a second behind, but slipping to 2 1/2 by the 1,500-meter mark. Their finishing sprint was enough to hold off the changing French, but not the Germans, who captured the silver.

There was a second U.S. boat hunting the Canadians on Lake Banyoles — the women's four.

Shelagh Donohoe and Cindy Eckert were the silver medalists in the four at the 1992 World Championships. Amy Fuller and Carol Feeney, veterans of the eight, completed the boat. "The strong point in our boat was that we all got along really well," Eckert said. "I think that was one of the keys to our success. We had a lot of trust in each other, and we all worked hard."

The U.S. four had finished second to the Canadians in the preliminary heat, but won its way to the finals with a strong repechage race. Once again, the preliminary heats were no indication of the speeds medal crews were capable of producing in the

ABOVE / *Out on the reflective waters of Lake Banyoles, the men's eight oars with coxswain gives a colorful impression. Canada barely defeated silver medalist Romania by .14 seconds.* (ALLSPORT / CANNON)

ABOVE / *Patrick Manning, Jeff McLaughlin, Tom Bohrer and Doug Burden caught a fast-starting Slovenian crew by the 1,000-meter mark but couldn't catch the Australian "Awesome Foursome," which crossed the finish line 1 1/2 seconds ahead of the Americans.* (ALLSPORT / M. POWELL)

SUCCEEDING PAGES / *Carol Feeney, Amy Fuller, Cindy Eckert and Shelagh Donohoe make up the U.S. women's four without coxswain. The crew finished 1.01 seconds behind the powerful Canadians to capture the silver.* (ALLSPORT / RONDEAU)

finals. The U.S. four trailed their northern neighbors throughout the final, getting as close as 1.06 seconds, but never closer. "The first 1,000 passed incredibly fast," Feeney said. "In fact, the whole race did. In the last 20 strokes, I couldn't feel my legs at all."

"We were shooting for the gold," Eckert said. "Trying to get off the line fast and hopefully pass them in the middle 1,000. But they're tough." So were the Americans, who, after battling for 1,800 meters, had enough at the finish to hold off both the Chinese and Germans for the silver.

Three U.S. crews fought for the bronze and finished fourth, including single sculler Anne Marden. The men's four with coxswain finished fourth in a final with a time that would normally have been fast enough for a men's four without coxswain. And the U.S. men's eight, still in search of its first Olympic gold medal since 1964, finished

> **"The first 1,000 passed incredibly fast. In fact, the whole race did. In the last 20 strokes, I couldn't feel my legs at all."**
> **—Carol Feeney**
> silver medalist of the U.S. women's four

behind the medalists Canada, Romania and Germany.

The Canadian women repeated their 1991 World Championships coup — gold medals in the women's pair, four and eight by women who rowed two events each. Not to be outdone, the Canadian men's eight ended the German's four-year domination of the event.

There were medals, too, for the Australians and Great Britain, who won not only the expected medal in men's pair, but the unexpected gold by the young Searle brothers, Jonathan and Greg, in the pair with coxswain, beating the legendary Abbagnales brothers, Carmine and Giuseppe, of Italy. Cuba made the finals for the first time in its rowing history — the men's pair with coxswain — and placed fifth. And the French were knocking at the door with a growing, impressive program. ❖ **MO MERHOFF**

SHOOTING
Barcelona's big shootout

Predictions may be an impossibility, or so it seems after 440 of the world's top guns took aim at 39 medals awarded in shooting events at the 1992 Olympic Games.

Who would have guessed that an unknown Korean — Yeo Kab-Soon — would win the first gold medal of the Games in women's air rifle by a healthy three-point margin. Among the stunned: the USA's Launi Meili and Debra Sinclair, who tied at 11th place, one point short of berths in the final round. "I've never heard of her before in my life," Meili said.

It was the first surprise of the world's greatest shootout, but happily for Meili and Team USA, definitely not the last.

Meili bounced back quickly from her air rifle defeat, firing a perfect 200 prone en route to triumphing in women's three-position with a near world-record score of 683.4. "I didn't want to ever let up. I wanted to shoot 10's until the end," said the 29-year-old American shooting star. "Right now this is hard for me to comprehend. It's the dream of a lifetime come true."

Meili's victory marked the USA's first gold in the history of the event, and only the third Olympic crown ever won by an American markswoman.

Within 24 hours of her stellar performance, 34-year-old U.S. rifle sensation Bob Foth had also achieved a lifelong goal. Ranked third after the 120-shot men's three-position match, Foth fired a steady 97.6 in the final round to win silver-medal honors. He finished eight-tenths of a point behind Olympic champion Gracha Petikian of the Unified Team.

"It was so tight today," Foth said. "The lead seemed to change every shot. In these crazy matches there are 1309.9 points, and I ended up losing the gold by eight-tenths of a point. That's probably three one-hundredths of an inch on the target. At that margin, I guess it really doesn't matter what color your medal is."

Others were also close to Olympic glory. One missed target took skeetshooter Matt Dryke and trap star Jay Waldron out of medal contention in their respective events. "One target got away, and that's all it takes," Dryke said after his final. "If you're a long jumper, you've got two or three chances, and they take your best try. Out here we've got to be perfect 200 times." The skeet gold medal went to China's Zhang Shan while Dryke claimed sixth. Waldron was also sixth in the trap competition as Czechoslovakia's Petr Hrdlicka took the gold.

Darius "Doc" Young posted the USA's best Olympic free pistol performance since 1968, but fell two points short of Swedish bronze medalist Ragnar Skanaker. "My goal was the gold, but I'm still happy because I shot above my average. There's no limit; at least I haven't found mine yet," said Young, who at 54 was the oldest member of the U.S. Olympic contingent. Konstantine Loukachik of the Unified Team struck gold in the free pistol.

Shooting at a bull's-eye smaller than a dime, Bill Meek missed the 10-ring only four times, but fell a point short of the men's free rifle prone final. He finished ninth overall as Korea's Lee Eun-Chul won the gold.

"I am devastated to have shot a 596. It was perfect out there. The wind wasn't doing anything," the 39-year-old Meek said. "I just had some 'where'd that come from?' shots. I expected to shoot at least a 598 and get in the final. Realistically, I thought I'd be third behind [Norwegian Harald] Stenvaag and whatever Russian showed up."

Rapid-fire pistol shooter John McNally also expected a medal, but the gold went to Germany's Ralf Schumann. McNally scored 781/800 points to place fifth after a total of 88 seconds on the firing lines. "Everything's happening so fast. In the semifinals and finals you're shooting five shots in four seconds," said the three-time Olympian and U.S. Army Captain. "When you say 'ready' on the line, that's it. There's no turning back."

Rusty Hill ranked 11th in the Olympic debut of 10-meter running target, which was won by Germany's Michael Jakosits, while Ben Amonette checked in at 14th in men's air pistol, which China's Yifu Wang won. Connie Petracek and Roxane Thompson placed 24th in women's air pistol and sport pistol, respectively. Marian Logvinenko of the Unified Team swept the gold medals in both women's events.

In all, Team USA boasted of six athletes in Olympic finals, while three American marksmen advanced to semifinal rounds. Teams from China, Germany and the Unified Team led the way in the medal count while the story of the Games belonged to China's Zhang, who became the first woman to win an Olympic gold medal in a combined event. Zhang won the skeet shooting competition ahead of Juan Giah of Peru and Bruno Rossetti of Italy. Ironically, skeet shooting will be divided into men's and women's categories for the 1996 Games at Atlanta. ❖ **KAREN MUTKA**

RIGHT / *The pressure was off. Launi Meili had the gold, an Olympic record of 684.3 points and the time to reflect on her long-sought victory in the three-position rifle competition. (ALLSPORT / MORTIMORE)*

OPPOSITE / *Bob Foth of the United States shot 1,266.6 to capture the silver in the three-position rifle. He also competed in the air rifle event in which he placed seventh.*

LAUNI MEILI

Tears To Triumph

BY MIKE SPENCE

From tears in 1988 to triumph in 1992, Launi Meili's Olympic experience runs a wide spectrum of emotion.

As a neophyte Olympian at the Seoul Games in 1988, Meili stunned the competition by firing a world-record preliminary round in the women's 10-meter air rifle competition.

But new to the pressure and unable to cope, Meili lost her composure and her lead in the 10-shot final. She finished a tearful sixth.

"I just remember being really nervous," the 29-year-old Meili said. "I had put every ounce of mental energy into the first part of the match. By the final, I was numb. I was shaking so much I couldn't follow through on my shots."

Four years later, Meili made the most of a second chance.

This time she triumphed, setting an Olympic record of 684.3 points in winning a gold medal in the women's three-position rifle competition.

"I didn't want to ever let up," Meili said. "I wanted to shoot 10s until the end."

The difference in Barcelona was Meili's mental edge, which had been hardened by her traumatic experience in 1988.

"In Seoul, I prepared myself as well as I could, but I just couldn't handle it in the final," Meili said. "This time I was nervous, but I felt like I was going to be able to control it."

Meili cooled her raging nerves by concentrating on the target, blocking out everything else, including memories of Seoul.

"I knew the only thing I could do was shoot the match I've had in my mind for so long," she said. "I think it took a lot of struggling over the years to finally put it together, but now I know I can trust myself with my goals and dreams."

Meili became the first U.S. woman to win a gold medal in the three-position event and the first U.S. shooter since 1960 to win using American-made ammunition.

"This was the culmination of every win I've ever had," Meili said. "I'm not ever going to be afraid to set my goals too high any more. This is a dream of a lifetime come true." ◆

S O C C E R
Putting the right foot forward

Making itself right at home, Spain's Olympic soccer team won the gold medal in the Barcelona Games, defeating Poland 3-2 in the final at Nou Camp Stadium in front of nearly 100,000 mostly native and delirious fans.

As the win sent the citizens of Barcelona into a night-long celebration, it also demonstrated just how competitive the first-ever under-23 Olympic tournament had been. In 17 days of competition, contested by teams from 16 nations, one-goal outcomes were common. Routs were scarce and virtually every team that started the tournament could imagine being where Spain wound up, if only for a break or two — and maybe a home crowd.

Such was the feeling of a U.S. squad that failed by the barest of margins to make it into the second round. Needing a win in its final qualifying match against the eventual silver medalists from Poland, the Americans had to settle for a 2-2 tie that eliminated them from the tournament. Until the loss to Spain in the final, Poland would not have a closer game than the one with the U.S. In the medal round, the Poles first defeated Qatar, 2-0, and then beat Australia, 6-1, to advance into the finals.

Spain's route to the final included a 1-0 win over Italy in the quarterfinals and a 2-0 win over Ghana — which went on to win the bronze with a 1-0 win over Australia — in the semifinals.

The U.S. team was armed with virtually the same squad that had captured the gold medal at the 1991 Pan American Games. Buoyed by that triumph, U.S. head coach Lothar Osiander's soccer team entered the Olympic Games in Barcelona with high hopes.

The 1992 Games marked the 10th time that the U.S. had qualified for the Olympic soccer tournament, which trails only Italy

ABOVE / *Playing before a flag-waving, chest-beating crowd, Spain downed Poland, 3-2, sending the nearly 100,000 soccer-crazed fans into a frenzy. The gold is Spain's first in soccer.* (ALLSPORT / CANNON)

(11) and Yugoslavia (11) in most appearances since the 1924 Games. And yet, under the present format, the U.S. had never advanced to the second round. Osiander's talented squad came into the competition fully intent on taking the program to the next level. In addition to the Pan Am gold medal, the U.S. had posted an impressive 8-1-1 record in Olympic qualifying play.

The luck of the draw certainly was not on the side of the U.S. when it was placed in Group A, arguably the strongest of the tournament's four groups. The U.S. would face powerful Italy in the tournament opener in Barcelona, then venture to Zaragoza to meet Kuwait and Poland.

After falling behind 2-0 in the tournament opener against Italy, the U.S. dominated the final 45 minutes of the contest. Midfielder Joe-Max Moore brought the U.S. to within a goal on a picture-perfect free kick at the 65th minute that caught the upper right corner of the net. The U.S. almost got the equalizer on a shot by midfielder Cobi Jones that was just tipped over the crossbar, but the Italians withstood the U.S. onslaught down the stretch to escape with the victory.

The U.S. bounced back in style with a 3-1 victory over Kuwait, after trailing 1-0 at the half. Midfielders Dario Brose and Manuel Lagos, along with forward Steve Snow, found the back of the net in the second half. The win propelled Osiander's squad into a showdown against the undefeated Poles with a spot in the coveted second round at stake.

Poland had already defeated Kuwait, 2-0, and Italy, 3-0. The impressive victory over the Italians, in particular, had raised more than a few eyebrows. The determined U.S. contingent went on top 1-0 when Erik Imler tallied a goal at the 20th minute, the first goal that Poland had allowed in more than 200 minutes of action. It also marked Imler's first goal for the U.S. in international play.

When Poland struck back to take a 2-1 lead, Osiander's never-say-die squad knotted things up on a goal by Snow at the 51st minute.

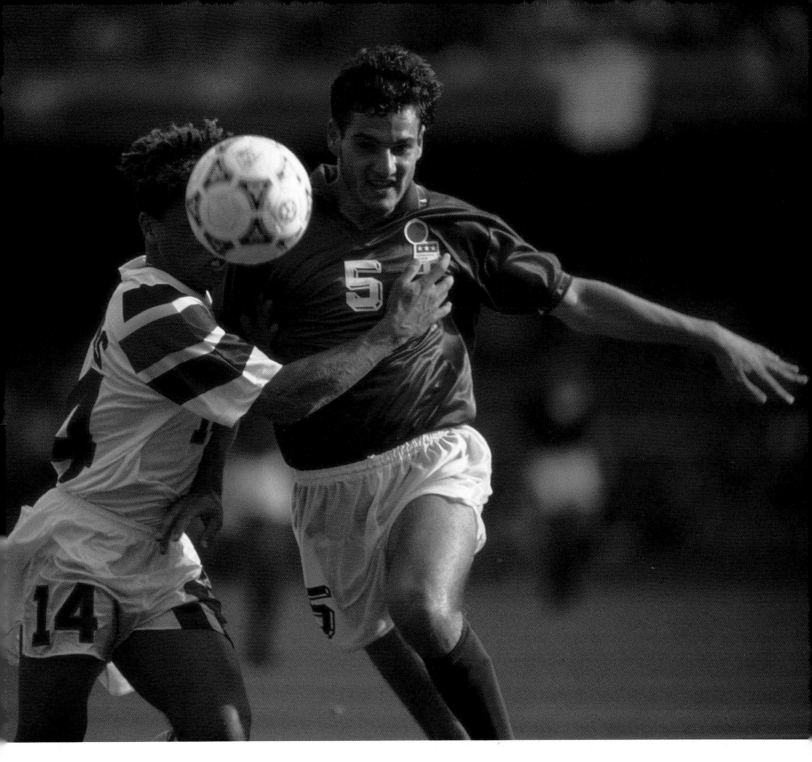

Both teams had numerous chances to score the game-winner the rest of the way, but the contest ended in a tie. Goalkeeper Brad Friedel, who did not miss a start in both Olympic qualifying and Olympic Games play, was sensational in the nets as the U.S. finished pool play with a 1-1-1 record and three points.

With a 2-0-1 record and five points, Poland had secured the top seed out of Group A for the second round. Despite FIFA Rule 26 that states that "the final two games in each group shall take place at the same time," Italy went into its final match with Kuwait fully aware of the outcome of the USA-Poland encounter. When the Italians came away with a 1-0 victory over Kuwait to end up 2-1 with four points in pool play, the U.S. was once again denied a second-round berth.

"I think that Group A, with the two strong European teams,

Italy and Poland in there, was the toughest of the four groups," Osiander said. "We came close, but we needed a little bit of luck to go on to the next round. I'm proud of my guys. We did the best we could."

Injuries to key players were also a big factor for the Americans. Midfield star Chris Henderson, the only member of the team to split his duties with the U.S. National Team and the Olympic Team, did not play in the Olympic Games due to a sprained knee. Defender Alexi Lalas, who suffered a broken left foot the week before the start of the Games, "miraculously" came back to start in the final Olympic contest against Poland.

The six goals scored by the U.S. in pool play was the most ever by a U.S. squad in Olympic Games action. The previous record was four set back in 1984. The three points earned tied the record for a U.S. team. The 1984 team also went 1-1-1 at Los Angeles. Osiander's squad certainly turned some heads with its fine play in Barcelona and set the stage for a prosperous future for the U.S. soccer program down the road. ❖

ABOVE / *Midfielder Cobi Jones of the U.S. gave a stellar performance against the Italians — a match that the U.S. lost 2-1 — that had even raised the international scouts' eyebrows.* (ALLSPORT / M. POWELL)

MARC RYAN AND DEAN LINKE

SWIMMING
The six greatest days

Simply stated, the 1992 Olympic swimming competition at Barcelona's Bernat Picornell pool produced the greatest six days in the history of the sport. In non-swimming parlance, the 1992 Olympic Games were an Ali-Frazier fight, or the 1971 Oklahoma-Nebraska football game — they were just that good.

When the waves had calmed, American swimmers owned 27 Olympic medals (11 gold, 9 silver and 7 bronze) and 30 swimmers on the 40-person squad would head home to a hero's welcome with at least one Olympic medal. Those medals didn't come easily, however. While the Americans outdistanced the second-place Unified Team, which won a total of 10 medals, six of them gold, it was clear that

ABOVE / *A favorite at the 1988 Games, Melvin Stewart came in a disappointing fifth. To Stewart, Barcelona meant unfinished business in the pool. This time, Stewart set the record straight with a gold-medal win in the 200-meter butterfly and an Olympic record to boot. (*ALLSPORT / VANDYSTADT*)*

OPPOSITE / *Anita Nall was one of the victims of upsets that cropped up all over the venues in Barcelona. The world record-holder in the 200-meter breaststroke, Nall finished second in the 100 and third in the 200. (*ALLSPORT / BRUTY*)*

Olympic level swimming had truly matured on a global scale.

Germany was second in the total medal count with 11 (1-3-7), but was listed fifth behind Hungary and China in the gold medal tally. Hungary won five golds along with three silvers and a bronze as triple gold medalist Krisztina Egerszegi (400 IM, 100- and 200-meter backstroke) and Tamas Darnyi, a double gold winner (200 and 400 individual medley), provided all of the Hungarian gold.

The new Russian front

THE UNIFIED TEAM'S effort was led by Sadovyi Evgueni, who became the first Russian since the great Vladimir Salnikov to hold the world record in the 400-meter freestyle. Evgueni won the 200 freestyle and anchored the Unified Team's 800 freestyle relay to return home a triple gold medalist. When the Russians won the 800 free relay with a world-record time of 7:11.95, it ended a U.S. Olympic unbeaten streak in that event that stretched all the way back to 1956 in Melbourne.

Russia also unleashed Alexander Popov on the swimming world. This amazing 20-year-old won the 100 free with a winning

time of 49.02 and took just 17 strokes to win the 50-meter freestyle in 21.91 seconds. He not only ended the reign of Americans Tom Jager and Matt Biondi in the 50 free, but he became the first swimmer to break the 22-second barrier in a full field.

The meet's most prominent theme had to be the roller coaster of extreme emotions highlighted by the likes of Pablo Morales, Janet Evans, Biondi and Ron Karnaugh.

A roller coaster ride

MORALES, THE 27-YEAR-OLD team co-captain, who was a silver medalist in Los Angeles but missed making the '88 U.S. team, won the 100-meter butterfly by .03 seconds. Just to make the Olympic team, Morales had to take a year off from Cornell Law School and endure the death of his mother, Blanca, last September.

Evans, America's sweetheart from 1988, had won 18 straight world-class 400-meter freestyle races since the summer of 1986. But, in Barcelona, she was outtouched by former East German Dagmar Hase and denied the chance to become the first woman since Martha Norelius in 1924 and 1928 to win the Olympic 400 free twice. Evans went out in style two days later, however, becoming the first woman ever to win the 800-meter freestyle in back-to-back Olympics with a winning time of 8:25.52.

Biondi, the world record-holder in the 100 free and former world record-holder in the 50 free, won his ninth, 10th and 11th Olympic medals, tying him with Mark Spitz and shooter Carl Osburn for the most Olympic medals in history. But his only individual medal was a silver in the 50 freestyle. His golds came in the 400 freestyle relay and as a prelim alternate in the 400 medley relay. Biondi and his teammate, Jager, became the first U.S. swimmers in history to win a gold medal in three different Olympic Games. Both won relay golds in '84 and, in Seoul, Biondi picked up five golds while Jager won a gold on the 400 freestyle relay.

Karnaugh wasn't slated to swim the 200 individual medley until the final day of the meet, so he was one of only a handful of swimmers able to march in the spectacular Opening Ceremonies. As he marched in at the front of the assembled American delegation, he saw his father, Peter, at the stadium's railing taking pictures and waving. It would be the last time Ron saw his father, as the elder Karnaugh died minutes later of a massive heart attack. With six days to finish his taper and think about the tragedy, Ron qualified fourth

in his event and finished sixth.

"This meet was like a war," said U.S. Swimming National Team Director Dennis Pursley, and he wasn't far off with his simile. The list of casualties included some of the greatest swimmers in the world. In fact, eight world record-holders, six of them Americans, could not win gold medals in their specialities. The list of American world record-holder casualties included Biondi and Evans in the 100 and 400 freestyles, respectively, Jager in the 50 freestyle, Jenny Thompson in the 100 freestyle, Anita Nall in the 200 breaststroke and Jeff Rouse in the 100 backstroke.

Among the Americans, only Evans in the 800 free and Olympic Village roommates Mike Barrowman and Melvin Stewart could remain in control of their world-record events. Barrowman won the 200-meter breaststroke with a world record of 2:10.16 and then announced that his coach, Joszef Nagy, would be required to sleep with the medal that night. It seems that whenever Barrowman didn't accomplish what Nagy had expected of him during a meet, the coach would make him sleep with the lesser place medal. Turnabout is fair play they say.

Stewart easily outpaced the field in the 200 butterfly to firmly establish himself as the new owner of the crown worn for the last decade by the incomparable Michael Gross. Stewart, who is known for his antics away from the pool, then proceeded to meet the Olympic press where he held court with a mixture of one-liners and serious remarks for almost 40 minutes.

Rouse, who saw Canada's Mark Tewksbury win the gold medal in the 100 back by .06 seconds over him, set a world record in the 100 backstroke the same way he got it in the first place: leading off the U.S. 4x100-meter medley relay. Rouse swam the first leg of the relay in a time of 53.86 seconds and the rest of the American team — 100 breaststroke gold medalist Nelson Diebel, Morales and Jon Olsen — won the event and tied the world record of 3:36.93.

ABOVE / *Nelson Diebel gave the U.S. its first gold medal of the Barcelona Games. Diebel outtouched Hungary's Norbert Rozsa by .18 seconds, winning in an Olympic record time of 1:01.50.* (ALLSPORT / BRUTY)

CLOCKWISE FROM TOP / *Pablo Morales has his prayers answered* (ALLSPORT / B. MARTIN); *Krisztina Egerszegi, Hungary's swimming sensation who took home three of its five golds, gives a shy teenage grin* (ALLSPORT / VANDYSTADT); *American Matt Biondi* (right) *passes the 50-meter Olympic crown to 20-year-old Aleksandr Popov of the Unified Team* (ALLSPORT / VANDYSTADT), *and Nicole Haislett and Dara Torres go for the gusto, cheering teammates Angel Martino and Jenny Thompson to a U.S. victory in the 4 x 100-meter freestyle relay.* (ALLSPORT / VANDYSTADT).

Best laid plans...

Before Breaking Training camp in Narbonne, France, on July 21, Pursley addressed the U.S. swimmers and told them that their success in Barcelona would depend on four things: the ability to adapt to less than perfect conditions, training and preparation; the ability to take a punch; and mental toughness. "The greatest team efforts," he said, "come from overcoming difficulties, not when everything goes according to plan."

Nothing could have been closer to the truth. The conditions on top of Barcelona's scenic Montjuic were extremely hot and humid. After each session, the team and spectator seating areas were littered with thousands of plastic water bottles. In the first week of the Games, buses sometimes didn't run on time and sleeping conditions in the village were often difficult because of the oppressive heat and humidity.

Almost every race came down to a blink of an eyelash finish, and in that blink, some of America's brightest hopes for gold medals were dashed. In other blinks, American swimmers owned a gold medal that had seemed destined for someone else.

Hangin' tough

The Americans' Key was their ability to hang together as a team and keep fighting back. After taking a disappointing fourth in the 100 free on the first night, Nicole Haislett came back the next night to win the 200 freestyle in spectacular fashion. She stayed on the hip of 14-year-old rising star Franziska VanAlmsick for 150 meters and then in the final 50 meters of the race sprinted by the young German — the last product of the old East German sports machine — to win by .10 seconds.

Summer Sanders, the most decorated U.S. swimmer in Spain with four medals, picked up a bronze in her first race — the 400 individual medley on the first night of the meet — with an American record of 4:37.58 and a silver behind the world record of China's Lin Li in the 200 IM with another American record of 2:11.91. Her 400 IM time was faster than the gold-medal time posted by Janet Evans in the 1988 Olympics. Finally, on the last night of the meet, Sanders outraced China's Wang Xiaohong and Australia's Susan O'Neill to win the 200 butterfly in 2:08.67. Sanders got her fourth gold as a member of the prelim team of the 4x100 medley relay.

Anita Nall went into her first race — the 200-meter breaststroke — as a prohibitive favorite. She was the world record-holder and her best time was over three seconds faster than anyone else in the field. In a stunning upset, she was beaten by Japan's Kyoko Iwasaki and outtouched by .03 seconds by China's Lin Li, leaving

Nall with a bronze medal. Two night's later, Nall was back to win a silver medal behind Elena Roudkovskaia, of the Unified Team, and set an American record in the 100 breaststroke in 1:08.17. One night later, she got her gold on the women's 400 medley relay.

The huge scoreboard at the pool originally flashed Jon Olsen's name as the bronze medalist in the 100 freestyle, in 49.51 seconds, but a touch pad error had left Brazil's Gustavo Borges without a place. A review of the overhead back-up video showed Borges taking second in 49.43, knocking Olsen to fourth.

Olsen came back the next night to anchor the U.S. 400 freestyle relay of Joe Hudepohl, Biondi and Jager to a gold medal. Even that didn't go according to plan as he had to hold off Popov, the Russian superstar, with a 48.28 second relay leg, the eighth fastest in history, to preserve the gold medal for the U.S. and keep the American Olympic unbeaten streak in that event unblemished. Popov swam a 47.83 second relay leg himself, the third fastest in history. That swim earned Olsen the anchor leg of the U.S. medley relay in the finals on the last night of the meet.

The women's 400 medley relay may have been the most cathartic event of the meet. Backstroker Lea Loveless, the bronze medalist

LEFT / *Summer Sanders avenged her sixth-place finish in the 100-meter butterfly by winning, at last, the gold in the 200-meter event. She beat Xiaohang Wang, another of the up-and-coming Chinese swimmers, by a touch.* (Allsport / Bruty)

ABOVE / *Tom Jager, Matt Biondi and Jon Olsen celebrate as Joe Hudepohl finishes first in the 4x100-meter relay with a time of 3:16.74.* (Allsport / Bruty)

OPPOSITE / *Racers take your mark, get set, bang.* (Allsport / Vandystadt)

When he wasn't practicing, Mike Barrowman mostly kept to himself while he waited for his event: the 200-meter breaststroke. The low-key strategy spelled success for Barrowman, who set a world record of 2:10.16. (ALLSPORT / BRUTY)

ABOVE / *Making a comeback at 27 years old, Pablo Morales put away the law books and climbed back into the pool. He accomplished what most thought was impossible and in an atmosphere where even the favorites were falling — a gold medal in the 100-meter butterfly.* (ALLSPORT / BRUTY)

OPPOSITE / *Back in 1988, Janet Evans was the 17-year-old sweetheart of America. She returned to Barcelona a young woman to defend her 400-meter and 800-meter freestyle titles. She won back-to-back golds in the 800, but Evans was stung by Dagmar Hase of Germany in the final 50-meter leg in the 400.* (ALLSPORT / COLE)

Pablo Morales finally had his golden moment at the Olympic Games.

Before an emotionally-charged crowd, eight years after settling for a silver medal in the 100-meter butterfly, the 27-year-old Morales of Santa Clara, Calif., won the event in which he owns the world record.

The top morning qualifier in the preliminaries, Morales just outtouched Poland's Rafal Szukala to win in 53.32. He got to the wall first by three one-hundredths of a second, less than half a finger's length.

Morales called it a "dream come true" as he floated on his back, hands clasped across his chest in prayer, after he finished his last competitive race.

Morales had quit swimming after failing to make the 1988 U.S. Olympic

PABLO MORALES

A Dream Come True

BY SHARON ROBB

Team. It was a stunning setback for someone so unfamiliar with failure.

Motivated by the death of his mother, Blanca, in 1991, after a four-year battle with colon cancer, Morales came out of retirement and put law school on hold to train for the Olympic Trials.

It was Blanca Morales who made her only son learn how to swim at a local YMCA pool in Chicago. His parents immigrated from Cuba to Chicago in 1956, eight years before Pablo was born. Blanca had nearly drowned off a beach in Havana, and was determined to have her children learn how to swim. Pablo learned well.

Morales remembered the emotion and inspiration when he and his mother watched television shows about Olympians. They were especially touched by the stories that focused on the lives of the athletes, not just their races.

Now it's my time at last, Morales thought. He said he wished his mother could have been at the Olympic Games to be a part of his story, to watch his race, and share his emotion, but he said he knew she was there in spirit. ◆

in the 100 back, led off the race with an American record in the 100 back before turning it over to Nall. In the butterfly leg, team co-captain and silver medalist Crissy Ahmann-Leighton split 58.58, the third fastest in history, to avenge an eyelash finish earlier behind China's Hong Qian in the 100 fly.

Anchoring the relay was Thompson, one of the greatest relay swimmers in history. After a silver in the 100 and not qualifying for the finals in the 200 free, Thompson posted the fastest and third-fastest relay splits in history during the Olympics. She anchored the 400 medley relay in 54.47 (third all-time split) and gave the U.S. women their first world record in this race since 1978.

The U.S. tandem of Thompson and Angel Martino expected strong competition from the rest of the world in the 50 freestyle, and they got it. In a race where the slightest mistake can make all the difference, Martino took the bronze in 25.23 and Thompson, the American record-holder, was sixth. Winning the race was China's world record-holder Yang Wenji, who lowered her own mark to 24.79 seconds and remained the only woman to break the 25-second barrier in the race.

A pacesetter's meet

GOING INTO THE 400 IM, no one gave the American record-holder, Erik Namesnik, much of a chance against Hungary's Tamas Darnyi, but with 300 meters gone in the race, 'Snik, as he is known to his teammates, was eyeball to eyeball with the world record-holder. In the end, however, Darnyi got the gold in 4:14.23 and Namesnik the silver, just 1.34 seconds back.

For sheer noise, nothing beat the Spanish partisans when Martin Lopez-Zubero won the 200-meter backstroke. Zubero, the world record-holder and a native of Jacksonville, Fla., with dual U.S./Spanish citizenship, followed in his brother David's footsteps by electing to swim for Spain rather than the U.S. An appreciative local crowd cheered loudly as he won the gold medal in 1:58.47 over Vladimir Selkov of the Unified Team. William "Tripp" Schwenk, the lone American in the final, was fifth.

Australia's Kieren Perkins was another world record-holder who showed he could fight back. He was the world record-holder in the 400, 800 and 1,500-meter freestyles coming into the meet, but found himself a silver medalist in the 400 free to Evgueni's new world record. On the final day of the meet, Perkins blistered the field in the 1,500 freestyle and won in a world record time of 14:43.48, taking an incredible 4.92 seconds off his own mark. Finishing second in the race and giving Australia a one-two sweep was Glen Housman in 14:55.29.

The 1992 Olympic swimming competition set the tone for the sport in the next decade. No one country may ever again totally dominate the sport as the Americans did in the 1960s and early '70s. And, FINA, the sport's international governing body, will conduct worldwide out-of-season testing on swimmers beginning in 1993 with the objective being to keep the sport clean and above reproach.

In all, the meet saw 10 world records, 21 Olympic records and five American records set. The average margin of victory in all the events was only 1.19 seconds, and when Perkins' 12.04-second win in the men's 1,500 freestyle is factored out, the margin shrinks to .83 seconds. A true measure of the meet's competitiveness is that 21 of the 31 races in the meet were won by less than .46 seconds, and 12 were decided by less than two-tenths of a second. ❖ **JEFF DIMOND**

Hard to say who adopted whom. Florida resident Martin Lopez-Zubero, who is more at ease speaking English than his "native" Spanish, competed for Spain. He broke the Olympic record of the USA's Rick Carey in winning the 200-meter backstroke. (ALLSPORT / COLE)

SYNCHRONIZED SWIMMING
Everything in sync

When the U.S. Olympic synchronized swimming team selects music for its next competition, the theme music should come from the show "Solid Gold." Nothing would be more appropriate after the U.S. captured gold medals in both the solo and duet events at the 1992 Olympic Games, becoming the first U.S. team to sweep those events at the Games.

Soloist Kristen Babb-Sprague got things started for the U.S. team. After celebrating her 24th birthday only a few days earlier, the Pleasanton, Calif., resident won the compulsory figures competition over Canadian rival Sylvie Frechette, 92.808 to 92.557. The U.S. duet specialists, Sarah and Karen Josephson, finished second at 92.587, and third at 92.564, respectively. The U.S. team's technical prowess

Sylvie Frechette of Canada speaks out:

"Come to the pool. Try it once. Practice one day. Believe me, you'll quit before me, I promise you. Try to keep both hands out of the water without sinking, feel that burning in your legs. It's a lot of hard work, but hidden."

in the 1-2-3 finish allowed the Americans to head into the routine finals more confident than ever.

In the solo finals, the pressure was on Babb-Sprague, a four-time U.S. national solo champion. Frechette had beaten Babb-Sprague in each of their meetings in 1991. In their last encounter, Babb-Sprague lost by less than one-tenth of a point in the very same pool they were competing in at the Olympic Games. However, Babb-Sprague had vowed that things would be different in Barcelona this year.

Swimming seventh in the order and performing to "Rodeo," "Amazing Grace" and "Cowboys," she took to the water performing 33 360-degree vertical spins, including her patented drag spin. She earned two 10's for technical merit and one for artistic impression for a routine score of 99.040.

Frechette, the current world champion and last swimmer of the day, earned two 10's for technical merit and three 10's for artistic impression to total 99.160. When the compulsory figures were added in however, it wasn't enough for Frechette's total of 191.717 to overtake Babb-Sprague's 191.848. Japan's Fumiko Okuno was third with 187.056 points.

"I'm convinced I had the performance of my life," Babb-Sprague said. "That's what I came here for. I've played this day out 400 times in my head, and it's better than I ever imagined."

It was an emotional win for Babb-Sprague, who a little less than three years ago was sidelined for nine months with a back injury. Unable to practice and her muscles atrophied, she had to rebuild and develop them so she could compete again.

"Every athlete who has ever been injured always has doubts," she said. "But I think it's doubts that get us back in the pool."

In the duet competition, 1988 Olympic silver medalists Karen and Sarah Josephson had a lot on the line. Following the 1988 Games in Seoul, the J's, identical twins from Bristol, Conn./Concord, Calif., had retired for a year but decided to re-enter the competitive arena in search of Olympic gold. Since that time, they had compiled a 15-meet win streak, adding a duet world championship crown and a FINA world cup title to their trophy case.

Oddly enough, their toughest competition would come from another set of identical twins, Canadians

Penny and Vicky Vilagos, who had also come out of retirement with the sole intent of making the Olympic team.

The J's, considered the true technicians of the sport, proved it once again when they compiled a hefty 2.221 compulsory figures lead over the Canadians heading into the routine finals. Performing to excerpts from "An American Salute," "City Slickers," "Appalachian Spring," "Rhapsody in Blue," and "Allegro Agetato," the J's opened up their routine with a daring handstand walkover entry into the pool. They went on to perform 24 perfectly synchronized 360-degree vertical spins and a mirror image tandem hybrid. The J's routine received four 10's for technical merit and four 10's for artistic impression.

Their final routine score of 99.600, out of a possible 100 points, was enough to lock up the gold medal before the Canadians even swam. The Vilagos, however, did receive one 10 for technical merit and three 10's for artistic impression. The final totals were 192.175 to 189.394. Japan's Fumiko Okuno and Aki Takayama placed third with a mark of 186.868.

"We had a good performance in '88, but we wanted to better that," Karen Josephson said. "I think we did today."

"It took 20 years of hard work, but we definitely made the right decision to come back after '88," Sarah Josephson said. "Winning the gold medal made it all worth it."

The 1992 Games in Barcelona marked the last time the solo and duet events were held. A team event will replace both at the 1996 Olympic Games in Atlanta. Although the idea of winning a team gold medal at the 1996 Games seems enticing, all three 1992 U.S. Olympic champions have vowed permanent retirement. ❖ **LAURA LaMARCA-SHATKOWSKI**

OPPOSITE / *Kerry Shacklock of England takes a breather from training.* (ALLSPORT / COLE)

ABOVE / *A big smile of relief for Kristen Babb-Sprague, who squeaked by Sylvie Frechette of Canada to capture the gold.* (ALLSPORT / NEWKIRK)

TOP / *The 28-year-old Josephson twins take a deserved break from the pool. After capturing the gold in the duet event, the double gold medalists announced their retirement from competition.* (ALLSPORT / NEWKIRK)

TABLE TENNIS
Stomping on Asian turf

Appearing as a medal sport in the Olympic Games for only the second time, the table tennis competition in Barcelona clearly showed the international interest that can develop in a sport that gains Olympic approval.

While competitors from the Orient, table tennis' traditional hotbed, found success, so, too, did players from Europe and, to a greater extent than ever before, from the United States.

This was a competition that saw a men's singles final without an Oriental player to be found. Sweden's Jan Ove Waldner, the leading light in his country's table tennis surge, defeated France's Jean-Phillipe Gatlen, 21-10, 21-18, 25-23, for the gold medal as Kim Taek Soo of South Korea took the bronze.

China led the nation's medal haul with five medals, three of them gold, while South Korea won four medals, all bronze, and North Korea won two bronze medals. Germany also found its way to the medal stand when Steffen Fetzner and Jorg Rosskopf collected a silver in the men's doubles.

As for the team from the U.S., including returning Olympians Sean O'Neill, Diana Gee and Insook Bhushan, while it was unsuccessful in breaking through for medal success, it nonetheless showed improvement on the international scene, recording two upsets in pool play qualifying and drawing attention in two other matches against the world's best players.

Bhushan, 40, became the first U.S. performer to win a match with a 21-19, 21-17 upset victory over Barbara Chiu of Canada in the first round of the Group A draw of women's singles. Bhushan, an 11-time U.S. national champion, entered the match ranked No. 68 in the world, while Chiu was ranked No. 64.

Jim Butler, who entered the Olympics ranked No. 122 in the world, followed suit with a 22-20, 17-20, 21-18 triumph past Tomas Janci of Czechoslovakia in the opening round of the Group D draw of men's singles. Janci was ranked No. 37 in the world.

The assignments grew more difficult with Bhushan bowing to China's Deng Yaping, the world's top-ranked women's player, 21-14, 21-12, in the second round. Then it was O'Neill's turn to share the spotlight when he faced Nam Kyu Yoo of South Korea, the defending Olympic singles champion, in the second round. It could have been the ideal present for O'Neill, who was celebrating his 25th birthday. Nevertheless, O'Neill accomplished what he set out to achieve in earning respect during his hard-fought 21-10, 19-21, 21-19 setback.

"I'm not disappointed at all," said O'Neill, a five-time U.S. champion and holder of 18 U.S. Olympic Festival gold medals. "In

ABOVE / *American Lily Hugh teamed with Diana Gee in the doubles event. The first-time Olympian Hugh and returning Olympian Gee faced stiff competition in Barcelona.* (DUOMO / MITCHELL LAYTON)

the third game, I think everyone in the arena was watching my match, knowing Yoo could go down at any moment. It was a good effort. This guy is a professional player who trains seven days a week, six to eight hours a day.

"It would be comparable to me being a college basketball player trying to beat the Dream Team. I mean, you can come close...but toward the end most everyone will pick the favorite. But I don't think I'll lose any respect from the table tennis players here."

Butler was the highest seeded U.S. men's player, at No. 43, in the 64-player Olympic singles draw. He finished with a 2-1 record. While it might have been Butler's first trip to the Olympic Games, it wasn't his first flirtation with big-time competition. At 14, he was the youngest finalist ever to play for the U.S. national championship in 1985.

"I think Jim can become a Top 30 player," said his coach, Zhenshi Li. "He's much stronger mentally now, and he really wants to be a great player. I think he can."

Bhushan finished with a 2-1 record in her draw, while Gee and Lily Hugh posted 1-2 marks in their respective pools.

Deng and Qiao Hong of China upset their top-seeded compatriots and the world champions, Chen Zihe and Gao Jun, 21-13, 14-21, 21-14, 21-19, to capture the women's doubles gold. Li Bun Hui

ABOVE / *In a sport traditionally dominated by the Asians, Jan Ove Waldner of Sweden surprised the field by taking the gold in men's singles.* (ALLSPORT / CHRIS COLE)

and Yu Sun Bok of North Korea and Hong Cha Ok and Hyun Jung Hwa of South Korea received bronze medals.

Deng became the first double gold medalist in Olympic table tennis history, beating her teammate Qiao, 21-6, 21-8, 15-21, 23-21, in the women's singles championship.

Lu Lin and Wang Tao of China won the men's doubles gold medal, defeating Fetzner and Rosskopf of Germany, 26-24, 18-21, 21-18, 13-21, 21-14. ❖   **MIKE MAHON**

TEAM HANDBALL
Going one better

The United States sent one of its most experienced and talented handball teams ever to the Olympic Games in Barcelona. Many of the women on the team had been competing within the elite level since the mid-1980s, with eight returning members from the 1988 Olympic Team. The women had finished seventh in Seoul and were anticipating a much stronger showing in Spain.

These hopes were not unfounded hopes. The team had won the gold medal at the 1991 Pan American Championships in Brazil, qualifying as the only North or South American team in the tournament. The women also displayed strong form in international tournaments prior to the Olympic Games, particularly at the Cheb Tournament in February, where they defeated the Russian team, somewhat of an unexpected victory.

But the 1992 Games would be a different story. The U.S. team found itself in a tough pool, consisting of the defending world champion Unified Team, and a very strong German squad, bolstered by the reunification of the East and West. While the odds were stacked against the Americans, the U.S. was optimistic heading into the tournament.

However, the U.S. lost the opener to the Unified Team, after putting up a tough battle. The U.S. was leading with 11:31 in the first half when two U.S. players were ejected less than a minute apart. The Unified Team capitalized on the player-up advantages and turned the game around, charging to a 15-10 lead. The American squad could not turn the tide, losing 23-16.

"We started out so well," said three-time Olympian Cindy Stinger. "They capitalized on our mistakes. Then it seemed almost impossible."

The loss put the U.S. in a tough position. In order to advance to the medal round, the Americans would have to beat the German team, considered one of the best in the Olympic field. The Germans lived up to their reputation, outscoring the U.S. by a 32-16 margin.

In the medal round, the women's team from South Korea surged

ABOVE / *In 1988, the former Soviet Union dominated the team handball competition, and in 1992, the divided states joined for one last effort as the Unified Team to win the tournament.* (ALLSPORT / HEWITT)

ABOVE / *Three-time Olympians Leora "Sam" Jones and Kim Clarke help defend their goal from a unified attack. The U.S. lost to the Unified Team, 23-16.* (ALLSPORT / RONDEAU)

to the gold medal, its second in a row after a stunning upset over the Soviet Union in Seoul in 1988. Norway lost to the Koreans in the gold-medal match to claim the silver medal while the Unified Team finished as the bronze-medal winner.

Once they were out of medal contention, the next goal for the American women was to improve upon their 1988 Olympic showing. They needed to beat Nigeria in their third game to advance to the fifth-place game. Nigeria had also lost to the Germans and the Unified Team.

The U.S. got in the win column with a 23-21 win over Nigeria, advancing to meet Austria for fifth place.

"Now the pressure is gone," said U.S. head coach Vojtech Mares. "We had some high expectations and that created a lot of pressure. I know the girls. They know how to play handball."

The U.S. entered the Austria game in what would likely be the final game for a group of veterans, including three-time Olympian Leora "Sam" Jones and team captain Carol Peterka.

Austria led 11-6 at halftime, and the Americans pulled within 13-10 in the second half before succumbing by a final 26-17 margin. The U.S. finished in sixth, its highest placing at an Olympic Games and one better than its performance at the 1988 Olympic Games.

"This time around we really wanted to be here and take home a medal," Peterka said. "It didn't happen."

Jones was the leading scorer for the United States team in the tournament with 18 goals, followed by Peterka with 13 and Laura Coenen with 10.

In the men's division, the Unified Team dominated the field to win the gold medal, theoretically its second straight following a Soviet Union triumph in Seoul. Sweden took the silver medal and France the bronze. The U.S. men's team did not qualify for the Olympic Games in Barcelona. ❖ **STEVE PENNY**

TENNIS
Serving up gold medals

While the tennis draw had the look of a Grand Slam event with the eligibility of professional players, the tournament definitely had the feel of the Olympic Games on the clay courts at Vall d'Hebron.

"There's more pressure here than the Grand Slams," Gigi Fernandez of the U.S. team said. "There's only one Olympics. You can't get used to it, like you can the Slams. Also you're representing your country which is really something. Normally getting to the quarterfinals is no big deal, but here you're playing for a medal. It's nerve-wracking."

The mantle of the gold-medal favorite weighed particularly heavy on the American men's shoulders at the outset of the tournament with the world's number one player Jim Courier as the top Olympic seed followed by third-seeded Pete Sampras and sixth-seeded Michael Chang.

With the presence of defending Olympic champion Steffi Graf of Germany on the women's side, the U.S. contingent didn't figure to send too many ripples through the draw with Jennifer Capriati as the third seed, Mary Joe Fernandez as the fourth seed and 1988 Olympic bronze medalist Zina Garrison as the 12th seed.

But the American women had the impact of a tidal wave, winning three medals as Jennifer Capriati took the gold medal in singles over Graf while Mary Joe Fernandez tied for the bronze. Team Fernandez, the USA pair of Mary Joe and Gigi Fernandez, captured the gold medal in women's doubles.

Meanwhile the U.S. men, along with top players such as Stefan Edberg of Sweden and Boris Becker of Germany, were washed away in the early rounds, leaving the singles gold medal to hard-serving Marc Rosset of Switzerland. Jordi Arrese of Spain won the silver and Croatia's Goran Ivanisevic and Andrei Cherkasov of the Unified Team tied for the bronze. Becker bounced back in doubles, teaming with Michael Stich to win the gold medal over Wayne Ferreira and Piet Norval of South Africa.

Certainly the biggest smile of the Olympic Games was on the face of a beaming 16-year-old Capriati. After beating Spaniard Arantxa Sanchez Vicario in front of the King and Queen of Spain in the semifinals, Capriati was poised to write a new chapter in her development as one of the great tennis players in the world.

Two days later, in the women's final against Graf, who had already knocked out Mary Joe Fernandez, Capriati topped the German star for the first time in five career attempts, 3-6, 6-3, 6-4.

The American journey to the gold medal in women's doubles was just as difficult. In the second round, Mary Joe and Gigi Fernandez had to subdue Germany's Graf and Anke Huber. In the finals, the Fernandez duo had to overcome the hometown favorites Conchita Martinez and Sanchez Vicario for the gold.

The men's bracket followed the course of the roll of the dice. The U.S. had formed the most impressive group of players from any country at the Olympic Games. But no American made it to the quarterfinal round, and, in fact, only one player in the top 24 world rankings advanced to the quarterfinals.

Courier and Sampras were both knocked out in the third round as Courier fell to Rosset and Sampras was eliminated by Andrei Cherkasov of the Unified Team. Michael Chang fell in the second round to Jaime Oncins of Brazil. The U.S. doubles team of Sampras and Courier also hit hard times, losing to Spain's Sergio Casal and Emilio Sanchez. ❖

STEVE HATCHELL

BACKGROUND / *Croatian Goran Ivanisevic was bounced from gold-medal contention along with seeded players Jim Courier, Stefan Edberg and Boris Becker.* (Allsport / Rondeau)

PAGE 156 / *Americans Gigi and Mary Joe not only share the same last name — Fernandez — but the joy of bringing home the gold in the doubles competition.* (Allsport / Bruty)

When she arrived at the Olympic Games, Jennifer Capriati hadn't made it to the final of a tournament all year. In her career, she had never beaten Steffi Graf in the four times they had played. What's more, she didn't have a regular coach and she found herself having to deny rumors that, at age 16, she already was burned out on professional tennis.

So it came as a bit of a surprise that when she left the Olympics, Capriati had a gold medal in her possession.

After braving a partisan and unfriendly crowd — including the King and Queen of Spain — to defeat Arantxa Sanchez Vicario of Barcelona in the semifinals, Capriati upset Graf, 3-6, 6-3, 6-4, to win the gold medal in women's singles.

She battled back into the match with a flurry of baseline drives and steady backhands that finally wore down Graf, the winner of the 1988 Olympic gold

JENNIFER CAPRIATI

BY CHRISTINE BRENNAN

medal in Seoul.

"It was definitely one of my greatest matches in terms of fighting for everything, running down balls, and really grinding it out," said Capriati, who became the youngest player to win an Olympic tennis gold medal.

There has been much discussion about whether tennis should be in the Olympics, about whether the pros care enough about winning a gold medal in the midst of their Grand Slam events, but there was no doubt that winning the gold medal had a great impact on Capriati.

"It was so emotional," she said about receiving her medal and listening to the national anthem. "I had the chills the whole time. I just can't believe it. All week, I watched the other athletes up there and I was with them and I thought, 'Wow, that would be so cool.'"

Capriati's victory proved she would not wilt under pressure, gave her the most meaningful victory of her short career and added immediate luster to her stagnating resume.

Said Graf, who, at age 15, won the 1984 gold medal when tennis was a demonstration sport: "It helped me to believe in myself. I'm sure for Jennifer, it's going to help her a lot, even more." ◆

Sixteen-year-old Jennifer Capriati served up an unbeatable game and showed the world she could beat Steffi Graf.

VOLLEYBALL
Double dip of bronze

After an Olympic volleyball tournament punctuated by narrow, five-set matches, the men of Brazil and the women of Cuba ruled the world, if only barely. Just a notch below them were the men's and women's teams from the United States, who met the eventual champions in the semifinals and only reluctantly sent the winners on their way.

In the subsequent bronze medal matches, the U.S. got a measure of revenge when the women's team defeated Brazil and the men's team defeated Cuba. It left the Americans with a pair of bronze medals and a consolation prize of sorts — as the nation with the most volleyball medals.

Other countries figuring in the medals were the Netherlands' men's team and the Unified Team's women's squad. Both won silvers.

The U.S. women came to Barcelona as one of the medal contenders along with Cuba, China and the defending Olympic champion Unified Team. U.S. head coach Terry Liskevych felt his veteran squad was the most talented team he had coached during his eight campaigns with the U.S. national team. Plus, the program was looking to amend its seventh-place finish in Seoul in '88.

Led by '84 Olympic silver medalist Paula Weishoff and '91 world MVP Caren Kemner, the team showed flashes of brilliance throughout the tournament. But things did not start off with a bang for the "stars and stripes" squad following a disappointing 3-2 loss versus Japan.

Liskevych and the U.S. women remained confident about their chances versus the Unified Team — reigning world champions — in the next preliminary match.

The U.S. utilized Weishoff's savvy and Lori Endicott's setting talents to rally and defeat the Unified Team in five games to regain its medal hopes. They fought off a pair of set points in game two (trailing one set to none), which provided confidence to the squad.

In the fifth and deciding set, the U.S. led 3-2 before the Unified Team scored five of the next six points. However, the score was deadlocked at 11-11 when Kemner and Endicott provided the key points in making the U.S. the only country other than Japan to defeat the former Soviet Union in Olympic competition.

Following a 3-0 whitewash of Spain and a four-set victory over the Netherlands in the quarterfinals, the Americans faced Cuba in what many felt should have been the gold-medal matchup. Another grueling five-set match saw the momentum change like a seesaw, as the teams alternated games until the fifth set.

In the tight final stanza, the lead changed five times and the score was tied on seven occasions before Cuba recorded six of the last eight points to win the match.

Less than 12 hours later, the U.S. returned to Palau Sant Jordi for the bronze-medal encounter versus Brazil. They came out with fire in their eyes, and Elaina Oden's block of an Ana Moser attack sealed the bronze medal.

The Americans also brought some additional hardware home to San Diego, as Weishoff was crowned the most outstanding player of the tournament. She was joined by Kemner on the all-spectacular team, and Endicott was tabbed the best setter.

"This is a culmination of seven-and-a-half years of hard work and two weeks of upset stomachs," Kemner said.

Meanwhile, a successful protest by the Japanese, followed by the shaved heads, grabbed the headlines for the U.S. men's volleyball team throughout the Games. Almost forgotten were three key elements for head coach Fred Sturm — a chance to make Olympic history with a third consecutive gold, the knee injury to middle blocker Bryan Ivie and the return of the '88 Olympic trio of Steve Timmons, Jeff Stork and Bob Ctvrtlik from Italy.

Reserve middle blocker Bob Samuelson became the focus as he

ABOVE / *Brazilian Mauricio Lima is riding high after beating the Netherlands for the gold in men's volleyball.* (ALLSPORT / RONDEAU)

OPPOSITE / *Six-foot-one middle blocker Elaina Oden intends to give the ball a healthy hit back into Brazil's court. The U.S. won the match to seal a bronze-medal victory.* (ALLSPORT / DUFFY)

replaced Ivie in the third set of the Japan match. A 6-5 dynamic and flashy middle blocker, Samuelson exudes excitement and power, and proved to be an integral member of America's drive toward hopes of a "three-peat."

The match with Japan, which the Americans won on the court 3-2 but lost to a FIVB Control Committee's decision less than 24 hours later, could have been heartbreaking, but the Americans used it to their fullest advantage. At issue was a penalty point that, according to the official rules, should have been assessed to the Americans because of two unsportsmanlike conduct calls against Samuelson. The penalty point would have given the match to Japan, but it was not called.

With the "clean cut" look showing team unity and support for "Sammy," (who is bald), Timmons (34 kills) and Samuelson (23 kills, four blocks) thwarted a Canadian comeback by capturing a 15-12, 15-12, 10-15, 11-15, 16-14 decision. Two days later, in front of the home crowd, Spain continued to give its opponents trouble and forced the Americans to yet another five-set match before Timmons took control of the match in the final set to lead the U.S. to victory.

That match appeared to mark the end of the U.S. struggles, as the men needed just over one hour to shut out France before facing Italy, one of the gold-medal favorites.

In a match with no major importance to the standings, the Americans sent a message to the rest of the Olympic field — Watch Out. After dropping the initial set, the U.S. trailed until knotting the score at 10-10 in the second set. Samuelson, Timmons and Scott Fortune (the tournament's top digger) paced the U.S. attack.

The match also marked the return of Ivie (10 kills) and the emergence of Brent Hilliard, who replaced Timmons to start off the third game. The 22-year-old tallied 20 kills in the downing of one of the gold-medal favorites and the 1990 world champions.

"This match was real important to our team...more so than for Italy," said Ctvrtlik, who was named the top serve receiver of the '92 Games. "They know they are among the best, and we are still trying to re-establish ourselves and find our niche among the world's elite."

Following its quarterfinal triumph over the Unified Team, the Americans found themselves against the world's hottest team — unbeaten Brazil. After capturing the opening set, the Americans saw why Brazil had not lost a match, as it played a near-perfect match in the final three sets to advance to the finals and douse the U.S. dream of Olympic history.

"This is not a position I am used to — losing," said Timmons, only the second volleyball player to win three medals. "It felt awkward to me. Right now, it's a letdown. I haven't played in too many third-place matches in my career."

Not wanting to leave Barcelona empty-handed, the Americans rebounded with their decisive 3-1 bronze-medal victory over Cuba.

❖ **RICHARD WANNINGER**

OPPOSITE (TOP) / *First-time Olympian Tara Cross-Battle helps the U.S. women to a win over Brazil.* (ALLSPORT / DUFFY)

(BOTTOM) / *As the cameras turn to the victorious Brazilians, whose win over the U.S. sends them to the gold-medal game, Bryan Ivie (left) and Bob Samuelson take a moment to sort out the up-and-downs of Olympic competition.* (ALLSPORT / LEAH)

LEFT / *Six-foot-five Steve Timmons, 6-3 Jeff Stork and 6-6 Doug Partie stalk the front line, providing a towering defense and an attacking offense.* (ALLSPORT / LEAH)

"THE VOLLEYBALDERS"

Skin Is In

BY MIKE SPENCE

It was a "hair"-brained scheme to be sure. But the decision by the U.S. men's volleyball players to shave their heads in protest and in support of their bald teammate was one of the Games' most poignant moments.

"I don't know too many teams that would sacrifice their hair for what they believe," said Olympic veteran Steve Timmons. "But we were united."

The U.S. team decided to go with the Telly Savalas look after a hard-fought, five-set victory over Japan was overturned by international volleyball officials.

The controversy began with Japan leading 2-1 in games and at match point, 14-13, in game four.

Bob Samuelson was given his second yellow card for yelling at officials. Rules call for a red card to be issued and the awarding of a technical point to Japan.

If referee Ramis Samedov of Azerbaijan had followed those rules, Japan would have won the match at that point. But Samedov did not issue the red card and allowed play to continue. The U.S. fought back to win (or so they thought) 8-15, 15-11, 15-10, 15-13.

A Japanese protest was upheld after a 5 1/2-hour meeting, turning the U.S. victory into a defeat.

After the decision, the Americans called a team meeting. And hair began to fall.

"We were talking about doing it and some of the guys weren't so sure," said Timmons, who had sported a distinctive red flat top for years. "But once I did my hair, everyone else got in line."

The first the world learned of the protest was when the U.S. team showed up for its match against Canada the next day.

"I think the protest brought this team closer together than it had before or during the Games," Timmons said.

The Americans defeated Canada and cruised into the medal round before losing to Brazil in the semifinals.

Despite the semifinal loss, the Americans were able to regroup and defeat Cuba for third place.

And bald, but unbowed, the U.S. men's team left Barcelona with a bronze medal. ◆

WATER POLO
Pain in Spain

Almost nothing went as expected in the Barcelona Olympics water polo tournament. Right down to the last goal of the last match, when Italy shocked Spain with a 9-8 win in triple overtime to claim the gold medal, what the odds said should have happened...didn't.

With a capacity crowd consisting almost entirely of Spanish fans watching the gold-medal match, the Italians would have been excused for stepping aside in the name of popular opinion. But they stubbornly hung on to the end, silencing all of Barcelona, at least momentarily, in the process.

Equally as surprising as an Italy-Spain final was the U.S. team's out-of-the-medals fourth-place finish.

The U.S. team started strong enough — winning its first three games over Australia, Czechoslovakia and France for its best start since the sport's 1904 Olympic introduction.

A team with more than half its members boasting of Olympic silver-medal credentials, the team was certainly deemed a gold-medal candidate. The Americans had won their first major international title — the 1991 FINA Water Polo World Cup — in Barcelona at the same pool, the Piscina Bernat Picornell, a year earlier, setting the stage for the 1992 Games. The U.S. team had also collected Olympic silver medals in 1984 and 1988 behind Yugoslavia, which had been banned from the 1992 Games due to United Nations sanctions.

With three early-tournament wins, the Americans appeared poised for the gold medal. But their pace faltered down the stretch en route to a fourth-place finish.

Fate showed a glimpse of the final outcome during preliminary play when a strong and willful Unified Team came from behind to defeat the Americans. The difference in the contest was determined by extra-man situations. The Russians scored in six of nine extra-man opportunities, while the Americans managed only one goal in eight chances.

Thus, the Americans would be put to the test with a must-win-or-tie situation against Germany to advance to the semifinals. U.S. goalie Craig Wilson shined, registering 11 of his 16 saves in the first half as the U.S. club dominated Germany, 7-2, and earned a berth in the medal round. Germany converted only two of 28 shots against Wilson.

"Sometimes the ball looks like a beach ball, coming in slowly. Sometimes it looks like a golf ball, coming in quickly," Wilson said. "Today was a beach ball day."

But the semifinals would not be a day at the beach for the Americans, especially with 10,000 boisterous fans rooting and whistling for a Spanish team bristling with momentum.

A noisy, hometown crowd, some missed U.S. shots and a questionable referee call each contributed to knock the U.S. team out of a chance for the gold medal in a 6-4 loss to Spain.

ABOVE / *Nice accessories. The Italians are stylin' in their blue robes perfectly complemented by a gold medal around their necks. The Italians downed the Spaniards, 9-8, in the match for the gold.* (ALLSPORT / HEWITT)

ABOVE / *The U.S. water polo team suffered another disappointment in Olympic competition. Its usually tough defense crumbled in the game against Spain along with the hope of a gold medal. The U.S. bowed out of the competition in fourth place.* (ALLSPORT / BRUTY)

Wilson, with 15 saves in the game, was magnificent for the U.S. The crucial moment in the game came with 3:36 remaining when U.S. player Mike Evans was ejected by German referee Jeurgen Blan for kicking Spain's Jordi Sans. Evans was ahead of the Spaniard heading for the goal when Sans grabbed Evans by the suit and climbed on his back. Evans inadvertently kicked Sans, and was ejected from the game. Sans headed back toward the American goal and 11 seconds later put Spain up 5-3.

"That call was the turning point of the game," said U.S. Head Coach Bill Barnett. "Evans was going in for the score, and they came out of it a man-up and scored. It was basically a two-goal turn-around."

The loss knocked the U.S. team into a rematch with the Unified Team, a 9-8 loser to Italy in the semifinals.

In the bronze-medal match, the Unified Team outscored the U.S. by an 8-4 count. A case of "third-quarter blues" proved to be the Americans undoing. The Unified players, all of whom hail from the Russian Republic, outscored the Americans 4-1 in a crucial seven-minute frame, beginning late in the second quarter and lasting all of the third.

"We came out and played hard, but our shooting was way, way in outer space somewhere," Barnett said. "It was somewhere between here and Los Angeles."

"Fourth place to me is the same as 12th place," Wilson said. "Even second place would have been the same as 12th place to me because we came here to win the gold medal."

Wilson stopped 12 of the Russian shots on goal to raise his Olympic record saves number to 88 of 126 scoring attempts (70 percent). His 88 saves is considered a new Olympic record, surpassing his 1984 Olympic mark of 70. Unified player Dmitri Apasnassenko and Spain's Manuel Estiarte topped the scoring efforts with 22 goals each. Estiarte has now led the Olympic field in goal scoring in the last three Olympic Games as Wilson has led in goalie saves.

The fourth-place finish was especially difficult for four-time Olympian Terry Schroeder, who came out of retirement to help the U.S. qualify for the 1992 Games. "Over the last four years the competition has become better and gotten tougher," Schroeder said. "We didn't rise to the occasion." ❖ **EILEEN SEXTON**

WEIGHTLIFTING
An uplifting performance

For their last lifts as an organized team, the weightlifters from the former Soviet Union made certain they won't soon be forgotten. No other country came close to the domination of the Unified Team in the competition in Barcelona.

All told, the Unified Team collected nine of a possible 30 medals, including five of the 10 gold medals awarded. The total would have been higher if not for a tantrum thrown by Ibagim Samadov in the 181-pound division. When Samadov was presented with the bronze medal he refused it and walked off the podium. He had, in fact, tied with Pyrros Dimas of Greece and Krzysztof Siemion of Poland in the competition, each lifter totaling 370 kilograms. The three-way tie was broken by weighing the lifters. The lightest -- by less than a pound -- was Dimas, and that gave him the gold. Next lightest was Siemion, less than a quarter of a pound behind Samadov.

The Unified Team fared particularly well in the heavier divisions. In the super heavyweight class, where the "World's Strongest Man" was decided, Alexandre Kourlovitch of the Unified Team edged his teammate, Leonid Taranenko, for that distinction.

A total of 11 nations won medals in Barcelona. Bulgaria and China, with four each, were runners-up behind the Unified Team while Poland and Germany won three each.

The United States team was led by Tim McRae of Daytona Beach, Fla., and Mario Martinez of San Francisco. McRae, 22, went five-for-six and finished with a personal record performance. The 67.5 kg lifter equalled the American record in the snatch with 135 kg and hoisted 162.5 kg in the clean-and-jerk to finish with a 297.5 kg total, five better than his previous best. McRae placed eighth among 18 athletes.

"I wish my family could have been here," McRae said. "No telling how much I would have done. I was focused, but I still didn't have the fire in me you get when your family is watching."

McRae's family was unable to travel to the Games, but Ray and Abby Martinez settled in Barcelona for a few days to cheer on their son, Mario. Super heavyweight Mario led the U.S. team in 1984 with a silver medal and again in 1988 taking fourth place.

Now 35, Martinez snatched 170 kg and made a 215 kg clean-and-jerk. He finished eighth with 385 kg. Martinez had hoped to place higher, but he was pleased to add a third Games to his athletic career.

TOP / *Almost Ernesto! While Ernesto Aguero of Cuba struggles to lift his weight in the over 100-kilogram category, Alex Kourlovitch* (MIDDLE) *of the Unified Team goes for the gold with a total lift of 450 kilograms.* (ALLSPORT / BRUTY). *Meanwhile, Cedric Plancon of France* (BOTTOM) *wonders if he has a prayer of gold. He doesn't. He finishes seventh in the 90-kilogram division.* (ALLSPORT / BOTTERILL)

OPPOSITE / *Super heavyweight Mark Henry of the U.S. has made great gains in his short career and is being touted as a 1996 medal contender for Atlanta.* (DUOMO / DAVID MADISON)

Newcomer Mark Henry, 21, of Silsbee, Texas, bounded onto the Olympic scene in the super heavyweight division. Henry tipped the scales as the heaviest lifter ever to compete on the Olympic platform. Weighing in at 166.40 kg, the largest lifter surpassed the unofficial record of 164.95 kg set in 1988 by Jiri Zubricky of Czechoslovakia.

Henry snatched 165 kg and lifted a personal record 212.5 kg in the clean-and-jerk to equal his best total of 377.5 kg for 10th place in the +110 kg class.

"I was so scared when I walked out onto that stage," Henry said. "I wanted to turn around and go back down the stairs. I thought I was going to have a heart attack I was so scared."

Vernon Patao of Kahului, Hawaii, like Henry, also made big gains. The 22-year-old placed 10th in the 67.5 kg class with a 290 kg total. At the close of the Games, Patao had announced that he would return to his family in Hawaii and would train for the 1996 Games.

Like Patao, other young 1992 team members plan to use their experience in Barcelona as a springboard for '96. Bryan Jacob, a 23-year-old from Norcross, Ga., finished 18th in the 60 kg class but his 262.5 kg total was the best ever by a U.S. lifter at the Games. Wes Barnett of St. Joseph, Mo., finished 15th in the 100 kg class with the second best total of his career, 352.5 kg.

Rich Schutz of Mount Prospect, Ill., battled with a virus in Barcelona before competing on the platform and his performance was well below his best. Still Schutz lifted 347.5 kg to place 18th.

Bret Brian of Baton Rouge, La., turned in a gutsy effort in the 90 kg class. Nursing a back injury, Brian finished 13th with a 337.5 kg total.

Roberto "Tony" Urrutia of Hollywood, Fla., was the only lifter in 1992 who had appeared in the Olympic Games as early as 1976. He had competed for Cuba in '76 and for the U.S. in 1988. The 34-year-old had one of the best competitions of his life. He posted an impressive 340 kg total in the 82.5 kg class for 17th place and then announced his retirement from competitive weightlifting.

"Our super heavyweights came through at the end and the other team members weren't where we had hoped but they worked very hard," said USA head coach Roger Nielsen. "I think we've set ourselves up for a bright transition to 1996." ❖ **MARY ANN RINEHART**

WRESTLING
Grappling for gold

With three Olympic champions and six world champions on its 10-man roster entering the 1992 Games in Barcelona, the USA certainly fielded a freestyle wrestling squad of the ages — all ages, that is.

The United States' wrestling haul — eight medals won, including three gold — was exceeded only by the Unified Team's 16 medals, six gold. And with the dissolution of the Unified Team immediately after the conclusion of the Barcelona Games, that left the Americans in good shape for the next Olympics to be staged on their home mats.

John Smith, one of the winningest freestyle wrestlers in history, keyed the U.S. attack by defending the gold medal he won in 1988 in Seoul. Wrestling in the 136.5-pound division, the native of Stillwater, Okla., shut out Asgari Mohammadian of Iran, 6-0, in the gold-medal match.

Smith was one of three American freestyle wrestlers to win a gold medal in Barcelona.

At 180.5 pounds, 1991 World Champion Kevin Jackson of Ames, Iowa, edged Elmadi Jabrailov of the Unified Team, 1-0 in overtime at 6:54, in the gold-medal final. Jackson's victory was not without its share of controversy, however.

Early in the overtime period, Jabrailov attempted to take Jackson down and score what would have been the winning points. Officials ruled that Jabrailov failed to establish control before the two wrestlers skidded out of bounds, however, and refused to award any points.

Unified Team coaches jumped to the mat to protest the officials' decision, delaying the match for several minutes. Enraged by the

controversy, Unified Team athletes and fans threw shoes on the mat and booed during the U.S. National Anthem.

The remaining U.S. gold medalist, Bruce Baumgartner of Cambridge Springs, Pa., made history by winning top honors in the super heavyweight (286 pounds) class.

A gold medalist in the 1984 Olympic Games and a silver medalist in 1988, Baumgartner became the first American wrestler in history to win three career Olympic medals by taking the gold in Barcelona.

He also joined Smith (1988, 1992) and George Mehnert (1904, 1908) as the only American wrestlers in history to win two Olympic gold medals.

Baumgartner won the gold in Barcelona by knocking off Canada's Jeff Thue, 8-0, in the finals. On his way to the gold medal, Baumgartner also dropped 1991 World Champion Andreas Schroder of Germany and 1990 World Champion David Gobedjishvili of the Unified Team.

Americans Zeke Jones of Bloomsburg, Pa. (114.5 pounds), and Kenny Monday of Stillwater, Okla. (163), were both defeated in the finals and brought home silver medals.

Monday, a gold medalist in the 1988 Olympic Games, dropped a hard-fought, 1-0 decision to South Korea's Park Jang-Soon in the finals. Monday yielded just one point — Park's winning point — during the Olympic Games.

Jones, the 1991 World Champion at 114.5 pounds, was stopped

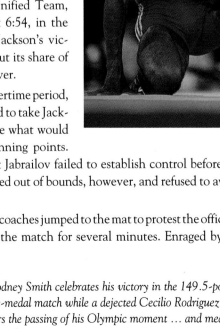

ABOVE / *American Rodney Smith celebrates his victory in the 149.5-pound Greco-Roman bronze-medal match while a dejected Cecilio Rodriguez Perez of Cuba ponders the passing of his Olympic moment ... and medal.* (ALLSPORT / M. POWELL)

OPPOSITE / *Thirty-seven-year-old Chris Campbell, a member of the 1980 U.S. Olympic Team, stepped back into the wrestling ring after a five-year retirement to finish some unfinished business: wrestling in the Olympic Games. Terrance Parker of New Zealand got a bitter taste of Campbell's comeback. Campbell won the match and the bronze in the 149.5-pound division.* (ALLSPORT / BOTTERILL)

by North Korea's Li Hak-Son, 8-1, in the finals.

The final American to medal in freestyle wrestling, Chris Campbell of Fayetteville, N.Y., proved that you're never too old to experience Olympic success by capturing the bronze in the 198-pound weight class.

A 37-year-old practicing corporate attorney, Campbell ended a five-year retirement from the sport of wrestling in 1989 with hopes of fulfilling his life-long dream of competing in the Olympics.

Campbell was stretched into overtime before downing rival Roberto Limonta of Cuba, 5-4 at the 7:14 mark, for the bronze medal.

Excluding the 1984 Olympic Games, in which the powerful Eastern bloc nations did not compete, it had been two decades (1972 in Munich, Germany) since the United States had won three gold medals in freestyle wrestling.

Additionally, the Barcelona Games marked the first time in U.S. history that all 10 freestyle wrestlers placed among the top 10 in their weight classes.

The United States' success on the mat wasn't limited to freestyle wrestling, however. In Greco-Roman, the U.S. won two medals, including a silver by Dennis Koslowski of St. Louis Park, Minn., and

> **"The Unified Team has six or seven different world champions. The Americans have six world champions. This will be the last great competition between what was the Soviet Union and America."**
>
> **— USA Head Coach Bobby Douglas**

doubled the medal output from the 1988 Olympic Games in Seoul.

Koslowski fell in the finals to Cuba's Hector Millian, 2-1 in overtime at 5:25. A bronze medalist in the 1988 Olympic Games, Koslowski ended a two-year retirement from the sport in 1991 in hopes of making another run at an Olympic medal.

In what was perhaps the biggest — and most pleasant — surprise for the U.S. Greco-Roman Olympic Team, newcomer Rodney Smith of Fort Benning, Ga., stunned Cuba's Cecilio Rodriguez, 6-3, to claim the bronze medal at 149.5 pounds. Smith, considered a long-shot to make the U.S. Olympic Team when the trials began in 1992, was competing in his first major international tournament.

For the first time in Olympic history, the United States had seven Greco-Roman wrestlers place among the top 10 in their weight classes.

Besides the success enjoyed by the U.S. and Unified Team wrestlers, teams from South Korea, Cuba, Turkey, Germany and Iran all won at least two medals apiece. In all, 18 nations split up the 60 medals up for grabs in Barcelona. The 20 gold medals were claimed by nine nations in what was arguably the most competitive Olympic wrestling meet ever. ❖ **DARRYL SEIBEL**

LEFT / *Five-time world champion John Smith gained a victory over Kim Gwang Kol of North Korea to advance to the third round in the 136.5-pound weight class. Smith, who won the gold in Seoul, cruised to another golden victory after manhandling Asgari Mohammadian of Iran in the finals.* (ALLSPORT / BOTTERILL)

OPPOSITE (TOP) / *Zeke Jones, the 1991 World Champion at 114.5 pounds, had problems shaking the wiry Li Hak-Soon of North Korea in the finals. Li's relentless attack won the match, 8-2, and relegated Jones to the silver.* (ALLSPORT / BOTTERILL)

(BOTTOM) / *His two-year-old son Bryan told him over the telephone to "win the gold, Daddy" and Bruce Baumgartner did. The 31-year-old American wrestler celebrates his third Olympic medal in the 286-pound class, while a disappointed Jeffrey Thue of Canada feels the weight of the moment.* (ALLSPORT / LEAH)

JOHN SMITH

Smith Overcomes Himself

BY MIKE SPENCE

After four world championships and one Olympic gold medal, John Smith was expected to coast through the U.S. Olympic Trials and waltz right up to the victory stand in Barcelona.

It didn't happen.

For the first time in recent memory, the man considered the finest U.S. wrestler ever found himself struggling.

He lost to an American opponent for the first time in five years at the trials. And he lost to a foreign opponent for the first time in two years at the 1992 Olympic Games.

Despite those unexpected setbacks, Smith won his second Olympic gold medal at 136.5 pounds in expected form, beating Iran's Asgari Mohammadian, 6-0, in the final.

The victory elevated Smith into select company, along with super heavyweight Bruce Baumgartner (1984 and 1992) and George Mehnert (1904 and 1908) as the only American wrestlers to win two Olympic gold medals.

Smith's 1992 Olympic gold medal may have been more satisfying than the one he won in 1988.

Coaching responsibilities at Oklahoma State, forced Smith to shift his attention from his career to those of the 25 wrestlers he was coaching.

As a result, Smith wrestled only five matches in the months leading up to the Olympic Trials. His rustiness showed.

"I won some tight matches that I felt a year ago I would have dominated," Smith said. "Right now, I'm at about 60 percent of what I'm capable of. My body is at 100 percent, but my mind is not. I've been battling myself in training. I've been battling myself mentally."

Smith questioned his preparations. He questioned his motivation. He wondered if he had lost a step.

Yet when it came time to wrestle for the gold medal, Smith left no questions unanswered.

He led 4-0 after 90 seconds. He frustrated Mohammadian's every move. With six seconds left in the match, the Iranian conceded the inevitable, standing motionless as the clock ran out.

"I felt like my old self out there," Smith said. "It's been a real tough year for me. It's worn me down at times. But all that matters is that I'm going home with the gold." ◆

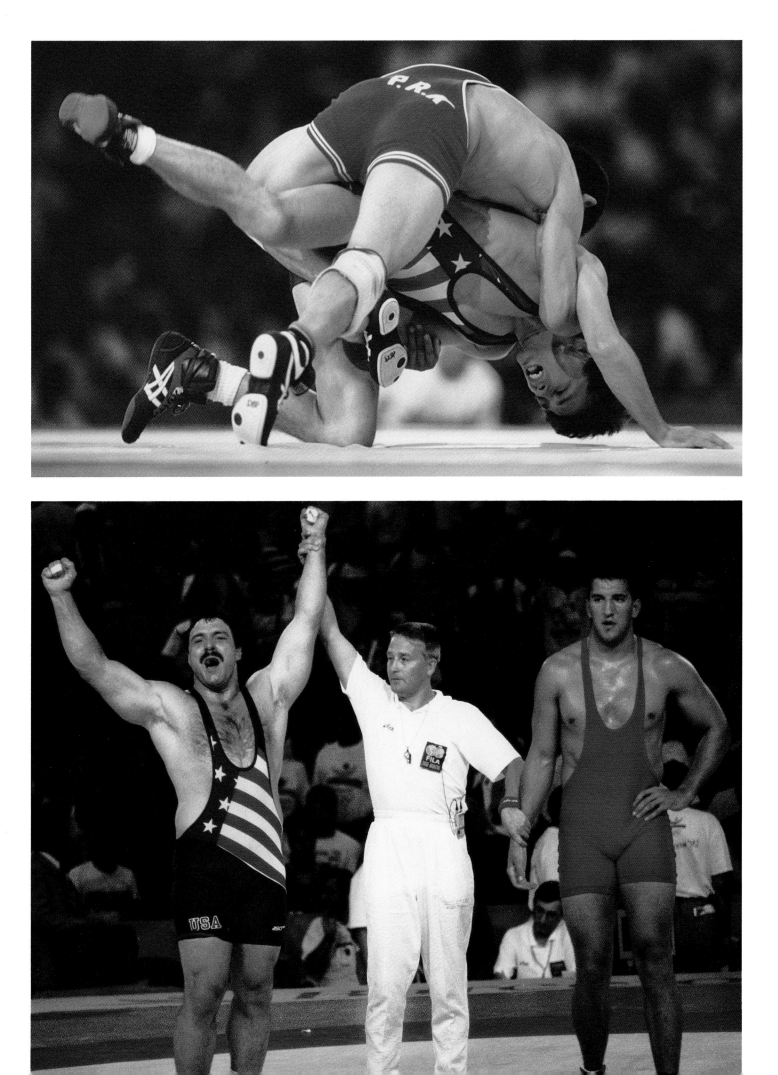

YACHTING
Sailing to the medal stand

When skipper Mark Reynolds stepped off his boat after clinching the gold medal in the Star class with teammate Hal Haenel, he walked directly into his wife's arms, kissed her and said, "All I want to do now is spend some time with my wife."

In those few words, Reynolds seemed to sum up the emotions of all Olympic sailors after more than two grueling weeks in the steamy summer sun of Barcelona for the 1992 Olympic Games.

Reynolds' and Haenel's lone gold medal for the U.S. team was especially significant, because the pair had been forced to settle for the silver medal in 1988 when the mast on their vessel broke in the final race.

The entire U.S. team's performance — nine medals in 10 events — topped any previous American effort in the history of the modern Olympic Games, and also topped all the countries that entered boats in Barcelona. No country came close to winning as many medals, although Spain, the runner-up with five, did use a home-water advantage in the Mediterranean Sea to make sure four of those medals were gold.

In the men's 470 event, Floridians Morgan Reeser and Kevin Burnham won the silver medal in a hard-fought battle. From one day to the next, the winds were as light as a knot or two or as strong as 17. By race four, the Reeser/Burnham scores read like the wind changes. "After winning the fourth," Morgan said, "it was a relief."

"When I think about how much work it took to get here from Pusan, it's unbelievable," said Finn class silver medalist Brian Ledbetter, who raced at the 1988 Games in Seoul but did not medal. In the final race, Ledbetter needed to beat four opponents to guarantee the silver medal. At the first mark, he was in 12th place and behind all four boats. "I just chipped away, stayed on their heels, and passed them one by one," Ledbetter said. "At the end of the race, I was in sixth and they were all behind me."

World champions Paul Foerster and Steve Bourdow seemingly had a lock on the gold medal until the fifth race, when they started poorly and finished 17th. That dropped the duo to the silver medal in the Flying Dutchman class despite winning three races in the regatta.

ABOVE / *Were it not for exceeding the four-hour time limit in the seventh race of the Tornado event, Randy Smyth and Keith Notary would have gone home with the gold. A new race was scheduled for the following day, but their luck didn't hold out. The U.S. sailors took the silver medal behind France's Yves Loday and Nicolas Henard. (ALLSPORT / BILOW)*

ABOVE / *Barbara Kendall of New Zealand turned in the best score of 10 races to capture the gold in women's windsurfing.* (ALLSPORT / VANDYSTADT)

Californians JJ Isler and Pamela Healy, the reigning world champions, edged out their closest competitors in a come-from-behind finish for the bronze medal in the women's 470 event.

Julia Trotman's bronze medal-performance in the Europe Dinghy, which made its Olympic debut in 1992, was the surprise of the U.S. team. Trotman led the fleet early in scoring but lost a shot at the gold and silver medals on a disqualification for a premature start. After the final race, Trotman talked about her grandfather who taught her to sail. "He died about three months after I decided to campaign for the Olympics," she said. "I think he thought I was wasting my education. I'd like for him to see me now."

The Soling regatta was the most publicized and promoted of the 10 Olympic yachting events. With live television coverage of the match racing medal rounds, 1992 Soling world champions Kevin Mahaney, Jim Brady and Doug Kern raced brilliantly into the gold-medal round, only to be defeated in the final best-of-three series by Jesper Bank, Steen Secher and Jesper Scier of Denmark.

The Tornado, the Olympic catamaran, yielded a silver medal for Randy Smyth and Keith Notary. Smyth, a 1984 Olympic silver medalist in the same event, and Notary, the youngest world champion ever in the Tornado class, had the regatta won in the seventh race until the race was canceled for exceeding the four-hour time limit. Re-racing the following day, the U.S. sailors took the silver medal behind France's Yves Loady and Nicolas Henard.

For the first time in the Olympic Games, the Windsurfer class was divided into two events for the men and women. In the women's event, American Lanee Butler finished the regatta in fifth place overall despite finishing first in two of the 10 races. Mike Gebhardt, the 1988 Olympic bronze medalist, captured a silver in the men's division, which featured 44 countries, the largest fleet of the meet. ❖ **CONNIE SMITH**

Curtain Call

Taekwondo, roller hockey and pelota played a part of Olympic history in Barcelona by becoming the last sports to compete as demonstration sports in the Olympic Games. Demonstration sports, part of the Olympic Games since 1900 when men's basketball was featured in the Olympic Games in Paris, will no longer be part of the schedule after the International Olympic Committee's vote last year brought an end to those sports not on the official program.

Demonstration competitions have played an important role in previewing sports for potential Olympic inclusion. The list of sports that have joined the official Olympic program after debuting as demonstration sports includes badminton, baseball, basketball and canoe/kayak.

Taekwondo, still a strong candidate for inclusion in future Olympic Games, was the most successful of the demonstration sports in Barcelona for the United States. The team brought home six medals in eight weight classes, including a gold medal by Herb Perez, two silver and three bronze medals.

Perez defeated the hometown Spanish favorite before a noisy and boisterous crowd, including the King of Spain, to claim the gold medal in the middleweight class. The Palisades Park, N.J., resident scored on sharp, quick kicks in a 3-2 victory over Juan Solis Godoy at Palau Blaugrana.

Perez grew up in New York City in a Puerto Rican neighborhood with a Puerto Rican father and a Polish mother. "They called me a Polarican," he said of his youth. When he was 12 his father was murdered trying to stop a burglary and his mother died of diabetes in 1990.

"I wish they could have seen me win the gold and go to law school," Perez said.

Perez runs a taekwondo school in New Jersey. He provides free memberships for neighborhood youths who can't afford the cost of the school. Many of those kids went on to make the national team trials this year and others have gone on to lead successful lives after overcoming a troubled youth.

"The Olympics is only a small part of what taekwondo is," Perez said. "It is a 60-year-old woman taking up the sport. It is a five-year-old boy who got beat up by the neighborhood bully. Those are the people I think about when I fight. I can go back to them and smile."

Juan Moreno of Zion, Ill., and Diane Murray of Citrus Heights, Calif., won silver medals for the American team.

Moreno won his second consecutive silver medal at the Olympic Games, duplicating his feat of 1988 when he finished second in his first international competition. Moreno lost to the world champion from Denmark, Gergely Salim, in the finals and announced his retirement from the sport after the match.

Murray, a former telegram singer, bellydancer and owner of two 10-foot snakes, narrowly missed the gold medal in the bantamweight class. She lost by a judges' decision after the match ended 1-1 after three rounds.

Bronze-medal winners included Terry Poindexter in the women's flyweight, Danielle Laney in the women's welterweight and Lynette Love in the women's heavyweight.

Korea and host Spain led the medal charts with five and four gold medals, respectively. Korea led the field with a total of seven medals overall in the competition while Spain and the U.S. tied for second with six each.

IOC President Juan Antonio Samaranch was a former roller hockey player in Spain, and it was natural that the sport would

ABOVE / *Diane Murray kicked her way through the taekwondo tournament in the 112-pound division, finishing second to Hwang Eun-Suk of South Korea.* (ALLSPORT / RONDEAU)

OPPOSITE/ *To many Americans, the fast-paced game of pelota is a mystery, but to Spain, which had the license to select one of the demonstration sports, pelota is a national pastime of its Basque people.* (ALLSPORT / LEAH)

appear on the program of the Olympic Games in Barcelona. The game is extremely popular in Spain, and the home team rode the frenzy of the crowd to the gold-medal game before losing to Argentina in the finals.

The U.S. team was knocked from the medal round by Portugal, the eventual fourth-place finisher. The Americans began the competition with a 10-1 win over the Japanese, tied eventual gold medalist Argentina 4-4, lost to bronze medal-winner Italy 13-2, beat Switzerland 5-2, and dropped the final game 7-3 to Portugal to keep from advancing.

The U.S. finished with a 2-2-1 record and had the honor of being the first American team in history to compete in the Olympics.

Spain was once again a power in the third demonstration sport of pelota. The host country led with 10 total medals followed by Mexico with seven and France with six. The United States did not enter a team in the competition. ❖ **BOB CONDRON**

ALBERTVILLE

winter blahs turned oh! là! là!

BY LEE BENSON

The venues stretched from one end of the Savoie to the other, through spectacular, picture-book terrain, on roads that never straighten, and over mountain passes that spend their summers causing bicycle racers in the Tour de France to ponder the meaning of life.

Spread over 640 square acres punctuated by jagged mountains and ski resorts, the XVIth Olympic Winter Games showed off the French Alps all right.

In all, 14 villages and/or ski resorts tucked here and there in the region of southeastern France called the Savoie (pronounced "Salve-wah") were used as Olympic venues in varying capacities.

These were the Games where you couldn't tell the contestants without an odometer.

Since the International Olympic Committee awards the Games to cities, not areas, states, countries, or famous mountain ranges, Albertville, the lowest-lying and most-easily accessible of the 14 venues with a population of about 20,000 (providing Kristi Yamaguchi wasn't performing at the new Albertville Ice Hall), became the official host of the 1992 Olympic Winter Games.

BACKGROUND / *The French Alps served as an impressive backdrop for the XVIth Olympic Winter Games and were, in fact, a congenial host, delaying only the women's super G event (and by only one day) with bad weather.* (ALLSPORT/VANDYSTADT)

But in reality, these Games were no more the Albertville Olympics than the American League is just the New York Yankees. Albertville was a stop, and an important one, of the Games in the Savoie, but still just one stop. Its chief purpose was to provide the temporary grandstands (30,000 capacity) for the Opening and Closing Ceremonies, the outdoor ice rink for the speedskaters, the indoor ice hall for the figure skaters and to serve as a launching pad to the Alps beckoning just beyond the city limits.

Albertville's designation as the alpha and omega of these Games did provide a certain symmetry, however. It was at the Opening Ceremonies in Albertville on Feb. 8 that the more than 1,800 Olympians from 64 countries paraded together, getting the go-ahead from French President Francois Mitterand and a glimpse of Jean-Claude Killy, the most famous son of the Savoie and co-president of the Albertville organizing committee.

From there, the athletes went their separate ways until 16 days later on Feb. 23, when they returned to Albertville for the Closing Ceremonies and for directions to Lillehammer, Norway, the site of the 1994 Olympic Winter Games.

Indeed, there were complex logistics involved in staging the third Winter Games on French ice and snow, logistics far different from those of the Games of Chamonix in 1924 and the Games of Grenoble in 1968. Chamonix is a little more than an hour from Albertville on the way east to Switzerland; Grenoble is a little more than an hour from Albertville on the way south to Spain.

At Chamonix, the site of the first Winter Olympics ever held, 16 countries attended, represented by 294 athletes. They competed in 13 events, all of them within reach of the Chamonix village square.

At Grenoble, the site of the Xth Winter Games (and the site where Killy won his three gold medals), 1,293 athletes from 37 countries assembled to compete in 35 events held in the ski resorts in the mountains beyond the city and in the arenas built in the city.

With its 1,808 athletes, 64 nations, 57 events and far-flung venues, Albertville went well beyond the combined scope of

Chamonix and Grenoble Olympic Winter Games.

Two factors were necessary for success — agreeable weather and an efficient transportation system.

Albertville was fortunate. It got both.

Only one event, the women's super G skiing race, had to be delayed because of the weather (and at that, by just one day), and a venue-wide, bus-only system was successful in avoiding the massive traffic jams it was feared might develop (and never go away) on the two-lane mountain roads. No less than 1,500 buses were brought into service, available free of charge to spectators (who couldn't drive their private cars to the events even if they wanted to), as well as to officials, journalists and the competitors themselves. And so the Games of Albertville negotiated the French Alps, from Les Saisies in the northeast, near Chamonix and Mont Blanc, Europe's highest peak, to Les Menuires in the southwest, toward Grenoble, on the right flank of Les Trios Vallees, the three-resorts-in-one skiing conglomerate. It was at Les Saisies that the first medal of these Olympic Winter Games was won, by

INSET / *From the Opening to the Closing Ceremonies, Albertville unfolded a futuristic theme, beginning with this graphic ski jumper flying in the air* (ALLSPORT/COLE) *and ending with some creature of sorts flying across the ice* (**ABOVE** - ALLSPORT/VANDYSTADT).

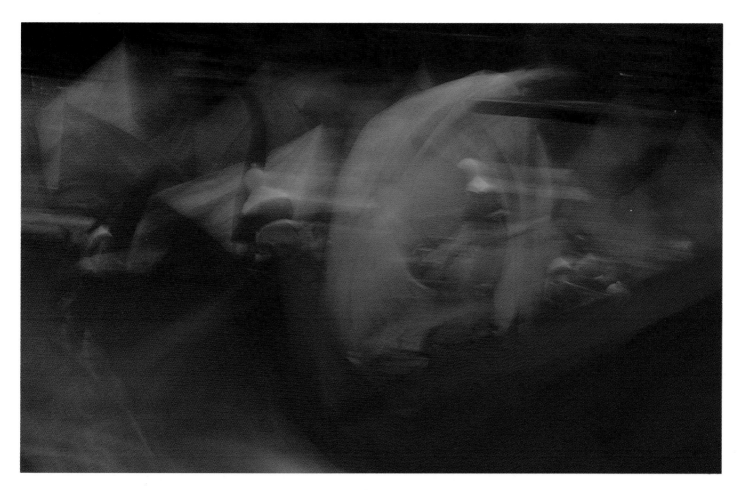

nordic skier Lyubov Egorova of the Unified Team.

It was at Les Menuires that the last skiing medal was won, by slalom racer Finn Christian Jagge of Norway.

At these places, and at the rest, the Savoïe spirit was ever-present, accented by pine boughs, harvested in anticipation of the Games, that were placed everywhere, and by the red ribbons that could be seen tied around light poles, fences, window panes, and masts holding flags of France and the Savoie.

There had been cost overruns and controversies (most notably at the bobsled/luge venue in La Plagne, where they passed out gas masks to locals in case the ammonia-fueled track refrigeration system malfunctioned) but when the Games came they were largely non-issues and well out of the glare of the CBS television cameras that paid $243 million for the rights to beam the Games back to the United States. Long forgotten was Killy's short-lived resignation early in the development process, some six years before, when there was grumbling about the way he went about awarding some of the venues. They talked Killy back into office and then they talked out the details as to which village would do this and which resort would do that.

In the aftermath of the Games, much vanished. The 30,000-seat stadium in Albertville was dismantled, the speed skating oval next door was turned into a track and field facility, and the ice hall across the street was trimmed from a 9,000-seat arena to one of more modest, 2,000-seat proportions.

The bobsled/luge run at La Plagne remains, as does the ski jump at Courchevel, and the famous Bernhard Russi designer downhill courses at Val d'Isere and Meribel. The nordic tracks at Les Saisies will live on and forever be remembered as the place from which the Norwegians finally ruled the world.

But the hockey rink at Meribel, built to look like a ski chalet, was turned back into a ski chalet, and the Main Press Center at La Lechere was largely dismantled, the part that remained turned into a hotel conveniently located adjacent to the hot springs. At Moutiers, the site of the broadcast center, and Brides-les-Bains, the site of the athlete's village, similar transformations took place.

In the end, Albertville and the Alps kept the memories and went back to what they were, which wasn't bad to begin with. ❖

ABOVE / *A blur of colored scarves becomes a visual delight at the Opening Ceremonies.* (ALLSPORT/COLE)
INSET / *Dusk falls on the town of Les Arcs, which hosted the demonstration sport of speed skiing.* (ALLSPORT/RONDEAU)

ALPINE SKIING
Austria reigns but U.S. grabs a silver lining

ABOVE / *Hilary Lindh's 17th-place showing in the super G was, well, not unexpected. What was, was the Alaskan native's glorious silver-medal finish in the downhill on Meribel's long (1 3/4 miles) and difficult course nicknamed "Le Roc de Fer" — the Iron Rock.*
(ALLSPORT / RONDEAU)

OPPOSITE / *Sixth in the super G, Canadian Kerrin Lee-Gartner surprised the downhill field by taking the gold in the tightly won race, where .18 seconds separated the first-place finisher from the fifth.*
(ALLSPORT / BRUTY)

When the alpine skiing events came to a close at the 1992 Olympic Winter Games, the ever-so strong Austrians reigned supreme in the Savoie region, taking home eight of 30 total medals. Switzerland was no longer the team to beat as in the 1988 Winter Olympics in Calgary. The Swiss won only one medal at the 1992 Games compared to 11 in 1988. Swiss racers Maria Walliser and Pirmin Zurbriggen were no longer around to bring home those medals while two-time Olympic medalist Vreni Schneider would go home empty-handed.

The Nation's Cup-leading Austrians took care of business. Two medals went to Petra "the Great" Kronberger. The two-time overall World Cup champion opened with a gold in the combined while teammate Anita Wachter took the silver and France's Florence Masnada captured the bronze.

Kronberger returned to the podium, winning the slalom while Julie Parisien of Auburn, Maine, was the U.S. heartbreak kid. She led the race after the first run but finished fourth overall when the sun set.

"Fourth is the worst position to be in at the Olympics," said a disappointed Parisien. "In a World Cup, it would be great, but just 5/100ths out of a medal. What a headache that is."

New Zealand's Annelise Coberger achieved a first by winning her country's first Winter Olympic medal with a silver in the slalom. Blanca Fernandez-Ochoa mastered a bronze for Spain's only alpine medal at the Games and the third Winter Olympics medal in her country's history.

In the men's combined, some of the favorites such as Switzerland's Paul Accola did not finish the treacherous course and opened the door for the one-two Italian finish of Josef Polig and Gianfranco Martin. Bronze medalist Steve Lochner claimed Switzerland's lone Olympic alpine skiing medal.

"Of course a single medal is a great disappointment," said Swiss men's coach Jean-Pierre Fournier. "We had the possibility to take medals in all disciplines. I think we have been under a jinx here."

A pre-race prediction on the medalists for the women's downhill would have excluded the North American duo of Canada's Kerrin Lee-Gartner and Hilary Lindh of Juneau, Alaska. But the pair shocked the field. Lee-Gartner, who had never won a World Cup race in her career, garnered the gold while Lindh, the 22-year-old Alaskan, brought home a silver medal for the U.S.

Lindh's silver medal was the first for the U.S. women in downhill since 1976 when Cindy Nelson took the Winter Olympics bronze at Innsbruck. It also marked the first alpine medal for the U.S. since the 1984 Sarajevo Games.

"When I came through the finish line, the crowd was so quiet and I didn't think I had done that well," Lindh said. "Then, I turned around and looked up and saw second. I couldn't believe it."

> The pair shocked the field. Lee-Gartner, who had never won a World Cup race in her career, garnered the gold while Lindh, the 22-year-old Alaskan, brought home a silver medal in the downhill.

The U.S. notched its second alpine medal of the 1992 Games when Diann Roffe-Steinrotter took all the chances she needed and tied Austrian Anita Wachter for the silver in the giant slalom. Roffe-Steinrotter thought her Olympic dream had slipped away after finishing ninth in the first run.

"I wasn't going to be excited until I saw the board, and then I saw I was in the medals," Roffe-Steinrotter said. "Seven years ago (when she won the giant slalom at the World Championships), I was 17 years old and a dark horse. Nobody expected me to win the gold medal. It's much different when you know a medal is possible and you start to apply pressure to yourself."

Sweden's Pernilla Wiberg took the gold with a pair of incredible runs.

Making its second appearance in the Winter Olympics, the women's super G event along with the men's giant slalom were held on the same day — a day that will be long-remembered by Italians.

Alberto Tomba made it look easy defending his Olympic gold in the giant slalom. In the valley of Meribel, Deborah Compagnoni captured the women's gold in the super G. France's Carole Merle won the first medal of her career — a silver — while Germany's Katja Seizinger won Germany's only alpine medal with the bronze.

Marc Girardelli, a one-man squad known as Team Luxembourg, won the second Olympic medal of his career behind Tomba in the giant slalom. The bronze went to Norway's Kjetil Andre Aamodt, who captured one of Norway's four alpine medals.

Earlier in the men's competition, Aamodt handily won the super G by 73/100ths of a second with Girardelli second. Aamodt's Norwegian teammate Jan Einar Thorsen rounded out the top three.

The men's alpine events opened with the prestigious men's downhill on the course designed by Olympic downhill champion Bernhard Russi. The course, highly criticized for its tight turns, tested even the best downhillers.

American AJ Kitt of Rochester, N.Y., had the experts wonder-

On February 18, 1992, the day of the men's giant slalom and women's super G, Alberto Tomba and Deborah Compagnoni gave their fellow Italians something other than *calcio* — that is, soccer — to talk about.

ing if could win again in Val d'Isere. Just two months before the Winter Olympics, Kitt became the first American male since 1984 to win a World Cup downhill in Val d'Isere. But Kitt's win came on the old downhill course, not the site of the Olympic downhill.

Another Austrian Patrick Ortlieb had his day on the Bellevarde face at Val d'Isere. Until the Olympic downhill, Ortlieb had never even won a World Cup race, but he walked away with the Olympic gold medal around his neck.

The French had trained on the Olympic downhill course for a couple of weeks prior to the event and led the pack quite frequently during the training runs. So when Franck Piccard took the silver in front of his hometown crowd, it was no surprise. Ortlieb's teammate Guenther Mader (a giant slalom specialist) captured the bronze. Kitt had a respectable ninth as the top American.

With only two days remaining in the Winter Olympics, the final alpine event — the men's slalom — took place.

With one medal already firmly in his grasp, Tomba wanted to defend his slalom gold medal from the 1988 Winter Olympics.

After one run, Tomba found himself more than one and one-half seconds behind the leader Finn Christian Jagge of Norway.

Usually that amount of time isn't easily made up, but Tomba was skiing. When he came storming into the finish area, the 30,000-plus

On February 18th, compatriots Alberto Tomba and Deborah Compagnoni (**ABOVE**) gave Italy two solid golds — his in the giant slalom and hers in the super G.

OPPOSITE (BELOW) / Four days later, Tomba hoped to achieve another Olympic double, but he ended up with the silver in the slalom (ALLSPORT / M. POWELL) and hugs from his sister and a friend (**OPPOSITE / ABOVE**). First-place honors went to Finn Christian Jagge (**RIGHT**), who along with Kjetil Andre Aamodt, gave Norway its first pair of alpine golds — a long wait since Stein Eriksen's gold medal 40 years ago. (ALLSPORT/VANDYSTADT)

The U.S. sported two alpine silver medalists: Downhiller Hilary Lindh (**RIGHT** - ALLSPORT / STEWART) and Diann Roffe-Steinrotter (**OPPOSITE/ TOP** - ALLSPORT / M. POWELL), who overcame a knee injury in 1991 to place second in the giant slalom in 1992.

OPPOSITE (BOTTOM) / Julie Parisien was the U.S. heartbreak kid, coming in fourth in the slalom, just .05 seconds from the bronze medal. In the giant slalom (**PICTURED**), she placed fifth while being disqualified in the super G. (ALLSPORT / S. POWELL)

DIANN ROFFE-
STEINROTTER
&
HILARY LINDH

SILVER SURPRISES

BY LEE BENSON

After their silver-medal performances at Meribel, alpine ski racers Diann Roffe-Steinrotter and Hilary Lindh assured their positions in history as prime examples of what can happen when you're patient, long-suffering, and are willing to hang in there even when your knee has been reconstructed.

For years to come, Roffe-Steinrotter and Lindh will be exhibits A and A-plus when U.S. Ski Team coaches give their adversity speeches. They'll be the prototypes of patience. Not only for those who are looking for their first taste of success, but, more importantly, for those looking for their second taste of success.

Both Roffe-Steinrotter, 23 at the time of the 1992 Winter Olympics, and Lindh, 22, came to Albertville with vast ski-racing histories. Both had been child prodigies.

Roffe-Steinrotter, of Potsdam, N.Y., won the world giant slalom championship in 1985 when she was just 17. In 1986, Lindh, of Juneau, Alaska, won the world junior downhill champion-ship and placed 13th in her first World Cup downhill race when she was all of 16.

But ski racing has a way of collecting its dues, and with Roffe-Steinrotter and Lindh those dues came in the form of hard luck and hard knocks soon after their dizzying debuts.

Coming into Albertville, Roffe-Steinrotter had neither won another in-ternational race in seven long years, nor medaled in another world championship or Olympic Winter Games. For her part, Lindh had finished better than 13th in

the downhill, her specialty, only spar-ingly, and her best finish of the 1991-92 season was 11th.

Too, both had endured career-threat-ening knee injuries, Roffe-Steinrotter early in the 1990-91 season when she was rounding into top form, and Lindh in 1987 just as she was emerging on the international scene.

It would have been easy for Roffe-Steinrotter and Lindh to figure their time had come and gone. But on separate days on the slopes of Meribel, they didn't reach back, they reached forward. Roffe-Steinrotter caught up an astonishing 1.15 seconds after the first run of the giant slalom to rush into a tie for second with Austria's Anita Wachter, barely behind the winner, Pernilla Wiberg of Sweden. In the downhill, Lindh came within 6/100ths of a second of winning, quali-fying for the silver medal behind winner Kerrin Lee-Gartner of Canada.

In their eighth and ninth seasons, respectively, as members of the U.S. Ski Team, Lindh and Roffe-Steinrotter fi-nally collected what they had coming. ◆

BACKGROUND / *The men's downhill course — that is, the Face Bellevarde in Val d'Isere — was a bag of controversy for its technical difficulty and Patrick Ortleib of Austria one of its sternest critics. Ortleib walked away with the gold and the hope of never having to race the course again.* (ALLSPORT / S. POWELL)

TOP / *AJ Kitt was a U.S. favorite in the downhill, with plenty of talk of a chance for a medal, but the course prevailed and Kitt came in a disappointing ninth place.* (ALLSPORT / BRUTY)

MIDDLE / *You've got to congratulate Lamine Gueye of Senegal — a country that doesn't even see snow — of his gutsy attempt of Face Bellevarde, which had even the favorites complaining. He came in last in the downhill with a time of 2:12.84.* (ALLSPORT / COLE)

BOTTOM / *From this view point, the downhill course looks mildly tame as American Reggie Crist attacks. But Crist, who finished 28th, can attest otherwise.* (ALLSPORT / BRUTY)

crowd cheered him. Jagge was the last skier with the ability to better Tomba's time. Jagge didn't falter to win the final alpine medal of the Games and took the gold by 28/100ths of a second. Tomba had the silver with Austrian Michael Tritscher the bronze. That brought the Austrian tally to eight and indicated why the Austrians were at the top of the hill for these Olympic Winter Games. ❖ **JOLENE AUBEL**

ABOVE / *After all the favorites had fallen, Italians Josef Polig and Gianfranco Martin were left standing 1-2 in the men's combined.* (ALLSPORT / COLE)
RIGHT / *They call her "Petra the Great," the most versatile female skier on the slopes these days. Kronberger from Austria competed in all five events, winning two golds, one in the combined, the other in the slalom, and finished a respectable fourth in the super G and fifth in the downhill.* (ALLSPORT / VANDYSTADT)

BIATHLON
Shooting stars make tracks at Les Saisies

Adrenalin raced through Joan Smith's veins as the skilled biathlete stepped up to the starting position for the 7.5-kilometer sprint race at the scenic Les Saisies trails. Smith shot out of the gate and was the first U.S. finisher.

Smith's departure was a historic one as women's biathlon made its official debut in the Olympic Winter Games.

In the men's events, Germany's Mark Kirchner dominated the competition, winning three medals — a pair of golds and one silver. He captured the 10-kilometer sprint, skied a leg on the winning 4x7.5- kilometer relay team and placed second behind the Unified Team's Evgueni Redkine in the 20-kilometer individual race.

Kirchner's teammate, Ricco Gross, left Les Saisies with two medals. He claimed a silver behind Kirchner in the 10 kilometers and skied a leg on Germany's overpowering gold-medal relay team.

As expected, the top performer for the U.S. team was three-time Olympian Josh Thompson, who celebrated his 30th birthday during the final week of competition. The Gunnison, Colo., biathlete improved with each outing in the 1992 Games, placing 32nd in the opening 10 kilometers (27:53.2), skiing the best segment on the relay (22:12.0) and finishing a strong 16th in the 20-kilometer finale

(1:00:05.4).

Thompson's 16th-place finish in the 20 kilometers tied him with Charles Akers for the third best result in U.S. history in the event. It also was significantly better than his 25th-place finish four years ago in Calgary.

Thompson and teammate Curt Schreiner of Day, N.Y., also broke into the U.S. overall Olympic Top 10 performance list in the 10-kilometer sprint as Thompson posted the fifth-best finish (32nd) and Schreiner had the sixth-highest placing (37th).

Erich Wilbrecht of Jackson, Wyo., and Duncan Douglas of Lake Placid, N.Y., joined Thompson and Calgary veteran Schreiner in the events at Les Saisies. Schreiner finished 37th, and was the only U.S.

ABOVE / *Anfissa Restzova* (**FOREGROUND**) *of the Unified Team confessed she wasn't very good at shooting, making three mistakes, but she stormed through the 7.5-kilometer trek to beat silver medalist Antje Misersky of Germany by 15 seconds.* (ALLSPORT / VANDYSTADT)
OPPOSITE / *Shooting well, skiing well and buoyed by a roaring crowd, the French women's relay team snatched the gold from the Germans.* (ALLSPORT / MARTIN)

man to shoot clean in the 10-kilometer sprint. Wilbrecht finished 49th and Douglas finished 55th in the sprint race, while Schreiner took 51st and Douglas took 59th in the 20 kilometers. Jon Engren of Billings, Mont., who was on the 1988 U.S. Nordic Team, took 70th in the 20 kilometers.

The women, meanwhile, thrilled appreciative crowds with their debut on the Olympic program. Anfissa Restzova of the Unified Team won the first women's gold medal, sweeping to first place in the 7.5-kilometer race on opening day.

France got a stirring gold-medal performance in the second women's event, the 3x7.5-kilometer relay, when Corinne Niogret, Veronique Claudel and Anne Briand teamed for an emotional win over runnerup Germany.

Germany finally got its women's gold in the 15 kilometers as Antje Misersky, who took a silver in the 7.5 kilometers, bested Svetlana Pecherskaia of the Unified Team, while the bronze medal went to Myriam Bedard of Canada.

Misersky was the standout among women biathletes at the Winter Olympics, collecting one gold medal and two silvers. Restzova finished with a gold and a bronze.

The inaugural appearance of the U.S. women biathletes in the Winter Olympics was a tough one, even though all of them had

The origins of the biathlon are linked to reindeer hunting in Scandinavia, but it was Germany and the Unified Team — not the Nordic countries — who took home 13 of the 20 medals.

competed in World Cups and World Championships. A top relay performer, Patrice Anderson of Nordic Valley, Utah, was hampered by a neck injury and the fastest national team member did not make the Olympics.

The highest individual finish was Smith's 21st place out of 69 competitors in the 7.5 kilometers with a 26:54.5 time.

Smith and Nancy Bell of Stowe, Vt., were the only women to compete in all three events. Smith also finished 55th in the 15 kilometers (1:01:15.2) and was on the 3x7.5- kilometer relay team, which wound up 15th out of 16 entries.

Bell, meanwhile, posted the highest finish in the 15-kilometer finale, skiing a 57:55.2 for 34th place, and was 44th in the 7.5 kilometers (28:20.6). Mary Ostergren of Norwich, Vt., was 25th in the 7.5-kilometer race (27:05.7) and was the third member of the relay team. Joan Guetschow of Minnetonka, Minn., placed 64th in the 7.5 kilometers (31:30.6), Anderson placed 42nd in the 15 kilometers (1:01:15.2) and Beth Coats of Breckenridge, Colo., came in 47th in the 15 kilometers (59:36.1).

Overall, it was a barometer-type performance for the United States team, and while no medals were won — and none were predicted — the seven men and seven women gained valuable experience that will most certainly help them in two years in Lillehammer. ❖   **JOE BROWNING**

BACKGROUND / *To the observer the scene is deceivingly peaceful. In truth, biathlete Saso Glajf of Slovenia will raise his pulse to 170-190 beats — the average heart rate for elite athletes — on the cross-country track, then, as quickly as possible, drop it to at least 130 beats at the shooting range to ensure a steady shot.* (ALLSPORT / BRUTY)

INSET / *The top performers of the U.S. Biathlon Team were Joan Smith, who shot clean in the 7.5-kilometer sprint to finish 21st* (**ABOVE** - ALLSPORT / BILOW) *and Josh Thompson* (**BELOW** - ALLSPORT / BRUTY), *a three-time Olympian. Thompson, who turned 30 at the Games, placed 32nd in the 10-kilometer sprint.*

BOBSLED
A drive with destiny

The bobsled competition in La Plagne threw out a few curves both on and off the ice. The 19-turn course, stiff European competition and the residual turmoil from the team selection process left the U.S. with a slippery climb to the medal platform. But the U.S. responded with its best finish in the two-man event since 1980 and then placed two sleds in the top 11 in the four-man competition.

Bobsledding is a drive with destiny as sleds careen down an icy chute at speeds reaching 90 mph. Competition is based on the accumulative time of four runs over a two-day span. In this sport, the start is crucial and the U.S. team had signed up its swiftest and strongest to move its sleds off the hill.

The Olympic Winter Games heralded the participation of one of America's most intriguing sports personalities in professional football running back Herschel Walker. Joining the team in January after his NFL season with the Minnesota Vikings, Walker dominated the push-off trials and was tabbed as the brakeman for both the USA I two-man and four-man teams.

"I love to compete, but people don't always take me seriously," Walker said. "Someone asked me about a gold medal, that's the only reason I'm here. I didn't come all the way over here to be in the Olympics. I don't need a uniform. I'm here to win. That's all I'm here for."

The high aspirations of USA I driver Brian Shimer, a two-time Olympian, and Walker were put to test on the track. After sitting in ninth place after the first three runs, the Florida/Georgia duo improved to seventh place overall among the 46 competitors. Shimer and Walker finished with an accumulative time of 4:03.95, which was 32/100ths of a second out of a bronze medal.

ABOVE / *Shimer, who has his sights set on Lillehammer, shares a hug with push partner Herschel Walker.* (ALLSPORT / COLE)

OPPOSITE / *Built for speed, the 440-pound, two-man bobsled careens around a hairpin curve at a hair-raising speed. One error in judgment on the driver's part can flip a sled, giving new meaning to every bobsled driver's favorite phrase: "I want to control my own destiny."* (ALLSPORT / RONDEAU)

LEFT / *In the quest for the fastest push times, pilot Brian Shimer teamed up with football player and athlete extra-ordinaire Herschel Walker. The match-up, which had only a handful of practice runs, produced a seventh-place finish in the two-man bobsled.* (ALLSPORT / COLE)

HERSCHEL WALKER

Herschel Knows Snow

BY LEE BENSON

Herschel Walker, a self-described "competition junkie," found just the cure for his winter season.

He joined the United States Bobsled Team.

The 6-foot-1, 220-pound running back who won the Heisman Trophy at the University of Georgia prior to a career in the National Football League, didn't know what to do with himself when he wasn't, well, competing, so while other football players were back home getting serious about the off-season, Walker was at the Olympic bobsled venue in La Plagne, getting serious about pushing driver Brian Shimer's sled.

American spectators among the crowd in La Plagne were soon wearing t-shirts that read, "Bo Knows Diddley, but Herschel Knows Snow."

At every opportunity, Walker made it clear that he wasn't in France for a frolic or for his vanity, but to be a team player and see about winning the gold medal. When the bobsled team made its way to France from Germany via van, Walker rode in the back and toted the gear; at the Opening Ceremonies in Albertville he marched in with the U.S. team, and he set up camp early in La Plagne with his fellow U.S. sledders, acting as the unofficial team barber in between his daily four-mile runs and routine of 2,000 sit-ups and 1,500 push-ups.

In the end, fitness and enthusiasm were not quite enough to make up for experience, however. The team of Shimer-and-Walker, with only a handful of competition runs together, finished seventh, ranking behind teams from Germany, Switzerland, Italy and Austria that had been practicing since the days when Walker was running for the Georgia Bulldogs and didn't know what snow was, let alone a bobsled.

Still, Shimer and Walker finished ahead of 39 teams and posted the best two-man finish for a U.S. team since the Lake Placid Games in 1980. ◆

"I'm definitely looking toward '94," Shimer said. "I guess that will ease this disappointment a little bit. In two years I'll have another shot, and I think we can pick up where we left off. I've learned a lot in my first Olympics as a pilot."

The USA II team of driver Brian Richardson and brakeman Greg Harrell, who also came from the pro football environs with the L.A. Raiders, placed 24th in the field in 4:08.17.

Traditional countries maintained their stranglehold on the final standings. The Switzerland I team of Gustav Weder and Donat Acklin moved from fifth place after the first day to the gold medal. The two sleds from Germany took the silver and bronze medals.

The four-man bobsled event followed the two-man competition, but the storyline developed during the practice rounds. Returning Olympian Randy Will, the driver of USA I, opted to change his brakeman from Walker to Chris Coleman two days prior to the official competition. Walker had been scheduled as the only athlete on the U.S. team to compete in both events.

"One of the major reasons we made this change is to make the pilot very comfortable," said Olympic team leader Jim Hickey. "Herschel is a great athlete and a great individual. Chris Coleman had ridden with Randy before, and they've been a team before. We decided to put them back together. It's clearly not because Herschel doesn't have the ability. We're just hoping we can go faster."

The change netted results as the USA I sled of Will, Coleman

ABOVE / With a wave of support, the USA-I four-man bobsled, piloted by veteran Randy Will, rode to a ninth-place finish. (ALLSPORT / RONDEAU)

and side pushers Karlos Kirby and Joe Sawyer recorded four world-class start times. But Will had problems negotiating curve 18 on the course, and the U.S. finished ninth overall with a four-run total of 3:54.92.

The USA II team of driver Chuck Leonowicz, side pushers Bryan Leturgez and Bob Weissenfels and brakeman Jeff Woodard claimed 11th place in the 31-sled field with a 3:55.23 clocking. The gold medal went to Ingo Appelt's Austrian team followed by Germany I, driven by Wolfgang Hoppe, and Switzerland I, with double medalist Weder as pilot.

"I think it's one of the strongest showings we've had with two sleds in the top 11," said Olympic team coach John Philbin. "With respect to one of our major goals to have the fastest push times in the world, we're one of the teams in that hunt. We've shown we can do it."

So the quest of the U.S. bobsled team, which has not garnered a medal since 1956, marches on to Lillehammer with more experience, an emphasis on technical improvements and a better understanding of the balancing act between professional athletes and full-time World Cup performers. ❖ **FRANK ZANG**

FIGURE SKATING
U. S. shows mettle to medal

In a sport often criticized for its predetermined results, the figure skating competition at the 1992 Olympic Winter Games produced a surprising slew of unlikely medalists. In each of the four events, the heavy favorites faltered, making way for the emergence of a number of new heroes.

The U.S. produced its share of heroes with the gold and bronze-medal performances of Kristi Yamaguchi and Nancy Kerrigan in the ladies' event, and with the emotional silver-medal effort of Paul Wylie in the men's event. In addition to the three medals, the U.S. figure skaters were responsible for providing some of the most intense drama of the Games.

LADIES
16 years later Kristi gives U.S. some enchanted evening

WHEN KRISTI YAMAGUCHI was five years old, she would skate around the rink clutching a Dorothy Hamill doll. Hamill, the 1976 Olympic champion, was her idol and the reason for taking up the

sport. Fifteen years and thousands of practice hours later, Yamaguchi found herself on the verge of becoming the next Hamill. Having unanimously won the original program with a flawless waltz to the Blue Danube, Yamaguchi stood poised to become the first American woman since Hamill to win the Olympic gold in figure skating.

As she waited backstage to take the ice for her final four-minute performance, Yamaguchi received an unexpected visitor. It was Hamill.

"She wanted to wish me the best," Yamaguchi said. "She reminded me of how hard I've worked to get here, and to go out there and have fun."

That she did. Performing a mesmerizing number to "Malaguena," Yamaguchi's every move was enchanting. Yamaguchi nailed her opening triple, triple combination followed by three more triple jumps. Difficulty on a triple loop jump halfway through her performance kept Yamaguchi from achieving perfection, but it wasn't enough to keep her from capturing the gold medal.

"I was really pleased with the way I skated and whatever the outcome, I would have been satisfied with my Olympic experience,"

OPPOSITE / *Paul Wylie, whose natural grace and athletic ability were, in the past, foreshadowed by inconsistency in competition, surprised and delighted the world with a flawless original and free skate program to earn the Texas native the men's silver medal.* (ALLSPORT / VANDYSTADT)

RIGHT / *Enchanting Kristi Yamaguchi of the U.S. recaptured the ladies' crown after a 16-year hiatus.* (ALLSPORT / VANDYSTADT)

KRISTI YAMAGUCHI

ICE PRINCESS

BY LEE BENSON

Figure skating has never been so much what you can do as what you can do when it matters. And so it was that Kristi Yamaguchi, all five feet and 93 pounds of her, entrenched herself as the best figure skater in the world — again — at the Winter Olympics.

As she had done at the 1991 World Championships and also at the 1992 U.S. Championships just a month prior to the Albertville Games, Yamaguchi was a picture of poise under pressure in the Albertville Ice Hall as she capped her triple-crown sweep of the three major titles by capturing the gold medal.

Twenty years old and skating for the first time in the Winter Olympics, Yamaguchi took the early lead after a flawless, no-falls, short program, and then she never looked back. In the long program she did slip on a triple loop halfway through her routine, but quickly composed herself for a strong finish that

clinched the title.

In the process, the fourth-generation Japanese-American from Fremont, Calif., held off her much-publicized rival, Midori Ito of Japan.

Ito, the 1989 world champion, came to Albertville as one of only two women in the world (American Tonya Harding, who finished fourth, was the other) who had landed a triple Axel — the three-and-a-half rotation jump that is figure

skating's equivalent of climbing Mount Everest — in competition. Since Yamaguchi hadn't ever landed, or attempted, a triple axel in competition, it was assumed Ito might have an athletic edge in Albertville.

But just as she had at the 1991 World Championships, where she finished fourth, Ito found that the triple Axel can taketh away as well as giveth. She missed her first try at her trademark jump at the start of her long program, and in the crucial short program she second-guessed even trying the triple Axel, scratched it from her routine, and then fell on an easier triple lutz.

By the time Ito finally landed a triple Axel near the end of her long program, it was only enough to win the silver medal.

The gold was by then locked away by Yamaguchi, a skater of style and substance; and, even more important, a skater who had once again been at her best precisely when she needed to be. ◆

Yamaguchi said. "I still can't believe what's happening to me."

Yamaguchi was co-favored to win the gold along with Midori Ito of Japan, but the long-awaited battle between the two failed to materialize after Ito skated to a disastrous fourth-place finish in the original program. In the final free skate, Ito ran into trouble early on with a fall on her trademark triple Axel, but rebounded with five solid triples. A gutsy second attempt at a triple Axel was successful, and the former world champion was able to pull up to second.

Nancy Kerrigan made an impressive Olympic debut, winning the bronze medal behind Ito with a faultless original program and an elegant final free skate. Originally in the running for the silver medal, Kerrigan made three mistakes in the free skate to drop to third overall.

Tonya Harding should have been pleased with her free skating performance. After a costly fall on a triple Axel in the original program, Harding finished just short of a medal in fourth place with a solid free skate.

"I tried to think of this as just another competition, but I was aware of the importance of it. It seems like everyone was counting on this one," Harding said. "I'm disappointed in myself for not landing the triple Axel in the short program."

MEN
Petrenko gets long-awaited gold; Wylie's pressure performance clutches silver

PAUL WYLIE'S ROAD to Albertville was anything but an expressway. By the time he reached the 1992 Games, he had competed in 14 U.S. Championships, three World Championships, and the 1988 Olympic Games. All without ever having won a major title. The 1992 Games were to be Wylie's last chance to show the world his exceptional talents.

> **"For seven years I thought he was one of the most magnificent skaters I had ever seen. I was praying that the world would see what I've seen for years, and they did."**
> —Coach Mary Scotvold

Under great pressure, Wylie came through with two spectacular performances. His final free skate showcased six triple jumps intertwined with exquisite artistry. Wylie's triumphant performance earned him the silver medal.

OPPOSITE / *The duel between American Kristi Yamaguchi* (ALLSPORT / MARTIN) *and Midori Ito* (TOP - ALLSPORT / STEWART) *of Japan never materialized. Ito's trademark jumps failed her in the original program, placing her fourth, and Yamaguchi, first after the original program, skated clean enough in the final free skate to take the gold.*
BOTTOM / *After winning the elusive gold, the charismatic Viktor Petrenko entertained the French during a gala skating exhibition.* (ALLSPORT / VANDYSTADT)

NANCY KERRIGAN
AND
PAUL WYLIE

MASS
connection

BY LEE BENSON

For figure skaters Nancy Kerrigan and Paul Wylie, practice partners and good friends for the past seven years, the Games of Albertville couldn't have been orchestrated much better: They each won a medal while the other was watching, they withstood the strongest of pressures and challengers along the way, and, for an encore, they got to skate their trademark pairs routine while a television audience of about one billion viewers looked on.

All in all, it was a rather rewarding Winter Olympics for the best friends from Massachusetts.

Wylie and Kerrigan first met in 1985 when Wylie and his coaches, Evy and Mary Scotvold, moved to Massachusetts and added Kerrigan, a native of Stoneham, Mass., to their line of proteges. Wylie, who was born in Texas and later moved to Denver, was 20 at the time; Kerrigan was 15, and, like soldiers in a foxhole, they forged a close bond while progressing through the often trying demands of world-class figure skating. Whenever practice would get a little too intense, they would unwind by skating together.

In Albertville, Wylie, who had finished well back in 10th place at the 1988 Winter Olympics in Calgary, got the Massachusetts pair off to a good start by overcoming long odds to win the silver medal, finishing barely in back of Viktor Petrenko of the Unified Team and ahead of such notables as three-time defending champion Kurt Browning of Canada and U.S. teammates Christopher Bowman and Todd Eldredge, both two-time U.S. champions. Inspired and encouraged by Wylie's performance, Kerrigan, skating in her first Winter Olympics, proceeded to win the bronze medal in the women's event, joining the heavily-favored twosome of Kristi Yamaguchi of the U.S. and Midori Ito of Japan on the winner's rostrum.

In the exhibition event that followed the medal competitions, Wylie and Kerrigan unwound as always — skating in unison to the music of "Miss Saigon." They wore the trademark skaters' smiles as they performed, but they were more than painted on. Six individual figure skating medals had been awarded at the Games of Albertville, and the best friends from Massachusetts had won two of them. ◆

OPPOSITE / *After the intensity of Olympic competition, bronze medalist Nancy Kerrigan and silver medalist Paul Wylie do what best friends do: unwind together. Skating together at the post-competition exhibition, the pair relaxed and just had fun.* (ALLSPORT / BRUTY)

"For seven years I thought he was one of the most magnificent skaters I had ever seen," coach Mary Scotvold said. "I was praying that the world would see what I've seen for years, and they did."

"This is the happiest moment of my life," Wylie said. "This medal certainly vindicates my decision to continue skating after Calgary."

Perennial runnerup Viktor Petrenko of the Unified Team finally emerged a winner with a victorious performance in Albertville. The charismatic Petrenko barely edged out Wylie for the gold medal with a well-choreographed free skate that included five triple jumps.

Petra Barna of Czechoslovakia completed a soaring quadruple toe loop en route to winning the bronze medal over Christopher Bowman. Bowman, hampered by a costly seventh-place finish in the short program, fought back with a solid long program to finish in fourth.

"I gave everything that I had for my fans, for the crowd," Bowman said. "I'm thrilled to death. I had a perma-grin the entire time."

Todd Eldredge, battling a back injury, finished in 10th after missing a double Axel in the short program and encountering a myriad of difficulties in the long.

"Nobody knows how hard it is to be out there and to complete every jump," Eldredge said. "I think I skated very well considering the pressure. I found out what kind of a person I am — how strong-willed I am."

PAIRS

Poetry in motion by gold medalists Mishkutionok and Dmitriev

CRITICS WHO SAY figure skating is moving in the direction of ice hockey — all athleticism and no artistry — should have been quieted by the gold medal-winning performances of Natalia Mishkutionok and Artur Dmitriev. Representing the Unified Team, the duo was mesmerizing, skating

RIGHT / *Olympic champions Natalia Mishkutionok and Artur Dmitriev of the Unified Team were a study in grace and balance as the flexibility and strength of the pairs produced imaginative and mesmerizing moves.* (ALLSPORT / BRUTY)

OPPOSITE / *At the post-competition exhibition, Isabelle and Paul Duschesnay returned to their inventive, athletic style of ice dancing that captivated audiences worldwide. Unfortunately, the French brother-sister team opted for a safe, conservative Olympic program, and in doing so, lost the gold to the provocative grace of Marina Klimova and Sergei Ponomarenko* (SUCCEEDING PAGES) *of the Unified Team.* (ALLSPORT / VANDYSTADT)

its way to straight first-place marks from all nine judges in both phases of competition.

Elena Betchke and Denis Petrov, representing the Unified Team, easily won the silver medal over early gold-medal favorites Isabelle Brasseur and Lloyd Eisler of Canada, whose error-laden free skate held them down in third place.

The top American finishers were 1991 U.S. champions Natasha Kuchiki and Todd Sand, who finished in sixth place after running into difficulties in both the short and long programs. Sand, who was struck with the flu just prior to competing, stumbled on double Axels in both performances.

Calla Urbanski and Rocky Marval, the American media's favorite waitress and truck driver, also experienced problems with their double Axels in both the short and long programs. In seventh place after the original program, the pair dropped to 10th place after making a series of costly mistakes in the free skate.

"This performance was definitely not up to our standards," Urbanski said. "We're not pleased with it, but it's something to learn from."

The most refreshing American performances came from Jenni Meno and Scott Wendland. With great enthusiasm, the rookie pair skated two flawless performances to finish a respectable 11th.

ICE DANCE
Husband and wife team up for the gold

SINCE WINNING THE world title in 1991, the French brother and sister team of Paul and Isabelle Duchesnay had been heavily favored to win the 1992 Olympic gold medal. Ice dancing legends in France, the Duchesnays had become famous for their bold, innovative approach to the sport. But in Albertville, the duo was unable to compete with its own past, performing a surprisingly conservative and unimaginative free dance to "West Side Story." The free dance earned them a silver medal behind Marina Klimova and Sergei Ponomarenko of the Unified Team.

Ironically enough, it was Klimova and Ponomarenko who presented the most imaginative performance of the week. Once considered strictly classical dancers, their provocative free dance to music from Bach earned the husband and wife team a string of 5.9's for artistic impression and the Olympic gold medal.

Maia Usova and Alexander Zhulin, the heir apparents to Klimova and Ponomarenko, captured the bronze medal.

April Sargent-Thomas and Russ Witherby were the top American finishers in 11th place. It was a personal victory for the team just to compete in Albertville after Sargent-Thomas was forced to undergo emergency surgery just three weeks prior to the U.S. Championships and seven weeks prior to the Games.

The Olympic Games marked the world debut of current U.S. silver medalists Rachel Mayer and Peter Breen. The newcomers finished 14th in the compulsory dances and original dance, but dropped to 15th after a fall in the free dance. ❖ **KRISTIN MATTA**

ABOVE / *Rachel Meyer and Peter Breen's debut at the Olympic Games brought the ice dancing pair a taste of world competition and an appetite for more. The American pair finished 15th after an unfortunate fall.* (ALLSPORT / MARTIN)

ABOVE / *Representing the Unified Team, Maia Usova and Alexander Zhulin captured the bronze in pairs and, with the retirement of the gold and silver medalists, look to be favorites in Lillehammer.* (ALLSPORT / VANDYSTADT)

FREESTYLE SKIING
Queen of the bumps, King of the hill

United States skier Donna Weinbrecht and France's Edgar Grospiron entered the freestyle moguls skiing competitions as overwhelming favorites for the gold medals and with good reason.

In Weinbrecht's case, the two-time World Cup champion and current world champion had been given the label of best shot at gold medal since Jean-Claude Killy at the 1968 Olympic Winter Games.

"I feel free in the air."
—Edgar Grospiron
Olympic mogul champion and helicopter pilot

"There was pressure and I just tried to remain focused," Weinbrecht said. "I wanted to be in the gate. That's where I wanted to be. I didn't worry about the outcome."

For Grospiron, coming from nearby La Clusaz, France, he was his country's best hope for a gold. Grospiron had won last season's World Cup title and World Championship title as well.

In trimming the field to 16, Grospiron and French teammate Raphaelle Monod won the men's and women's elimination rounds. Weinbrecht took second and Nelson Carmichael of Steamboat Springs, Colo., claimed fourth.

More than 15,000 spectators lined the Olympic course in Tignes to witness a possible French sweep. The sky opened up and dumped a blanket of snow on the competition, but the weather never stopped the crowd from backing the French skiers.

Weinbrecht, the 26-year-old skier from West Milford, N.J., posted the score to beat at 23.69 with only one skier left. It was all up to Monod to take the gold from Weinbrecht as she waited anxiously in the finish area. But the 23-year-old skier from Annecy, France, lost control about two-thirds of the way down the course and finished eighth. Weinbrecht went down in the history books as the first gold medalist in women's moguls. Elizaveta Kojevnikova of the Unified Team won the silver and Stine Hattestad of Norway captured the bronze.

Grospiron, a showman like alpine racing's Alberto Tomba, did not disappoint the predominately French crowds as his teammate

ABOVE / *He's the quintessential showman, a Frenchman with the inherited taste for good food and an unwavering zest for life. He's an unabashed show-off and was the undisputed favorite coming into the moguls competition. And true to form, Edgar Grospiron did not disappoint.* (ALLSPORT / VANDYSTADT)

Olivier Allamand set the score to beat at 24.87. Grospiron's piston-like skiing ability made it a one-two French finish putting down a score of 25.81 and turning Tignes upside down.

Carmichael took the bronze after watching his score topped first by Allamand and then by Grospiron.

Other top American finishers were Liz McIntyre, who was sixth in the women's competition while Chuck Martin of Killington, Vt., placed 15th and Craig Rodman of Park City, Utah, in 13th in the men's division. ❖ **JOLENE AUBEL**

LEFT / *Like Grospiron, Donna Weinbrecht of the United States was considered a shoo-in for the gold in the women's moguls event. The 26-year-old skier and former waitress bore the pressure and collected the gold.* (ALLSPORT / COLE)

LEFT / *After placing 10th in Calgary, where the moguls competition was an Olympic demonstration event, Nelson Carmichael pushed to come back to the Olympics, where, at Tignes, moguls skiing became a full-fledged medal event. "I never felt it was the wrong decision," Carmichael said. Indeed. The American went home with the bronze.* (ALLSPORT / COLE)

DONNA WEINBRECHT & NELSON CARMICHAEL

Freestylin' Spirits

BY LEE BENSON

Out of breath at the bottom of the hill, her blonde pony-tail finally at rest, Donna Weinbrecht, a former waitress and art student all of 26 years old, didn't exactly look like a pioneer. But that's exactly what she had become after skiing the most righteous, radical, gnarly, outrageous, totally awesome bump run in women's moguls Olympic history.

Together, Weinbrecht and the Albertville Olympics made history.

Albertville offered the first medals to mogul skiers in Olympic history. And Weinbrecht, after a nearly flawless final run down the 253-meter course at Tignes, was in line to accept the first one.

Like any self-respecting bump skier, Weinbrecht chose her own free-spirited route to the top. As a teenager, she taught herself how to negotiate the icy moguls on the ski slopes in the eastern U.S., mostly in Vermont. Then, after winning every meet on the U.S. Ski Association's eastern schedule as a mere high school senior, she put mogul skiing aside for a time, in favor of art school. She returned to the bumps in 1985, however, won her first of four straight national titles in 1988, and by 1990 had established herself as the top women's mogul skier in the world.

The heavy favorite coming into the competition at Tignes, Weinbrecht nonetheless had to overcome a first-day advantage gained in the semifinals by former world champion Raphaelle Monod of France, who also enjoyed something of a home-bump advantage. Weinbrecht's aggressive response on her final run unnerved Monod, who, skiing immediately after Weinbrecht, bounced off course and finished last.

While Weinbrecht was able to unnerve her French rival, the same wasn't true for Nelson Carmichael, also 26 and America's other gold-medal moguls hope.

Skiing in front of French teammates Olivier Allamand and world champion Edgar Grospiron, Carmichael, the men's world champion in 1988 and 1989, turned in a solid final run, only to see it exceeded first by Allamand and then by Grospiron.

Still, Carmichael could claim distinction as the first bronze medalist in men's moguls Olympic history. ◆

ICE HOCKEY
Unified effort dashes U.S. "ray" of hope

xpectations were high. The American public carried high hopes and the U.S. Olympic Ice Hockey Team wanted to deliver. It had been 12 years since the Olympic gold medal performance of the 1980 U.S. hockey team. Since then the U.S. had posted seventh-place finishes in Sarajevo (1984) and Calgary (1988).

"This should be our most experienced team ever," 1992 U.S. Olympic head coach Dave Peterson said. "We've got a good blend of some very talented players who have a great deal of international, professional and collegiate experience. I like our team. We're fast. We're gritty and the American public should enjoy watching us play."

Five members of the 1988 Olympic team — Greg Brown, Clark Donatelli, Guy Gosselin, Jim Johannson and Scott Young — returned to assist Peterson in the U.S. bid for Olympic glory. The 1988

ABOVE / *C.J. Young gets in a tussle with a Swedish player in a game that had tempers flying. The game ended in a tie and with some sore feelings on both sides.* (ALLSPORT / M. POWELL)

head coach as well, Peterson was also returning, marking only the second time than anyone had coached two consecutive U.S. Olympic teams.

Much had changed in the Olympic hockey picture since 1988. Many of the top players from the European and Eastern bloc countries would be playing in the NHL and not representing their respective countries at the Olympic Games. In addition, the U.S. had steadily climbed higher in international competition.

An addition, an Olympic format change, which now featured preliminary round robin play followed by single elimination in the

RIGHT / *In the 3-0 win over Poland, the U.S. chalked up another statistic: The 1992 squad became the first U.S. team since 1932 to post more than one shutout in the Olympic Games. The other shutout came against Germany. (*ALLSPORT */ STEWART)*

BELOW / *Ray LeBlanc does what he does best: he stops the puck. The 3-3 tie won grudging admiration from the top-seeded Swedes and advanced the Americans to a first-round playoff with France, which the U.S. won handily, 4-1. (*ALLSPORT */ M. POWELL)*

medal round, figured to be advantageous for the Americans. Four teams from each pool would advance to the playoff and medal round.

Sweden was a pre-Olympic favorite to win the gold, followed by the Unified Team, Canada and Czechoslovakia. The U.S. bracket included Italy, Germany, Finland, Poland and Sweden.

As the preliminary round progressed, U.S. goaltender Ray LeBlanc emerged as an unlikely hero. LeBlanc had spent the last seven years in the minor leagues of the NHL. At the 1992 Olympic Winter Games, he recorded two shutouts in the preliminary round and only gave up seven goals in 15 periods of play.

The U.S. opened tournament play against Italy and needed four unanswered goals in the third period to overcome a 3-2 Italian lead. Donatelli, the team captain, scored the game-tying goal and Steve

Finland's goal in the second period broke LeBlanc's streak of 110 minutes and 57 seconds of shutout hockey.

Heinze popped in the game-winner as the U.S. posted a 7-3 win.

LeBlanc collected his first of two Olympic shutouts in a 2-0 win over Germany. Marty McInnis and Ted Donato scored on power plays to give the U.S. the victory margin. The shutout was the first for an American goaltender since the 1964 Games in Innsbruck.

"I was just thinking one shot at a time," LeBlanc said. "I was pleased with my play, but I wasn't the only one on the ice. It's my job to stop the puck and that's what I do. Just going one shot at a time. You always want to do like Jim Craig did in 1980 and be a hero."

Finland would fall to the U.S., 4-1, with LeBlanc turning in another sterling performance, pushing aside 24 shots. Finland scored in the second period, the first goal allowed by the U.S. in seven straight periods. LeBlanc had played 110 minutes and 57 seconds of shutout hockey.

LeBlanc's prowess came to the front once again as the U.S. won its next preliminary game over Poland, 3-0. LeBlanc turned away 24 shots and Shawn McEachern, Tim Sweeney and Marty McInnis scored for the U.S. The 1992 squad became the first U.S. team since 1932 to post more than one shutout in the Olympic Games.

ABOVE / *American support for the U.S. team was genuinely grand, with fans waving Old Glory and emblazoning their chests with encouragement.* (ALLSPORT / STEWART)

RIGHT / *A 1988 U.S. Olympic team member, Guy Gosselin provided veteran defense in front of goalie Ray LeBlanc.* (ALLSPORT / BRUTY)

RAY LEBLANC

The Puck STOPS Here

BY LEE BENSON

A goalkeeper whose name in French means "The Blank" found the French Alps a perfect place to live up to his surname.

And as Ray LeBlanc, a 27-year-old lifetime minor leaguer, turned into the most aptly named man in Meribel, not to mention the stingiest, he and his U.S. teammates turned into the team Nobody Wanted To Play.

The puck stopped at LeBlanc. With a 2-0 win over Germany in the team's second game, he became the first American goalie to register a shutout in the Winter Olympics since 1964. In the very next game, against Poland in a 3-0 win, he repeated himself.

After that, he almost LeBlanked Finland in a 4-1 U.S. victory. In all, the Fitchburg, Mass., native had gone on a 110-minute, 57-second scoreless streak before the Finns proved him human, if only barely.

Coming into the Winter Olympics, LeBlanc had international credentials of sorts. He'd seen every rink in the International Hockey League, an NHL-feeder circuit centered in the midwestern United States. In the five seasons leading up to the 1992 Games, LeBlanc wore the IHL uniforms of the Flint Spirits, the Saginaw Gears, the Fort Wayne Komets and the Indianapolis Ice, sometimes shuttling back and forth from franchise to franchise in the same season.

The world hockey community was thus hardly prepared for the roadblock the unknown LeBlanc—who wasn't added to the U.S. roster until the team was already two months into its 64-game training schedule—would throw at them in Meribel.

In all, LeBlanc allowed just 19 goals in eight games at the Winter Olympics. In five preliminary round games he allowed a mere seven goals, three to Italy in a 6-3 U.S. win, one to Finland and three to defending world champion Sweden in a 3-3 tie that clinched top-seed status for the United States going into the eight-team medal round. LeBlanc and the U.S. might have gone all the way were it not for a Unified Team that peppered the U.S. goal with a furious 55 shots in the semi-finals. LeBlanc was able to stop 50 of those shots—but there were enough left over for a 5-2 Unified Team win.

Nonetheless, the U.S. team placed fourth for its highest finish since 1980, and LeBlanc came home to renewed interest from the National Hockey League (and a one-game NHL appearance courtesy of the Chicago Black Hawks so he could qualify for the expansion draft at the end of the season). All in all, LeBlanc's visit to Les Alps had been one to remember. ◆

The win gave the U.S. a 4-0 pool play record, the best tournament start since the 1960 team went 4-0. It also set up a showdown against top-seeded and undefeated Sweden in the final game of pool play.

After the U.S. had scored a goal in each period, Sweden stormed back in the third with three goals of its own to the tie the U.S. The tie advanced the Americans to a first-round playoff game with host France. "Now we're one of the eight teams and now you have to prove yourself all over again," Peterson said.

A three-goal outburst in the second period gave the U.S. a 4-1 victory over France and put the Americans in medal contention. The victory only proceeded to raise the stakes higher with a matchup against the Unified Team that brought back vivid memories of 1980. The winner would advance to the gold-medal game.

The Unified Team scored the first goal, but less than a minute later, defenseman Sean Hill tied the game for the U.S. when he scored on a wraparound play from the right side. The teams exchanged goals again and headed into intermission with a 2-2 tie.

"We felt right in the game at that point," Peterson said. Penalties proved to be the demise of the U.S. when the Unified Team had four power plays and scored twice in the third period.

LeBlanc once again withstood a heavy barrage, facing 55 shots and turning away 50 as the Unified Team outshot the U.S. by a 55-18 margin.

The 5-2 decision against the Russians was the first defeat for the U.S. in the Olympic Games and sent the Americans into the bronze medal game against Czechoslovakia, which had lost 4-2 to Canada in the other semifinal.

Throughout the tournament, the U.S. had played with an emotional edge that seemed to soften after the loss to the Unified Team. Hopes for a bronze medal were dashed when Czechoslovakia scored a 6-1 victory. The Unified Team went on to clinch its third consecutive gold medal by defeating Canada 3-1.

The fourth-place finish was the best for the U.S. team since 1980, and it was well above the expectations of the world hockey community that had predicted a sixth or seventh-place showing. Once again, the U.S. public was excited about hockey and the emotions of the 1980 dream come true resurfaced.

Throughout the Olympic Games, the U.S. players had worn T-shirts with the slogan "Experience The Dream" and then proceeded to live the dream by recording the best Olympic outing since the 1980 "Miracle On Ice." ◆   **ANNE ABICHT**

LUGE
The ultimate sleigh ride

tories abounded from this part of the French Alps with the unfolding of high expectations for a pair of World Cup silver medalists, the retirement of the sport's all-time goodwill ambassador and happenings of historical note.

The day following Opening Ceremonies, the luge competition commenced in La Plagne, and the U.S. team had the mission of delivering its first medal in Olympic history. While the Americans did not fulfill that goal, their improve-

French for *sleigh*, luge has been dominated by German-speaking athletes, with this Olympic year being no exception.

ment was noteworthy for the steps of progress always get smaller but more significant when closest to the summit.

In each discipline of men's and women's singles plus men's doubles, the American contingent improved or equalled its previous best Olympic showing.

High hopes had accompanied the U.S. team on the road to Albertville, particularly after Duncan Kennedy and Cammy Myler, the top U.S. performers, had each closed out the World Cup circuit as silver medalists, just one point shy of first place.

Fortified by his five medals during the World Cup season yet forewarned by disappointing training runs, Kennedy, who stood in sixth place after the first heat, slipped back to 10th place and maintained that final position for the best finish ever by an American in men's singles. He had a four-run combined time of 3:03.852. That topped the previous best showing of 12th by Jeff Tucker in 1980 and Frank Masley in 1988.

Wendel Suckow, only the third U.S. luger to compete in both the singles and doubles events at the same Winter Olympics, placed 12th in his first Olympic competition, matching the previous best men's showing, with a combined time of 3:04.195.

After a poor first run that left him in the back of the 34-man

ABOVE / *Remaining calm and collected, as Czech Maria Jasencakova appears, is just part of the requirements of world-class lugers, who shoot down the icy track negotiating 16 curves with a nine percent grade at speeds of 70 mph.* (ALLSPORT / RONDEAU)

ABOVE / *American Wendel Suckow, who competed in both singles and doubles events, "feels" his way around one of the curves at La Plagne. Lugers, acutely attuned to the course conditions, stay on track and accelerate with subtle corrections by the body.* (ALLSPORT / MARTIN)

pack, 18-year-old Robert Pipkins, who was the red-hot U.S. slider fresh off his world junior championship in Japan, jumped 11 places in the standings to finish in 21st with a 3:06.899 clocking.

World Cup champion Georg Hackl of Germany won the gold medal with a winning time of 3:02.363 followed by two Austrians — silver medalist Markus Prock and bronze medalist Markus Schmidt.

In women's singles, Myler battled a stomach virus as well as the competition to record the highest finish ever for an American in luge by placing fifth in the 24-woman field. That topped the previous best showing of sixth place by Bonny Warner in 1988. Myler's total time of 3:07.973 was only 3/10ths of a second out of fourth place and 8/10ths of a second from a bronze medal.

"I really wanted to see her beat my finish in Calgary because that would show that our sport has improved," Warner said. "It took a

BONNY WARNER & CAMMY MYLER

Frequent Flyers

BY LEE BENSON

When Bonny Warner announced she would be hanging up her sled after the Albertville Olympics, it meant the retirement of one of America's finest-ever luge loyalists as well as perhaps its most entertaining story. But Warner didn't bow out without leaving women's luge in the capable hands of her heir apparent, Cammy Myler.

Warner's reign was a long and, by all American standards, eminently successful one. While her 18th-place finish in Albertville was below expectations, Warner will nonetheless always be remembered as the airline pilot who was converted to luge while watching it during the 1980 Lake Placid Olympics, where she was a torch-bearer; who then stayed in Lake Placid to train; who won a trip to Europe the next winter and used it to train on the luge tracks there; and who finished an eye-popping sixth in the Calgary Games in 1988, the highest finish ever for an American at that time.

All the while, Warner, from Palo Alto, Calif., promoted luge with a tireless enthusiasm that was infectious to all who followed in her path.

Among those followers was Myler, whose ninth-place finish as a teenager in Calgary happened to be the second-best Olympic finish ever for an American (even though it was overshadowed by the charismatic Warner's success).

Born in Plattsburgh, a small town in upstate New York, Myler had become a frequent flyer down the luge run in nearby Lake Placid since the age of 11.

Calgary stamped Myler, just 19 then, as a force to be reckoned with in the future. Albertville stamped her as a force to be reckoned with now. She placed fifth in women's singles — yet another highest-ever Olympic finish for an American. And at that it was something of a disappointment. Just prior to the Winter Olympics, Myler, a pre-med student at Dartmouth, had finished second on the World Cup circuit, only one point shy of the gold medal.

In the Lillehammer Games in 1994, Myler figures to be America's shining luge star — taking over for Bonny Warner, who, in a tearful retirement speech in the French Alps, said the thing she was most proud about was that her sport was in better shape as she was leaving than it was when she arrived. ◆

weight off my shoulders because that meant there was somebody to carry on the sport and get those medals."

A 12-year veteran of the sport, Warner had a tearful farewell to her competitive luge career at the Winter Games. The three-time Olympian announced her retirement prior to the competition and finished 18th in the field at 3:09.757. Warner, a groundbreaker and ambassador for her sport, moved on to pursue her career as a pilot with United Airlines.

Erica Terwillegar, another seasoned veteran who came back from retirement and injuries, joined Myler in the Top 10 final results. Terwillegar's ninth-place showing in 3:08.547 equalled the third best Olympic performance in women's singles history.

An Austrian sister tandem grabbed top overall women's honors as Doris Neuner won the gold in 3:06.696 followed by Angelika Neuner in second and Germany's Susi Erdmann in third.

The U.S. doubles team followed suit in posting noteworthy results. The tandem of Suckow and Bill Tavares matched the best finish ever for an American doubles team by claiming ninth overall with a 1:33.451 clocking. That equalled the ninth-place showing of Ron Rossi and Doug Bateman in 1984.

Meanwhile the 12th-place finish of Chris Thorpe and Gordy Sheer in 1:34.042 was the fifth best in U.S. Olympic history. Overall, the two German doubles teams garnered the gold and silver medals while the Italians took home the bronze.

"Our goal is to be in the medals in Lillehammer," U.S. head coach Wolfgang Schadler said. "We are close. With all the media attention, everyone had high expectations for a medal here, but I'm not disappointed." ❖ **FRANK ZANG**

ABOVE / *Duncan Kennedy, luging since the age of 12, does things decidedly different and always with an eye toward fun: He sports a U.S. luge tatoo on his left bicep, and when burnout symptoms appeared in 1989, the 25-year-old left the competitive circuit for the season to try snowboarding. He returned to luge a year later, refreshed, and in La Plagne finished 10th in the men's singles, the top finish for an American.* (ALLSPORT / STEWART)

RIGHT / *While a luger only concentrates on the next curve, the backdrop of the Alps gives the crowd plenty to focus their attention on as they wait for the next competitor to come shooting by.* (ALLSPORT / VANDYSTADT)

NORDIC SKIING
Norway's one-track mind: gold

For the cross country teams, the snow-laden, hilly terrain of Les Saisies proved both a challenge and a nemesis. For Norway, Les Saisies merely provided redemption.

Coming home empty-handed at Calgary had been a rude awakening to a country used to being on top. Back home, Norway got to work and four years later the men's team regained its crown, much to the dismay of its Nordic neighbors (who were having troubles of their own). The final tally: seven medals and the honor of first-place finishes in all five of the men's events.

Only the Italians provided the Norwegians with a run for the gold. But the dynamic one-two punch of Bjorn Daehlie and Vegard Ulvang held off the pesky challenges of Marco Albarello and Giorgio Vanzetta to bring home three golds and one silver each. Albarello, 19.2 seconds behind Ulvang, collected a silver in the 10-kilometer classical race and Vanzetta, less than one second behind Ulvang in the 15-kilometer freestyle leg of the new two-day pursuit race, had to settle for the bronze after Ulvang edged the Italian in a sprint finish. The race, of course, belonged to Daehlie, who, after five kilometers, was so far ahead he could not be caught.

Twenty-five-year-old Lyubov Egorova of the Unified Team dominated the women's events, winning the honor of the most decorated athlete at these Olympic Winter Games with three golds and two silvers. Egorova's teammate, Elena Valbe, who was predicted to turn the women's events into a gold-medal sweepstakes, had her own share of disappointments instead. Still weakened by a virus and overpowered by Egorova, the 23-year-old Russian left with four individual bronzes and the team gold. Finland, meanwhile, continued to command the five-kilometer sprint, winning its third consecutive Olympic title thanks to Marjut Lukkarinen's time of 14:13.8.

Stefania Belmondo, the 23-year-old Italian, was another standout in the women's events, capturing the gold in the 30 kilometers to

TOP / *Norwegians Bjorn Daehlie (silver), Vegard Ulvang (gold) and Terje Langli (bronze) were all smiles having achieved an amazing 1-2-3 sweep in the 30-kilometer race at Les Saisies.* (ALLSPORT / VANDYSTADT)

RIGHT / *Armed with three gold medals and two silvers, Nordic skier Lyubov Egorova of the Unified Team earned the honor as the most decorated athlete at these Winter Games.* (ALLSPORT / VANDYSTADT)

OPPOSITE / *Vegard Ulvang barrelled through the snowy course at Les Saisies to help Norway win the men's relay title and, in doing so, added another gold to his growing collection.* (ALLSPORT / COLE)

sweeten her cache of one silver and the team relay bronze.

Both the men's and women's U.S. teams trained high in the Italian Alps before arriving in the Savoie region, where they faced a stiff test of skill, fitness and endurance. "This is not Disneyland," first-time Olympian Pete Vordenberg of Boulder, Colo., quipped following the 50-kilometer marathon.

It was anything but a vacation for the nine men and eight women who made up the team. A grueling course and periodic snowfalls brought mixed results from the United States camp.

"In general, the men came out of the Olympics on a positive note," said U.S. head coach John Estle. "It wasn't a big step, but we're slightly ahead of last year."

Individually for the U.S. men, the team's newest citizen, John Aalberg of Salt Lake City,

He has climbed the Alps's Mont Blanc and Alaska's Mount McKinley, and in Albertville, Vegard Ulvang climbed to the top once again — three times.

Utah, continued to pace the American skiers. The Norway native competed in the most events of any of the nine Americans, skiing in four of the five races.

The best performance on the men's side came on the first day of the pursuit race when a 10-kilometer classical race was staged. The U.S. posted three Top 30 finishes as Aalberg placed 18th (29:47.6), John Bauer of Champlin, Minn., was 23rd (29:58.0) and Ben Husaby of Eden Prairie, Minn., came in 26th (30:06.0).

In addition, newcomer Luke Bodensteiner of West Bend, Wis., registered a 27th-place finish in the 30 kilometers (1:28:4 5.7), showing potential for the future.

TOP / *The Norwegian flag was a familiar site at Les Saisies, where supporters — including the trolls (* **BOTTOM** - ALLSPORT / FARRANT*) — celebrated their country's supreme triumph and left a traditional Nordic reminder of Lillehammer two years away. (*ALLSPORT / BOTTERILL*)

OPPOSITE / *Amidst the splendor of the Alps and mountain mist, two skiers plow their way through the hilly terrain of Les Saisies during the 30-kilometer men's race. (*ALLSPORT / BOTTERILL*)

In other U.S. finishes, Koch placed 42nd (1:30:4 1.6), John Callahan of Park City, Utah, placed 49th (1:32:07.9), and Vordenberg finished 51st in the 30 kilometers (1:32:24.7), while Jim Curran of Jackson, Wyo., finished 56th in the 50 kilometers (2:26:27.0).

Nancy Fiddler of Crowley Lake, Calif., was the only U.S. woman to compete in every race and set the pace for the Americans each time out: five-kilometer pursuit (15:19.2 / 25th), 10-kilometer pursuit (28:19.9 / 29th), 15-kilometers (46:42.4 / 27th), 30 kilometers (1:33:02.5 / 29th) and the 4x5-kilometer relay (15:36.1 on the first leg).

Individually, the best finishes for the other U.S women: Ingrid Butts of Park City, Utah, placed 47th in the five-kilometer pursuit (16:06.9); Sue Forbes of Valdez, Alaska, was 41st in the 15 kilometers (49:42.7); Nina Kemppel of Anchorage, Alaska, placed 52nd in the 10-kilometer pursuit (30:57.7); Leslie Thompson of Stowe, Vt., finished 41st in the 10-kilometer pursuit (28:51.1); Dorcas Wonsavage of Park City, Utah, ended up 44th in the 15 kilometers (50:00.5); Betsy Youngman took 43rd in the 30 kilometers (1:36:12.1); and Brenda White of Williston, Vt., finished 36th in the 15 kilometers (48:06.0).

"For the most part, the results were not what we were hoping for," said U.S. assistant coach Jim Galanes. "Nancy Fiddler skied solid, and we have some young people who got some good experience.

"I really believe we have four to six women who can score some World Cup points in one or two years. It will take a little work. We're not that far off. We just have to take that big step for Lillehammer." ❖ **JOE BROWNING**

ABOVE / *Bill Koch gave the U.S. Nordic team an early boost by carrying the flag in the Opening Ceremonies, the only Nordic skier to receive the honor. Competing in his fourth Olympic Games, the 1976 silver medalist finished 42nd in the 30 kilometers, second best of the American men.* (ALLSPORT / BRUTY)

BILL KOCH

The Comeback Kid

BY LEE BENSON

At 36, he was the oldest cross-country skier on the team. But he was also the new kid on the block. Bill Koch, unretired after all those years, represented the Winter Olympics both past and future at the Nordic venue in Les Saisies.

Koch needed no introduction when he rejoined the U.S. team. Everyone who had ever stepped into a pair of three-pin bindings knew that he was the only American cross-country skier in history to win a medal in the Winter Olympics with his silver-medal effort in the 30-kilometer race at the 1976 Games in Innsbruck. They knew he won the overall Nordic World Cup in 1982 and also competed in Lake Placid in 1980 and 1984 at Sarajevo, after which he retired to, as he put it, "settle down and become respectable."

Settling down and respectability didn't cure his longing to compete, however, and, after sitting out nearly seven years from active competition, he moved to Oregon and started to train again in the winter of 1990-91, with an eye on the Lillehammer Games in 1994.

To everyone's surprise, Koch included, his comeback came back faster than expected. At the U.S. cross country trials he raced his way onto his fourth Olympic team.

His reputation preceded him, and his fellow American Olympic teammates voted him to carry the U.S. flag in the Opening Ceremonies at Albertville.

Koch's 1992 Games were limited to only one event, the 30-kilometer classical race, the same event he placed second in 1976. He was 42nd this time, eight minutes behind the winner, Vegard Ulvang of Norway. But at that, he was the second best of four Americans, and he finished strong. Strong enough to make a fifth Olympic experience in Lillehammer appear to be a distinct possibility. ◆

RIGHT / *Topping the scales at less than 100 pounds and a hair over five feet, Stephania Belmondo of Italy's Dolomites region conquered the 30-kilometer course, beating out the steadfast Russian Lyubov Egorova by 22.1 seconds for the gold.* (ALLSPORT / STEWART)

BELOW / *With the help of Marjut Lukkarinen, Finland maintained its dominance in the five-kilometer sprint. Marjut, edging Lyubov Egorova of the Unified Team by less than one second, gave her country its third consecutive Olympic title in the event.* (ALLSPORT / RONDEAU)

ABOVE / *Betsy Youngman of the United States takes a breather at Les Saisies. The American finished 43rd in the 30-kilometer event with a time of 1:36:12.1.* (ALLSPORT / STEWART)

SKI JUMPING
"V" for victory

Youth was served and a local flavor illuminated the ski jumping and Nordic combined competitions. Two teen-agers replaced the old guard and soared above the field on the hills of Courchevel, while the French swelled with national pride after a gold-silver finish in the individual Nordic combined.

Austria and Finland have been the dominant countries on the normal and large ski jump hills in recent Olympic history, but while that remained the same in 1992 the faces were different. Finland's Toni Nieminen, a 16-year-old, proved to be a worthy successor to

> **"The V-style is estimated to increase distance by five to seven meters .... Nieminen took one month to learn the style."**

fellow countryman Matti Nykaenen, a two-time Olympic champion, with two gold medals and one bronze. Meanwhile, 17-year-old Martin Hollwarth from Austria showed amazing consistency with three silver medals.

The sport's rising youngsters improved in each event, as the Olympic competition progressed. On the normal (90-meter) hill, Hollwarth and Nieminen were the leaders after the first round only to see Austria's Ernst Vettori fly 87.5 meters on his final jump to capture the gold. The first-time Olympians were outdueled by less than six points, but they were quick to learn as time would tell.

All the experts predicted gold for the Austrians in the team event on the large (120-meter) hill, after placing four jumpers among the top six just five days earlier. Austria had a one-point lead heading into the final round, but that was before Nieminen would stun everyone with a clutch jump of 122 meters to move his team to the lead.

It all came down to Andreas Felder, as the former world champion had the day's final attempt. But Austria's 29-year-old hero could only muster 109.5 meters, and the Finns had flown to the upset. The difference in the 14-team competition was 1.5 points, and the young had replaced the sport's aging stars.

ABOVE / *Peering out of their well-placed windows, the judges scored the 120-meter ski jumping competition* (ALLSPORT / STEWART), *which this Olympic year was revolutionized by the popular V-style.* (**OPPOSITE** - ALLSPORT / BRUTY)

Nieminen, who uses the revolutionary "V-style" or Bokloev technique, added to his new-found lore with a dominating performance in the individual large hill event. He blasted 122- and 123-meter jumps to bury the field, and was only grounded by a dense fog which delayed the competition's start. Nieminen took one month to learn the style, where the skis are displayed in a "V" shape instead of held together. The V-style's development is estimated to increase distance by five to seven meters.

The 239.5 points accumulated by Nieminen topped Hollwarth, the only other jumper to carry past 120 meters during the meet, by a decisive margin. It marked the fourth consecutive Winter Olympics in which a Finnish jumper had won the large hill title.

"I'm convinced," said Jim Holland, who became the second U.S. skier to place in the top 15 on both hills in the same Olympics, and changed from the conventional style last summer. "Most of the top jumpers on the World Cup tour have gone to it." The "V" may define the next generation of jumpers, but for the youthful Nieminen it simply meant victory.

NORDIC COMBINED
The French give a rowdy welcome to their guy; Japan makes a golden impression

THE NORDIC COMBINED scene also featured new names and nations, as France's Fabrice Guy won the individual crown and Japan took the team competition.

Guy and teammate Sylvain Guillaume pulled off the unthinkable with a one-two finish in the individual event. Guy, the pre-Olympic favorite with several World Cup titles under his skis, was third after the first day's jumping competition. But the powerful

TOP / *Jim Holland gave the United States its best finishes in the hills of Courchevel, taking 13th in the 90-meter ski jump and 12th in the 120-meter event.* (ALLSPORT / BOTTERILL)

BOTTOM / *After placing third in the jumping competition, powerful Fabrice Guy of France made up a 42.7-second time difference in skiing to take the gold in the Nordic combined.* (ALLSPORT / VANDYSTADT)

OPPOSITE / *The 16-year-old Finn Toni Nieminen took the gold in the 120-meter event and, with a jump of 122 meters, won the gold for his country in the team event.* (ALLSPORT / VANDYSTADT)

Frenchman traveled through a soft, slushy course to capture gold by making up a 42.7-second time difference.

The boisterous French crowds were well prepared to welcome Guy at the Courchevel-La Praz finish line, but were completely surprised by his teammate's unexpected trip to the victory podium. Guillaume improved 11 positions during the 15-kilometer cross-country race to win the silver medal. Meanwhile, Austria's Klaus Sulzenbacher, who was second at the 1988 Games in Calgary, had to settle for the bronze.

West Germany, which now competed with East Germany as a unified team, had owned the team event throughout the 1980s. But as time and geography have changed the world's map, Japan has emerged as the force on the Nordic combined circuit. Norway moved up in the cross-country skiing from sixth place to capture the silver medal. Austria, the 1991 world champions, claimed third.

More up-and-coming Olympians helped the American team, fourth after the jumping phase, to end up in eighth place overall for its best Olympic finish. Ryan "Speck" Heckman, a 17-year-old who names his cross country skis after his favorite players from the NFL's Denver Broncos, and Tim Tetreault, another new face with a frog-legged, ski-jump style, hope to help the U.S. team breakthrough in the future like the Japanese. ❖ **BRIAN DePASQUALE**

SPEED SKATING
Double duty for Blair, Turner

The 1992 U.S. Olympic Long Track and Short Track Teams had their ups and downs at the Olympic Winter Games in Albertville, but in the end, the U.S. speed skaters had claimed more than a third of the country's overall medal haul and enhanced their reputation

With the exception of Bonnie Blair's dominance in the sprint events, the German women were obviously head, shoulders, and skates ahead of everyone else.

of producing more American medals than any other winter Olympic sport.

Bonnie Blair was considered a strong pre-Olympic favorite in two events — the 500 meters and 1,000 meters — and the strong-willed Champaign, Ill., native did not disappoint.

Blair, who had won the 500 meters and earned a bronze medal in the 1,000 meters in 1988 at the Winter Olympics in Calgary, entered these Games undefeated in those events in 1991-92 World Cup competition.

Following her performances in the Olympics, the intense Blair was still undefeated in those events as she picked up her third and fourth career Olympic medals when she again captured the gold in the 500 meters and then came back to claim her first 1,000-meter Olympic title.

"Both medals are very special in their own right," said Blair after winning back-to-back gold medals in the 500 meters in Calgary and Albertville. "The first time being the underdog and never having won before was a very special moment. This time I knew what to expect. But it's different when you can come back and win again. These are different memories, but ones I'll never forget."

Termed "a killer" by U.S. national team head coach Peter Mueller for her ability to put opponents away, Blair won her second gold medal in 1992 four days later in the 1,000 meters.

Not only was Blair's performance special in terms of American speed skating history, but she will go down as one of the most

LEFT / *The familiar posture of the speed skater reflected in golden light — the color most sought after at the Olympic Games.* (ALLSPORT / BOTTERILL)

ABOVE / *Gunda Niemann of Germany* (ALLSPORT / VANDYSTADT) *dominated the long-distance events, taking two golds home, while Bonnie Blair, America's strong-willed sprint queen, won two golds in the 500-and 1,000-meter events.* (**OPPOSITE** - ALLSPORT / M. POWELL)

decorated Olympic skaters of all time. By winning the 1,000 meters to claim her third gold medal, Blair became the first American woman ever to win three gold medals in Winter Olympic competition. Blair's four overall medals also rank as a best for any U.S. woman in Winter Olympic competition and ties her for second for most Winter Olympic medals — male or female. She is the first woman in the history of the Olympic Games to win two gold medals in the 500-meter event. She is the first U.S. woman to capture a gold medal in the 1,000 meters. Her two medals at these Games also

BONNIE BLAIR

AMERICA'S WINTER QUEEN

BY LEE BENSON

Bonnie Blair, America's Winter Queen, continued her assault on Eric Heiden's American record of five gold medals in the Winter Olympics. But Blair is taking her time, and, from all appearances, enjoying every minute of it.

It took Heiden one glorious Games to collect his five speed skating gold medals — at Lake Placid in 1980 when he won at every distance from 500 to 10,000 meters.

Blair, on the other hand, competed in her third Winter Olympics in Albertville. In the process, she upped her gold medal count to three after wins at 500 meters and 1,000 meters.

She could catch Heiden with two more golds in Lillehammer, Norway, in 1994, and pass him with three. She just might. Albertville left the distinct impression that, if anything, the fastest woman from Champaign, Ill., is nothing

if not resilient.

Already, she is the most prolific female medal winner in U.S. Winter Olympic history, and if she adds one more gold medal she will tie diver Pat McCormick and you can drop the word "Winter."

In other competitions, Blair has always acted human (her 1991 season leading up to the Games was fraught

with injury, for instance, and she didn't win any world titles), but in the Olympics she takes on an aura that is, well, Olympian. And more or less uncanny because of her ability to win the close ones.

Her Albertville victories were by 2/100ths of a second in the 500 and 18/100ths in the 1,000. Add in her win by 2/100ths in the 500 in Calgary in 1988 and Blair's gold medals combined place her 22/100ths of a second ahead of the world.

In the process, Blair has become every bit the household name Heiden was, and then some. Every few Februarys you can count on her skating into your living room, winning by the width of a skate blade, and smiling like she's on top of the world as they drape the gold medal around her neck. Slowly and surely, Bonnie Blair has turned herself into an American rite of winter. ◆

tive member of the national long track team in 1981 when she decided to concentrate on a professional singing career. In 1988, after watching short track speed skating debut as an Olympic demonstration sport, Turner decided to make a comeback, initially with the hopes of just becoming a member of the national team. Within three years Turner had become a world-class short track

"It's like when you're in the eye of a hurricane; you don't see, hear or feel anything. That's how it was for me."

— CATHY TURNER, upon winning the silver medal in the women's 3,000-meter short track relay.

OPPOSITE / In Calgary, Bonnie Blair took the bronze in the 1,000 meters, but in Albertville, the determined Blair once again beat out the 500-meter silver medalist Qiaobo Ye of China — this time by a mere .02 seconds — for the gold. (ALLSPORT / MARTIN)

ABOVE / An emotional Cathy Turner gives the U.S. its first Olympic gold in short track speed skating. (ALLSPORT / VANDYSTADT)

RIGHT / In the 3,000-meter short track relay, the U.S. women's team produced silver. (ALLSPORT / BRUTY)

brought the overall U.S. speed skating medal count to 44, more than any other sport in the history of the Winter Olympics.

"I wasn't really aware of the statistics coming, but it's nice," Blair said. "I'm very proud of that and I'm proud I could bring more medals back to America."

Another American speed skater, short tracker Cathy Turner, was also a proud contributor to the homeland's hardware coffers when she picked up a gold in the 500 meters and earned a silver as the anchor leg of the women's silver medal-winning 3,000-meter relay team.

Turner and her short track teammates provided an interesting story for the 1992 Games, coming in as relative unknowns and leaving with two top-three finishes.

Turner, a 29-year old native of Rochester, N.Y., was a prospec-

sprinter, but did not enter the Olympics as one of the favorites. By the end of the Games, Turner was the proud recipient of two medals — one a gold and another a silver. Through it all she maintained a unique "newcomer's" perspective on her Olympic accomplishments.

"When we won the silver medal (in the 3,000-meter relay), I had to remind myself that this was an Olympic medal," Turner said. "That's how far out of everything I was once I got to Albertville. It's like when you're in the eye of a hurricane; you don't see, hear or feel anything. That's how it was for me."

Turner and the 3,000-meter relay team consisting of Amy Peterson of Maplewood, Minn., Darcie Dohnal of Wauwatosa, Wis., and Nikki Ziegelmeyer of Imperial, Mo., captured a silver medal in the first "official" medal offered in short track speed skating in the Winter Olympics, finishing just over a second behind the gold medal team from Canada. Two other U.S. short track medal hopefuls, Amy Peterson and Andy Gable, did not advance past their heats.

With the exception of Dan Jansen, expectations for the men's long track team were not exceedingly high entering the Winter Olympics.

Jansen, who became known as the "hard luck kid" after falling in the 500- and 1,000-meter events at the 1988 Winter Olympics in Calgary, entered the Albertville Games as one of the favorites in the 500 meters. In World Cup competition leading up to the Games, Jansen and Germany's Uwe-Jens Mey had traded victories and taken turns breaking the record in the event. After the Olympic smoke had cleared, Mey had claimed his second consecutive 500-meter Olympic title, two Japanese skaters (Toshiyuki Kuroiwa and Junichi Inoue) went home with silver and bronze medals, respectively, and Jansen was relegated to a fourth-place finish.

"I knew it wasn't good enough when I crossed the line," Jansen said. "The first 100 was pretty good for the ice, the ice was slow, but

CATHY TURNER

TOP OF THE WORLD

BY LEE BENSON

She had retired from speed skating in 1980, when she was all of 18 years old, and decided that she might prefer life as a songwriter or a singer or a computer programmer or maybe a professional water skier.

But in 1988, after trying all of the above and more, she returned to speed skating, this time to the short track version. And by the time the Albertville Olympics had come around, so had Cathy Turner.

First she led the U.S. foursome of Amy Peterson, Darcie Dohnal, Nikki Ziegelmeyer and herself to the 3,000-meter relay silver medal and then, in the 500-meter individual event, she beat China's Li Yan by the width of a skate blade for the gold medal.

If short track — competing as a full-medal discipline for the first time in the Winter Olympics — was looking for someone to personify the twists, turns, bumps and comebacks peculiar to its rather unique discipline, it couldn't have drawn up a better profile than Turner.

A 29-year-old renaissance woman from Hilton, N.Y., Turner certainly hadn't taken a conventional straight line to Albertville. Her eight-year hiatus from speed skating had included a college degree, time on the road as a singer, selling several songs she wrote, and, in addition to a fling at tournament water skiing, a try at downhill ski racing.

It wasn't until she became aware of a long track speed skating friend who had switched to short track in 1988, about the time of the Calgary Olympics, that she determined to give the sport that is a combination of rugby, speed skating and roller derby her best shot.

She first learned the fundamentals of the sport and then, for nearly four years — an eternity in Turner years — she trained with an eye toward Albertville. After she'd survived crash after crash in the preliminary heats and then surged past Li Yan for her gold medal in the 500 final, she wore a smile as wide as the Alps as she skated a victory lap around the Albertville ice draped in an American flag. "I never made it to the top in anything else," Turner said. Clearly, she was enjoying the view. ◆

I think my main problem is that technically I'm a longer skater and the ice wasn't conducive to my kind of skating. But I have no excuses. Three guys beat me."

Another men's medal hopeful, Eric Flaim, who had won a silver in the 1,500 meters in Calgary, was the only other U.S. male to earn a Top 10 finish when he finished sixth in the 5,000 meters.

Taking a look at a country-by-country medal count at the 1992 Olympic speed skating events, the Norwegians and Dutch proved to be dominant in the men's distance events, while the Germans came to the forefront in the women's competition.

Leo Visser third. Geir Karlstad, another Norwegian, picked up the 5,000-meter gold, finishing ahead of two skaters from the Netherlands, Falco Zandstra and Visser. And after coming so close in the previous three events, a Dutch skater finally came out on top when Bart Veldkamp turned in the top time in the 10,000 meters.

With the exception of Bonnie Blair's dominance in the sprint events, the German women were obviously head, shoulders, and skates ahead of everyone else at these Games, winning a total of nine medals out of a possible 15. Gunda Niemann won both the 3,000 and 5,000 competitions and, in fact, led a one-two-three German sweep

...in the men's distance events, the Norwegians and Dutch swept the nine remaining gold, silver and bronze medals.

Along with Mey in the men's 500, another German, Olaf Zinke, captured the 1,000-meter gold medal. And in the men's distance events, the Norwegians and Dutch swept the nine remaining gold, silver, and bronze medals. Norway's Johann Koss, the world record-holder in the 5,000 and 10,000-meter events, unexpectedly claimed the top spot in the 1,500 and then came back to finish second in the 10,000 meters. Another Norwegian, Adne Sondral was second, and

in the 5,000-meter event. Teammate Jacqueline Boerner was the gold-medal recipient in the 1,500 meters, with Niemann claiming her third medal of the Games in this event when she finished second. And in the two shortest races, the 500 and the 1,000 meters, Germany's Christa Luding and Monique Garbrecht won bronze medals. ❖   **Paul Allan**

A demo, please

U.S. adds four bronze medals from demonstration events

Although they may not have received as much media attention, there were six demonstration events and one demonstration sport at the XVIth Olympic Winter Games in France that not only drew impressive crowds, but also provided some of the spectators in attendance with striking displays of finesse, style and speed. And the U.S. participants in the demonstration events combined to earn four bronze medals at the Games (that did not count in the overall medal standings).

In the demonstration sport of curling, a sport of strategy and delicate execution that resembles shuffleboard on ice, athletes threw (or "skipped") "rocks" at "houses" and earned medals, not reprimands, for their efforts.

While the freestyle skiing event of moguls was elevated to medal status on the 1992 Olympic Winter Games program, its freestyle discipline counterparts of aerials and ballet remained at the demonstration level. Competitors awed the onlookers with death-defying aerial stunts and gracefully choreographed routines to music. And, in the speed skiing events, participants roared down the mountainside, setting world records in a blur of color, often exceeding 200 miles per hour.

BACKGROUND / *Leaving a trail of snow spray, speed skiers start in an aerodynamic tuck to attain the greatest speed by the time they reach the course's "speed trap," a 100-meter section where the speeds of skiers are recorded.* (Allsport / Rondeau)

OPPOSITE (TOP) / *The men's U.S. curling team was a family affair: two fathers, two sons, all related. Brother-in-laws Bud Somerville, captain and the oldest Olympian to compete at 55, and Bill Strum, vice skip and lead rock, and their sons Tim and Mike beat France to qualify for the medal round. They won the bronze.* (Allsport / Rondeau)

(INSET) / *Jeff Hamilton of the U.S. earned the bronze medal with a speed of 226.700 kph in the men's skiing demonstration event.* (Allsport / Bilow)

CURLING

Switzerland and Germany rock the house

THIS SPORT, WHICH made its fourth appearance as an Olympic demonstration sport, was created in Scotland some 400 years ago. Curl is the termed used when one player of the four-member team throws the 42 1/2-pound polished granite "rock" down the ice. Meanwhile, two teammates sweep the ice in front of the rock to lower friction and make the rock go straighter, while the "skip" (team captain) stands at the end of the ice, pointing toward the house (a 12-foot diameter scoring area) which is 125 feet away. After curling eight stones per "end" (or inning), the team with the rock closest to the center of the house scores one point and one additional point for every rock nearer the center than the nearest opponent's rock. The team with the highest score wins.

It was a family affair for the USA men's team in Pralognan, as Superior, Wis., brothers-in-law Bill Strum and Raymond "Bud" Somerville and their respective sons (and cousins) Mike Strum and Tim Somerville pooled their genetic talents and experience to finish with a 3-2 overall record and the third-place medal in the eight-country tournament.

The U.S. men dropped their first "run" at the 1992 Games to Canada (7-3) after being called for a line violation that cost them a chance at three points in the second end. But, behind 55-year-old skip and team captain Bud Somerville (the oldest 1992 U.S. Olympic winter competitor among the 181-member delegation), the USA came back to win its next two round-robin matches against Sweden (8-4) and France (6-4), qualifying for the medal round.

In the medal round, the U.S. men lost to Norway, 8-3, in the semifinals, setting up the final, third-place match with Canada (an 8-4 loser to Switzerland in the other semifinal). The Americans finished on a strong note, winning the bronze medal by defeating the Canadians, 9-2, while the Swiss men edged Norway, 7-6, for the gold medal.

The U.S. did not qualify a women's team for the 1992 Olympic tournament in Pralognan, but North American counterpart Canada was favored for a medal in the competition. After the elimination round, the Canadian women stood with a perfect 3-0 record in its pool, while Germany and Norway were tied at 2-1 in the other pool. In the tiebreaker, Norway swept past Great Britain (9-4), while Germany earned a 5-4 victory against the British, leaving the semifinal match-ups of Canada vs. Norway and Germany vs. Denmark.

Norway and Germany won their respective semifinal games, staging a gold medal rematch reminiscent of the 1988 Winter Games. This time, however, Germany earned the gold with a decisive 9-2 win. Canada defeated Denmark, 9-3, in the bronze medal match and had to settle for third despite matching Germany's 4-1 overall record in the tournament.

SPEED SKIING

Winners exceed 200 miles per hour

THIS EVENT MADE its Olympic demonstration debut in Les Arcs and, although marred by competition delays because of too much snow and the death of Swiss skier Nicolas Bochatay in an out-of-competition accident, it drew large crowds who were fascinated by the sci-fi helmets and Lycra body suits and awed by the world-record speeds of 200-plus mph.

After a qualifying round was held, the field was split into two pools of athletes, with the fastest 15 men and four women from each of the two pools advancing to the semifinals. The final field featured five women and 20 men. In all, 45 men and 20 women competed in the event in France.

Both the men's and women's world record fell in the finals, as France's Michael Prufer went 229.299 kph and Tarja Mulari of Finland posted a 219.245 kph clocking in the women's race. Each had also owned the previous world record.

Jeff Hamilton of Truckee, Calif., earned the bronze medal in the men's event with a speed of 226.700 kph, as three U.S. men placed in the top 10 in the finals, with Jim Morgan and C.J. Mueller seventh and 10th, respectively. Morgan's fastest speed wa s 222.910 kph, while the 40-year-old Mueller, a previous world record-holder and the first person to ever ski more than 130 mph back in 1981, moved through the Les Arcs course at 221.811. France's Philippe Goitschel took the silver with a 228.717 clocking.

Norway's Liss Pettersen earned the women's silver medal (212.892) and Switzerland's Renata Kolarova won the bronze (210.526). Melissa Dimino-Simons led the American women with a fifth-place showing, and a speed of 203.620 kph in the final. The USA's Kirsten Culver, Amy Guras and Richelle Reichsfeld were eliminated in the preliminary round, finishing 10th, 14th and 18th overall, respectively, among the women.

AERIALS

High flying Canadians snatch the men's gold and silver

THE "QUEBEC AIR FORCE" of Philippe Laroche and Nicolas Fontaine swept the gold and silver medals in the men's event, as the two Canadians flew high over Tignes, site of the 1992 Olympic aerials competition. Laroche was very emotional after his 237.47-point win, because his older brother had been injured in a paraskiing accident in Tignes two years before.

France's Didier Meda earned the bronze medal in the men's event, while U.S. aerialists Kris Fedderson and Trace Worthington placed fifth and seventh, respectively, in the two-day competition. Fedderson earned a disappointing 82.27 points on the first jump and then scored the highest total of the second round with a 119.47.

"You win with two solid jumps at this level. I had a strong second jump, but that wasn't enough," Fedderson said.

On the women's side, Switzerland's Colette Brand took the gold medal and Sweden's Marie Lindgren earned the silver, followed by Germany's Elfie Simchen in third. American Sue Michalski, who had been somewhat bothered by nagging injuries going into the competition, finished a disappointing 12th after the first day of competition and did not advance to the final.

BALLET

Spina, Petzold grace U.S. with bronzes

THINGS WERE MORE positive for the U.S. team in the ballet event as Lane Spina, the Olympic silver medalist in Calgary, and Sharon Petzold won bronze medals in the men's and women's event, respectively. Spina, who announced his retirement following the Games, finished out an illustrious skiing career which included the 1991 world championship title.

France's Fabrice Becker skied a flawless run in the final to earn the gold medal with a score of 28.15, much to the delight of the French fans, while Norway's Rune Kristiansen took the silver. The USA's Jeff Wintersteen and Trace Worthington placed seventh and 11th, respectively, in the field.

Switzerland's Conny Kissling won the women's gold medal ahead of France's Cathy Fechoz and Petzold. American Ellen Breen placed sixth. ❖   **GAYLE PLANT**

TOP / *An aerialist flies off the platform high above the mountain resort town of Tignes. Making its second debut as an Olympic demonstration event, the aerials competition entertained the crowds with one death-defying act after another.* (ALLSPORT / RONDEAU)
BOTTOM / *Lane Spina, the 1991 World Champion, wound down a 10-year distinguished career in ballet skiing by earning the bronze behind Fabrice Becker of France and Norway's Rune Kristiansen . So, Lane, how'd the picture turn out?* (ALLSPORT / COLE)
OPPOSITE / *France's Fabrice Becker demonstrates the style and grace that won him the gold in the ballet event.* (ALLSPORT / VANDYSTADT)

PARTICIPATING NATIONS

ALBERTVILLE GAMES
64 COUNTRIES / 1,808 ATHLETES

BARCELONA GAMES
171 COUNTRIES / 10,563 ATHLETES

AHO	NETHERLANDS ANTILLES
ALB	ALBANIA
ALG	ALGERIA
AND	ANDORRA
ANG	ANGOLA
ANT	ANTIGUA
ARG	ARGENTINA
ARU	ARUBA
ASA	AMERICAN SAMOA
AUS	AUSTRALIA
AUT	AUSTRIA
BAH	BAHAMAS
BAN	BANGLADESH
BAR	BARBADOS
BEL	BELGIUM
BEN	BENIN
BER	BERMUDA
BHU	BHUTAN
BIZ	BELIZE
BOL	BOLIVIA
BOT	BOTSWANA
BRA	BRAZIL
BRN	BAHRAIN
BRU	BRUNEI
BUL	BULGARIA
BUR	BURKINA FASO
CAF	CENTRAL AFRICAN REPUBLIC
CAN	CANADA
CAY	CAYMAN ISLANDS
CGO	PEOPLE'S REPUBLIC OF CONGO
CHA	CHAD
CHI	CHILE
CHN	PEOPLE'S REPUBLIC OF CHINA
CIV	IVORY COAST
CMR	CAMEROON
COK	COOK ISLANDS
COL	COLOMBIA
CRC	COSTA RICA
CRO	CROATIA
CUB	CUBA
CYP	CYPRUS
DEN	DENMARK
DJI	DJIBOUTI
DOM	DOMINICAN REPUBLIC
ECU	ECUADOR
EGY	ARAB REPUBLIC OF EGYPT
ESA	EL SALVADOR
ESP	SPAIN
EST	ESTONIA
ETH	ETHIOPIA
EUN	UNIFIED TEAM
FIJ	FIJI
FIN	FINLAND
FRA	FRANCE
GAB	GABON
GAM	GAMBIA
GBR	GREAT BRITAIN
GEQ	EQUATORIAL GUINEA
GER	GERMANY
GHA	GHANA
GRE	GREECE
GRN	GRENADA
GUA	GUATEMALA
GUI	GUINEA
GUM	GUAM
GUY	GUYANA
HAI	HAITI
HKG	HONG KONG
HON	HONDURAS
HUN	HUNGARY
INA	INDONESIA
IND	INDIA
IOP	INDEPENDENT OLYMPIC PARTICIPANTS
IRL	IRELAND
IRI	ISLAMIC REPUBLIC OF IRAN
IRQ	IRAQ
ISL	ICELAND
ISR	ISRAEL
ISV	VIRGIN ISLANDS
ITA	ITALY
IVB	BRITISH VIRGIN ISLANDS
JAM	JAMAICA
JOR	JORDAN
JPN	JAPAN
KEN	KENYA
KOR	KOREA (SOUTH)
KSA	SAUDI ARABIA
KUW	KUWAIT
LAO	LAOS
LAT	LATVIA
LBA	LIBYA
LBR	LIBERIA
LES	LESOTHO
LIB	LEBANON
LIE	LIECHTENSTEIN
LIT	LITHUANIA
LUX	LUXEMBOURG
MAD	MADAGASCAR
MAL	MALAYSIA
MAR	MOROCCO
MAW	MALAWI
MDV	MALDIVES
MEX	MEXICO
MGL	MONGOLIA
MLI	MALI
MLT	MALTA
MON	MONACO
MOZ	MOZAMBIQUE
MRI	MAURITIUS
MTN	MAURITANIA
MYA	UNION OF MYANMAR (FORMERLY BURMA)
NAM	NAMIBIA
NCA	NICARAGUA
NED	THE NETHERLANDS
NEP	NEPAL
NIG	NIGER
NGR	NIGERIA
NOR	NORWAY
NZL	NEW ZEALAND
OMA	OMAN
PAK	PAKISTAN
PAN	PANAMA
PAR	PARAGUAY
PER	PERU
PHI	PHILIPPINES
PNG	PAPUA-NEW GUINEA
POL	POLAND
POR	PORTUGAL
PRK	DEMOCRATIC PEOPLE'S REPUBLIC OF KOREA
PUR	PUERTO RICO
QAT	QATAR
ROM	ROMANIA
RSA	SOUTH AFRICA
RWA	RWANDA
SAM	WESTERN SAMOA
SEN	SENEGAL
SEY	SEYCHELLES
SIN	SINGAPORE
SLE	SIERRA LEONE
SLO	SLOVENIA
SMR	SAN MARINO
SOL	SOLOMON ISLANDS
SOM	SOMALIA
SRI	SRI LANKA
SUD	SUDAN
SUI	SWITZERLAND
SUR	SURINAM
SWE	SWEDEN
SWZ	SWAZILAND
SYR	SYRIA
TAN	TANZANIA
TCH	CZECH AND SLOVAK FEDERATIVE REPUBLIC
TGA	TONGA
THA	THAILAND
TOG	TOGO
TPE	CHINESE TAIPEI
TRI	TRINIDAD & TOBAGO
TUN	TUNISIA
TUR	TURKEY
UAE	UNITED ARAB EMIRATES
UGA	UGANDA
URU	URUGUAY
USA	UNITED STATES OF AMERICA
VAN	VANUATU
VEN	VENEZUELA
VIE	VIETNAM
VIN	ST. VINCENT AND THE GRENADINES
YEM	YEMEN
YUG	YUGOSLAVIA
ZAI	ZAIRE
ZAM	ZAMBIA
ZIM	ZIMBABWE

The following former Soviet Union states were granted provisional NOC status by the IOC on March 9, 1992. They participated in the Games of the XXVth Olympiad as a Unified Team (EUN). If they meet all IOC requirements, they will each be recognized independently as of Jan. 1, 1993.

ARM	ARMENIA
AZE	AZERBAIJAN
BLS	BELARUS
GEO	GEORGIA
KGZ	KYRGHYZSTAN
KZK	KAZAKHSTAN
MLD	MOLDOVA
RUS	RUSSIA
TJK	TADJIKISTAN
TKM	TURKMENISTAN
UKR	UKRAINE
UZB	UZBEKISTAN

CODE:

ATTENDED BARCELONA ONLY — RED
ATTENDED BOTH GAMES — BLACK

MEDAL COUNTS

ALBERTVILLE GAMES

CTRY	GOLD	SILVER	BRONZE	TOT.
GER	10	10	6	26
EUN	9	6	8	23
AUT	6	7	8	21
NOR	9	6	5	20
ITA	4	6	4	14
USA	5	4	2	11
FRA	3	5	1	9
FIN	3	1	3	7
CAN	2	3	2	7
JPN	1	2	4	7
KOR	2	1	1	4
NED	1	1	2	4
SWE	1	0	3	4
SUI	1	0	2	3
CHN	0	3	0	3
TCH	0	0	3	3
LUX	0	2	0	2
NZL	0	1	0	1
ESP	0	0	1	1
PRK	0	0	1	1
TOTAL	**57**	**58**	**56**	**171**

BARCELONA GAMES

CTRY	GOLD	SILVER	BRONZE	TOT.
EUN	45	38	29	112
USA	37	34	37	108
GER	33	21	28	82
CHN	16	22	16	54
CUB	14	6	11	31
HUN	11	12	7	30
KOR	12	5	12	29
FRA	8	5	16	29
AUS	7	9	11	27
ESP	13	7	2	22
JPN	3	8	11	22
GBR	5	3	12	20
ITA	6	5	8	19
POL	3	6	10	19
CAN	6	5	7	18
ROM	4	6	8	18
BUL	3	7	6	16
NED	2	6	7	15
SWE	1	7	4	12
NZL	1	4	5	10
PRK	4	0	5	9
KEN	2	4	2	8
TCH	4	2	1	7
NOR	2	4	1	7
TUR	2	2	2	6
DEN	1	1	4	6
INA	2	2	1	5
FIN	1	2	2	5
JAM	0	3	1	4
NGR	0	3	1	4
BRA	2	1	0	3
MAR	1	1	1	3
ETH	1	0	2	3
LAT	0	2	1	3
BEL	0	1	2	3
CRO	0	1	2	3
IOP	0	1	2	3
IRI	0	1	2	3
GRE	2	0	0	2
IRL	1	1	0	2
ALG	1	0	1	2
EST	1	0	1	2
LIT	1	0	1	2
AUT	0	2	0	2
NAM	0	2	0	2
RSA	0	2	0	2
ISR	0	1	1	2
MGL	0	0	2	2
SLO	0	0	2	2
SUI	1	0	0	1
TPE	0	1	0	1
MEX	0	1	0	1
PER	0	1	0	1
ARG	0	0	1	1
BAH	0	0	1	1
COL	0	0	1	1
GHA	0	0	1	1
MAS	0	0	1	1
PAK	0	0	1	1
PHI	0	0	1	1
PUR	0	0	1	1
QAT	0	0	1	1
SUR	0	0	1	1
THA	0	0	1	1
TOTAL	**259**	**258**	**298**	**815**

RESULTS

WR = world record	DNQ = did not qualify
EWR = equals WR	DNF = did not finish
OR = Olympic record	AB = abandoned
EOR = equals OR	DNA = did not advance
FOR = Final OR	INJ = injured
DQ = disqualified	

XVIth OLYMPIC WINTER GAMES
Albertville, France
February 8-23, 1992

ALPINE SKIING

MEN'S DOWNHILL / February 9

RANK	CTRY	ATHLETE	TIME
1	AUT	Patrick Ortlieb	1:50.37
2	FRA	Franck Piccard	1:50.42
3	AUT	Guenther Mader	1:50.47
4	GER	Markus Wasmeier	1:50.62
5	NOR	Jan Einar Thorsen	1:50.79
6	SUI	Franz Heinzer	1:51.39
7	GER	Hansjoerg Tauscher	1:51.49
8	NOR	Lasse Arnesen	1:51.63
9	USA	AJ Kitt	1:51.98
16	USA	Kyle Rasmussen	1:52.71
20	USA	Tommy Moe	1:53.40
28	USA	Reggie Crist	1:54.54

MEN'S COMBINED / February 11

RANK	CTRY	ATHLETE	POINTS
1	ITA	Josef Polig	14.58
2	ITA	Gianfranco Martin	14.90
3	SUI	Steve Locher	18.16
4	FRA	Jean-Luc Cretier	18.97
5	GER	Markus Wasmeier	32.77
6	ITA	Kristian Ghedina	38.96
7	NOR	Ole Christian Furuseth	40.47
8	SUI	Xavier Gigandet	41.21
16	USA	Kyle Rasmussen	66.70
18	USA	Tommy Moe	82.15

MEN'S SLALOM / February 22

RANK	CTRY	ATHLETE	TIME
1	NOR	Finn Chr. Jagge	1:44.39
2	ITA	Alberto Tomba	1:44.67
3	AUT	Michael Tritscher	1:44.85
4	SUI	Patrick Staub	1:45.44
5	SWE	Tomas Fogdoe	1:45.48
6	SUI	Paul Accola	1:45.62
7	SUI	Michael Von Gruenigen	1:46.42
8	SWE	Jonas Nilsson	1:46.57
10	USA	Matthew Grosjean	1:46.94
23	USA	Kyle Wieche	1:51.12
—	USA	Joe Levins	DNF (1st run)
—	USA	Paul Casey Puckett	DNF (1st run)

MEN'S SUPER G / February 16

RANK	CTRY	ATHLETE	TIME
1	NOR	Kjetil Andre Aamodt	1:13.04
2	LUX	Marc Girardelli	1:13.77
3	NOR	Jan Einar Thorsen	1:13.83
4	NOR	Ole Christian Furuseth	1:13.87
5	ITA	Josef Polig	1:13.88
6	SUI	Marco Hangl	1:13.90
7	AUT	Guenther Mader	1:14.08
8	NOR	Tom Stiansen	1:14.51
13	USA	Jeff Olson	1:15.06
17	USA	Kyle Rasmussen	1:15.58
23	USA	AJ Kitt	1:16.31
28	USA	Tommy Moe	1:16.54

MEN'S GIANT SLALOM / February 18

RANK	CTRY	ATHLETE	TIME
1	ITA	Alberto Tomba	2:06.98
2	LUX	Marc Girardelli	2:07.30
3	NOR	Kjetil Andre Aamodt	2:07.82
4	SUI	Paul Accola	2:08.02
5	NOR	Ole Christian Furuseth	2:08.16
6	AUT	Guenther Mader	2:08.80
7	AUT	Rainer Salzgeber	2:08.83
8	SWE	Fredrik Nyberg	2:09.00
20	USA	Rob Parisien	2:12.03
25	USA	Paul Casey Puckett	2:13.25
—	USA	Christopher Puckett	DNF (1st run)
—	USA	Matthew Grosjean	DNF (2nd run)

WOMEN'S DOWNHILL / February 15

RANK	CTRY	ATHLETE	TIME
1	CAN	Kerrin Lee-Gartner	1:52.55
2	USA	Hilary Lindh	1:52.61
3	AUT	Veronika Wallinger	1:52.64
4	GER	Katja Seizinger	1:52.67
5	AUT	Petra Kronberger	1:52.73
6	GER	Katrin Gutensohn	1:53.71
7	AUT	Barbara Sadleder	1:53.81
8	EUN	Svetlana Gladishiva	1:53.85
12	USA	Krista Schmidinger	1:54.59
25	USA	Edith Thys	1:58.13

WOMEN'S COMBINED / February 13

RANK	CTRY	ATHLETE	POINTS
1	AUT	Petra Kronberger	2.55
2	AUT	Anita Wachter	19.39
3	FRA	Florence Masnada	21.38
4	SUI	Chantal Bournissen	24.98
5	NOR	Anne Berge	35.28
6	CAN	Michelle McKendry	39.02
7	SLO	Natasa Bokal	42.60
8	TCH	Lucia Medzihradska	47.43
11	USA	Krista Schmidinger	51.56
—	USA	Kristin Krone	DNF (1st run)

WOMEN'S SLALOM / February 20

RANK	CTRY	ATHLETE	TIME
1	AUT	Petra Kronberger	1:32.68
2	NZL	Annelise Coberger	1:33.10
3	ESP	Blanca Fernandez Ochoa	1:33.35
4	USA	Julie Parisien	1:33.40
5	AUT	Karin Buder	1:33.68
6	FRA	Patricia Chauvet	1:33.72
7	SUI	Vreni Schneider	1:33.96
8	NOR	Anne Berge	1:34.22
18	USA	Monique Pelletier	1:36.63
20	USA	Heidi Voelker	1:37.69
—	USA	Eva Twardokens	DNF (1st run)

WOMEN'S SUPER G / February 18

RANK	CTRY	ATHLETE	TIME
1	ITA	Deborah Compagnoni	1:21.22
2	FRA	Carole Merle	1:22.63
3	GER	Katja Seizinger	1:23.19
4	AUT	Petra Kronberger	1:23.20
5	AUT	Ulrike Maier	1:23.35
6	CAN	Kerrin Lee-Gartner	1:23.76
7	GER	Michaela Gerg	1:23.77
8	USA	Eva Twardokens	1:24.19
17	USA	Hilary Lindh	1:25.37
—	USA	Diann Roffe	DNF
—	USA	Julie Parisien	DQ

WOMEN'S GIANT SLALOM / February 19

RANK	CTRY	ATHLETE	TIME
1	SWE	Pernilla Wiberg	2:12.74
2	USA	Diann Roffe	2:13.71
2	AUT	Anita Wachter	2:13.71
4	AUT	Ulrike Maier	2:13.77
5	USA	Julie Parisien	2:14.10
6	FRA	Carole Merle	2:14.24
7	USA	Eva Twardokens	2:14.47
8	GER	Katja Seizinger	2:14.96
—	USA	Edith Thys	DNF (2nd run)

BIATHLON

MEN'S 10 KM / February 12

RANK	CTRY	ATHLETE	TIME
1	GER	Mark Kirchner	26:02.3
2	GER	Ricco Gross	26:18.0
3	FIN	Harri Eloranta	26:26.6
4	EUN	Serguei Tchepikov	26:27.5
5	EUN	Valeri Kirienko	26:31.8
6	GER	Jens Steinigen	26:34.8
7	ITA	Andreas Zingerle	26:38.6
8	CAN	Steve Cyr	26:46.4
32	USA	Josh Thompson	27:53.2
37	USA	Curtis Schreiner	28:08.4
49	USA	Erich Wilbrecht	28:41.1
55	USA	Duncan Douglas	28:49.2

MEN'S 20 KM / February 20

RANK	CTRY	ATHLETE	TIME
1	EUN	Evgueni Redkine	57:34.4
2	GER	Mark Kirchner	57:40.8
3	SWE	Mikael Lofgren	57:59.4
4	EUN	Alexander Popov	58:02.9
5	FIN	Harri Eloranta	58:15.7
6	FIN	Vesa Hietalahti	58:24.6
7	ITA	Johann Passler	58:25.9
8	NOR	Frode Loberg	58:32.4
16	USA	Josh Thompson	1:00:05.4
51	USA	Curtis Schreiner	1:03:34.2
59	USA	Duncan Douglas	1:04:17.5
70	USA	Jon Engen	1:06:18.4

MEN'S 4x7.5-KM RELAY / February 16

RANK	CTRY	ATHLETES	TIME
1	GER	Ricco Gross / Jens Steinigen / Mark Kirchner / Fritz Fischer	1:24:43.5
2	EUN	Valeri Medvedzev / Alexander Popov / Valeri Kirienko / Serguei Tchepikov	1:25:06.3
3	SWE	Ulf Johansson / Leif Andersson / Tord Wiksten / Mikael Lofgren	1:25:38.2
4	ITA	Hubert Leitgeb / Johann Passler / Pieralberto Carrara / Andreas Zingerle	1:26:18.1
5	NOR	Geir Einang / Frode Loberg / Gisle Fenne / Eirik Kvalfoss	1:26:32.4
6	FRA	Xavier Blond / Thierry Gerbier / Christian Dumont / Herve Flandin	1:27:13.3
7	TCH	Martin Rypl / Tomas Kos / Jiri Holubec / Ivan Masarik	1:27:15.7
8	FIN	Vesa Hietalahti / Jaakko Niemi / Harri Eloranta / Kari Kataja	1:27:39.5
13	USA	Jon Engen / Duncan Douglas / Josh Thompson / Curtis Schreiner	1:30:44.0

WOMEN'S 7.5 KM / February 11

RANK	CTRY	ATHLETE	TIME
1	EUN	Anfissa Restzova	24:29.2
2	GER	Antje Misersky	24:45.1
3	EUN	Elena Belova	24:50.8
4	BUL	Nadezda Alexieva	24:55.8
5	TCH	Jirina Adamickova	24:57.6
6	GER	Petra Schaaf	25:10.4
7	FRA	Anne Briand	25:29.8
8	BUL	Silvana Blagoeva	25:33.5
21	USA	Joan Smith	26:54.5
25	USA	Mary Ostergren	27:05.7
44	USA	Nancy Bell	28:20.6
64	USA	Joan Guetschow	31:30.6

WOMEN'S 15 KM / February 19

RANK	CTRY	ATHLETE	TIME
1	GER	Antje Misersky	51:47.2
2	EUN	Svetlana Pecherskaia	51:58.5
3	CAN	Myriam Bedard	52:15.0
4	FRA	Veronique Claudel	52:21.2
5	BUL	Nadezda Alexieva	52:30.2
6	FRA	Delphine Burlet	53:00.8
7	FRA	Corinne Niogret	53:06.6
8	FRA	Nathalie Santer	53:10.3
34	USA	Nancy Bell	57:55.2
42	USA	Patrice Anderson	58:59.6
47	USA	Beth Coats	59:36.1
55	USA	Joan Smith	1:01:15.2

WOMEN'S 3x7.5-KM RELAY / February 14

RANK	CTRY	ATHLETES	TIME
1	FRA	Corinne Niogret / Veronique Claudel / Anne Briand	1:15:55.6
2	GER	Uschi Disl / Antje Misersky / Petra Schaaf	1:16:18.4
3	EUN	Elena Belova / Anfissa Restzova / Elena Melnikova	1:16:54.6
4	BUL	Silvana Blagoeva / Nadezda Alexieva / Iwa Schkodreva	1:18:54.8
5	FIN	Mari Lampinen / Tuija Sikio / Terhi Markkanen	1:20:17.8
6	SWE	Christina Eklund / Inger Bjorkbom / Mia Stadig	1:20:56.6
7	NOR	Signe Trosten / Hildegunn Fossen / Elin Kristiansen	1:21:20.0
8	TCH	Gabriela Suvova / Jana Kulhava / Jirina Adamickova	1:23:12.7
15	USA	Nancy Bell / Joan Smith / Mary Ostergren	1:24:36.9

BOBSLED

TWO MAN / February 16

RANK	CTRY	ATHLETES	TIME
1	SUI-I	Gustav Weder / Donat Acklin	4:03.26
2	GER-I	Rudolf Lochner / Markus Zimmermann	4:03.55
3	GER-II	Christoph Langen / Gunther Eger	4:03.63
4	AUT-II	Ingo Appelt / Thomas Schroll	4:03.67
5	ITA-II	Gunther Huber / Stefano Ticci	4:03.72
6	GBR-I	Mark Tout / Lenox Paul	4:03.87
7	USA-I	Brian Shimer / Herschel Walker	4:03.95
8	AUT-I	Gerhard Rainer / Thomas Bachler	4:04.00
24	USA-II	Brian Richardson / Greg Harrell	4:08.17

FOUR MAN / February 22

RANK	CTRY	ATHLETES	TIME
1	AUT-I	Ingo Appelt / Harald Winkler / Gerhard Haidacher / Thomas Schroll	3:53.90
2	GER-I	Wolfgang Hoppe / Bogdan Musiol / Axel Kuhn / Rene Hannemann	3:53.92
3	SUI-I	Gustav Weder / Donat Acklin / Lorenz Schindelholz / Curdin Morell	3:54.13
4	CAN-I	Christopher Lori / Kenneth Leblanc / Cleve Langford / David Mac Eachern	3:54.24
5	SUI-II	Christian Meili / Bruno Gerber / Christian Reich / Gerold Loffler	3:54.38
6	GER-II	Harald Czudaj / Tino Bonk / Axel Jang / Alexander Szelig	3:54.42
7	GBR-I	Mark Tout / George Farrell / Paul Field / Lenox Paul	3:54.89
8	FRA-I	Christophe Flacher / Claude Dasse / Thierry Tribondeau / Gabriel Fourmigue	3:54.91
9	USA-I	Randy Will / Joseph Sawyer / Karlos Kirby / Christopher Coleman	3:54.92
11	USA-II	Charles Leonowicz / Robert Weissenfels / Bryan Leturgez / Jeffrey Woodard	3:55.23

FIGURE SKATING

MEN'S SINGLES / February 15

RANK	CTRY	ATHLETE	POINTS
1	EUN	Viktor Petrenko	1.5
2	USA	Paul Wylie	3.5
3	TCH	Petr Barna	4.0
4	USA	Christopher Bowman	7.5
5	EUN	Alexei Ourmanov	7.5
6	CAN	Kurt Browning	8.0
7	CAN	Elvis Stojko	10.0
8	EUN	Viatcheslav Zagorodniuk	13.0
10	USA	Todd Eldredge	15.5

WOMEN'S SINGLES / February 21

RANK	CTRY	ATHLETE	POINTS
1	USA	Kristi Yamaguchi	1.5
2	JPN	Midori Ito	4.0
3	USA	Nancy Kerrigan	4.0
4	USA	Tonya Harding	7.0
5	FRA	Surya Bonaly	7.5
6	CHN	Lu Chen	10.5
7	JPN	Yuka Sato	10.5
8	CAN	Karen Preston	14.0

PAIRS / February 11

RANK	CTRY	ATHLETES	POINTS
1	EUN	Natalia Michkouteniok / Artour Dmitriev	1.5
2	EUN	Elena Betchke / Denis Petrov	3.0
3	CAN	Isabelle Brasseur / Lloyd Eisler	4.5
4	TCH	Radka Kovarikova / Rene Novotny	6.0
5	EUN	Evguenia Chichkova / Vadim Naoumov	7.5
6	USA	Natasha Kuchiki / Todd Sand	9.0
7	GER	Peggy Schwarz / Alexander Konig	11.0
8	GER	Mandy Wotzel / Axel Rauschenbach	13.0
10	USA	Calla Urbanski / Rocky Marval	14.5
11	USA	Jenni Meno / Scott Wendland	15.0

ICE DANCING / February 17

RANK	CTRY	ATHLETES	POINTS
1	EUN	Marina Klimova / Sergei Ponomarenko	2.0
2	FRA	Isabelle Duchesnay-Dean / Paul Duchesnay	4.4
3	EUN	Maia Usova / Alexander Zhulin	5.6
4	EUN	Oksana Gritschuk / Evgeni Platov	8.0
5	ITA	Stefania Calegari / Pasquale Camerlengo	10.0
6	FIN	Susanna Rahkamo / Petri Kokko	12.4
7	HUN	Klara Engi / Attila Toth	13.6
8	FRA	Dominique Yvon / Frederic Palluel	16.6
11	USA	April Sargent-Thomas / Russ Witherby	21.6
15	USA	Rachel Mayer / Peter Breen	29.0

FREESTYLE SKIING

MEN'S MOGULS / February 13

RANK	CTRY	ATHLETE	POINTS
1	FRA	Edgar Grospiron	25.81
2	FRA	Olivier Allamand	24.87
3	USA	Nelson Carmichael	24.82
4	FRA	Eric Berthon	24.79
5	CAN	John Smart	24.15
6	SWE	Jorgen Paajarvi	24.14
7	CAN	Jean-Luc Brassard	23.71
8	SWE	Leif Persson	22.99
13	USA	Craig Rodman	21.18
15	USA	Chuck Martin	20.77
—	USA	Robert Aldighieri	elim.

WOMEN'S MOGULS / February 13

RANK	CTRY	ATHLETE	POINTS
1	USA	Donna Weinbrecht	23.69
2	EUN	Elizaveta Kojevnikova	23.50
3	NOR	Stine Hattestad	23.04
4	GER	Tatjana Mittermayer	22.33
5	GER	Birgit Stein	21.44
6	USA	Liz McIntyre	21.24
7	ITA	Silvia Marciandi	19.66
8	FRA	Raphaelle Monod	15.57
—	USA	Ann Battelle	elim.
—	USA	Maggie Connor	elim.

ICE HOCKEY

FINAL STANDINGS / February 8-23

RANK	CTRY	RECORD	—	USA GAME SCORES
1	EUN	7- 1- 0	—	USA vs. ITA 6-3
2	CAN	6- 2- 0	—	USA vs. POL 3-0
3	TCH	6- 2- 0	—	USA vs. GER 2-0
4	USA	5- 2- 1	—	USA vs. FIN 4-1
5	SWE	5- 1- 2	—	USA vs. SWE 3-3
6	GER	3- 5- 0	—	USA vs. FRA 4-1
7	FIN	4- 3- 1	—	USA vs. EUN 2-5
8	FRA	2- 6- 0	—	USA vs. TCH 1-6
9	NOR	2- 5- 0	—	
10	SUI	2- 5- 0	—	

USA TEAM: Greg Brown, Clark Donatelli, Ted Donato, Ted Drury, Mike Dunham, David Emma, Scott Gordon, Guy Gosselin, Brett Hedican, Steve Heinze, Sean Hill, Jim Johannson, Scott LaChance, Ray LeBlanc, Moe Mantha, Shawn McEachern, Marty McInnis, Joe Sacco, Tim Sweeney, Keith Tkachuk, Dave Tretowicz, C.J. Young, Scott Young

LUGE

MEN'S SINGLES / February 10

RANK	CTRY	ATHLETE	TIME
1	GER	Georg Hackl	3:02.363
2	AUT	Markus Prock	3:02.669
3	AUT	Markus Schmidt	3:02.942
4	ITA	Norbert Huber	3:02.973
5	GER	Jens Muller	3:03.197
6	AUT	Robert Manzenreiter	3:03.267
7	ITA	Oswald Haselrieder	3:03.276
8	GER	Rene Friedl	3:03.543
10	USA	Duncan Kennedy	3:03.852
12	USA	Wendel Suckow	3:04.195
21	USA	Robert Pipkins	3:06.899

MEN'S DOUBLES / February 14

RANK	CTRY	ATHLETES	TIME
1	GER	Stefan Krausse / Jan Behrendt	1:32.053
2	GER	Yves Mankel / Thomas Rudolph	1:32.239
3	ITA	Hansjorg Raffl / Norbert Huber	1:32.298
4	ROM	Ioan Apostol / Liviu Cepoi	1:32.649
5	ITA	Kurt Brugger / Willi Huber	1:32.810
6	SWE	Hans Kohala / Carl-Johan Lindquist	1:33.134
7	AUT	Gerhard Gleirscher / Markus Schmidt	1:33.257
8	EUN	Albert Demtschenko / Alexei Selenski	1:33.299
9	USA	Wendel Suckow / Bill Tavares	1:33.451
12	USA	Christopher Thorpe / Gordon Sheer	1:34.042

WOMEN'S SINGLES / February 12

RANK	CTRY	ATHLETE	TIME
1	AUT	Doris Neuner	3:06.696
2	AUT	Angelika Neuner	3:06.769
3	GER	Susi Erdmann	3:07.115
4	ITA	Gerda Weissensteiner	3:07.673
5	USA	Cammy Myler	3:07.973
6	GER	Gabriele Kohlisch	3:07.980
7	AUT	Andrea Tagwerker	3:08.018
8	EUN	Natalia Jakouchenko	3:08.383
9	USA	Erica Terwillegar	3:08.547
18	USA	Bonny Warner	3:09.757

NORDIC SKIING

MEN'S 10 KM CLASSICAL PURSUIT / February 13

RANK	CTRY	ATHLETE	TIME
1	NOR	Vegard Ulvang	27:36.0
2	ITA	Marco Albarello	27:55.2
3	SWE	Christer Majback	27:56.4
4	NOR	Bjorn Daehlie	28:01.6
5	SWE	Niklas Jonsson	28:03.1
6	FIN	Harri Kirvesniemi	28:23.3
7	ITA	Giorgio Vanzetta	28:26.9
8	AUT	Alois Stadlober	28:27.5
18	USA	John Aalberg	29:47.6
23	USA	John Bauer	29:58.0
26	USA	Ben Husaby	30:06.0
60	USA	John Farra	32:06.0

MEN'S 30 KM CLASSICAL / February 10

RANK	CTRY	ATHLETE	TIME
1	NOR	Vegard Ulvang	1:22:27.8
2	NOR	Bjorn Daehlie	1:23:14.0
3	NOR	Terje Langli	1:23:42.5
4	ITA	Marco Albarello	1:23:55.7
5	NOR	Erling Jevne	1:24:07.7
6	SWE	Christer Majback	1:24:12.1
7	SWE	Niklas Jonsson	1:25:17.6
8	SWE	Jyrki Ponsiluoma	1:25:24.4
27	USA	Luke Bodensteiner	1:28:45.7
42	USA	Bill Koch	1:30:41.6
49	USA	John Callahan	1:32:07.9
51	USA	Peter Vordenberg	1:32:24.7

MEN'S 50 KM FREE / February 22

RANK	CTRY	ATHLETE	TIME
1	NOR	Bjorn Daehlie	2:03:41.5
2	ITA	Maurilio De Zolt	2:04:39.1
3	ITA	Giorgio Vanzetta	2:06:42.1
4	EUN	Alexej Prokurorov	2:07:06.1
5	FRA	Herve Balland	2:07:17.7
6	TCH	Radim Nyc	2:07:41.5
7	GER	Johann Muhlegg	2:07:45.2
8	TCH	Pavel Benc	2:08:13.6
33	USA	John Aalberg	2:15:33.5
43	USA	Luke Bodensteiner	2:18:42.4
56	USA	James Curran	2:26:17.0
57	USA	Peter Vordenberg	2:26:25.8

MEN'S 15 KM FREE PURSUIT / February 15

RANK	CTRY	ATHLETE	TIME
1	NOR	Bjorn Daehlie	1:05:37.9
2	NOR	Vegard Ulvang	1:06:31.3
3	ITA	Giorgio Vanzetta	1:06:32.2
4	ITA	Marco Albarello	1:06:33.3
5	SWE	Torgny Mogren	1:06:37.4
6	SWE	Christer Majback	1:07:17.0
7	ITA	Silvio Fauner	1:07:34.9
8	EUN	Wladimir Smirnov	1:07:35.8
26	USA	John Aalberg	1:09:55.2
32	USA	John Bauer	1:10:37.7
46	USA	Ben Husaby	1:12:17.1
49	USA	John Farra	1:12:30.3

MEN'S 4x10-KM RELAY / February 18

RANK	CTRY	ATHLETES	TIME
1	NOR	Terje Langli / Vegard Ulvang / Kristen Skjeldal / Bjorn Daehlie	1:39:26.0
2	ITA	Giuseppe Pulie / Marco Albarello / Giorgio Vanzetta / Silvio Fauner	1:40:52.7
3	FIN	Mika Kuusisto / Harri Kirvesniemi / Jari Rasanen / Jari Isometsa	1:41:22.9
4	SWE	Jan Ottosson / Christer Majback / Henrik Forsberg / Torgny Mogren	1:41:23.1
5	EUN	Andrei Kirillov / Wladimir Smirnov / Mikhail Botvinov / Alexej Prokururov	1:43:03.6
6	GER	Holger Bauroth / Jochen Behle / Torald Rein / Johann Muhlegg	1:43:41.7
7	TCH	Radim Nyc / Lubomir Buchta / Pavel Benc / Vaclav Korunka	1:44:20.0
8	FRA	Patrick Remy / Philippe Sanchez / Stephane Azambre / Herve Balland	1:44:51.1
12	USA	John Husaby / John Bauer / John Farra / Luke Bodensteiner	1:48:15.8

WOMEN'S 5 KM CLASSICAL / February 13

RANK	CTRY	ATHLETE	TIME
1	FIN	Marjut Lukkarinen	14:13.8
2	EUN	Lyubov Egorova	14:14.7
3	EUN	Elena Valbe	14:22.7
4	ITA	Stefania Belmondo	14:26.2
5	NOR	Inger Helene Nybraten	14:33.3
6	EUN	Olga Danilova	14:37.2
7	EUN	Larisa Lasutina	14:41.7
8	NOR	Solveig Pederson	14:42.1
25	USA	Nancy Fiddler	15:19.2
47	USA	Ingrid Butts	16:07.9
52	USA	Leslie Thompson	16:27.8
56	USA	Nina Kemppel	17:12.9

WOMEN'S 15 KM CLASSICAL / February 9

RANK	CTRY	ATHLETE	TIME
1	EUN	Lyubov Egorova	42:20.8
2	FIN	Marjut Lukkarinen	43:29.9
3	EUN	Elena Valbe	43:42.3
4	EUN	Raisa Smetanina	44:01.5
5	ITA	Stefania Belmondo	44:02.4
6	FIN	Marja-Liisa Kirvesniemi	44:02.7
7	NOR	Inger Helene Nybraten	44:18.6
8	NOR	Trude Dybendahl	44:31.5
27	USA	Nancy Fiddler	46:42.4
36	USA	Brenda White	48:06.0
41	USA	Sue Forbes	49:42.7
44	USA	Dorcas Wonsavage	50:00.5

WOMEN'S 30 KM FREE / February 21

RANK	CTRY	ATHLETE	TIME
1	ITA	Stefania Belmondo	1:22:30.1
2	EUN	Lyubov Egorova	1:22:52.0
3	EUN	Elena Valbe	1:24:13.9
4	NOR	Elin Nilsen	1:26:25.1
5	EUN	Larisa Lasutina	1:26:31.8
6	ITA	Manuela Di Centa	1:27:04.4
7	SWE	Marie-Helene Westin	1:27:16.2
8	GER	Simone Opitz	1:27:17.4
29	USA	Nancy Fiddler	1:33:02.5
43	USA	Elizabeth Youngman	1:36:12.1
45	USA	Dorcas Wonsavage	1:36:39.8
49	USA	Brenda White	1:37:54.0

WOMEN'S 10 KM FREE PURSUIT / February 15

RANK	CTRY	ATHLETE	TIME
1	EUN	Lyubov Egorova	40:07.7
2	ITA	Stefania Belmondo	40:31.8
3	EUN	Elena Valbe	40:51.7
4	FIN	Marjut Lukkarinen	41:05.1
5	NOR	Elin Nilsen	41:26.9
6	SWE	Marie-Helene Westin	41:28.2
7	NOR	Inger Helene Nybraten	41:35.1
8	EUN	Larisa Lasutina	41:48.8
29	USA	Nancy Fiddler	43:38.9
41	USA	Leslie Thompson	45:18.1
48	USA	Ingrid Butts	46:12.7
52	USA	Nina Kemppel	48:09.7

WOMEN'S 4x5-KM RELAY / February 17

RANK	CTRY	ATHLETES	TIME
1	EUN	Elena Valbe / Raisa Smetanina / Larisa Lasutina / Lyubov Egorova	59:34.8
2	NOR	Solveig Pedersen / Inger Helene Nybraten / Trude Dybendahl / Elin Nilsen	59:56.4
3	ITA	Bice Vanzetta / Manuela Di Centa / Gabriella Paruzzi / Stefania Belmondo	1:00:25.9
4	FIN	Marja-Liisa Kirvesniemi / Pirkko Maatta / Jaana Savolainen / Marjut Lukkarinen	1:00:52.9
5	FRA	Carole Stanisiere / Sylvie Giry Rousset / Sophie Villeneuve / Isabelle Mancini	1:01:30.7
6	TCH	Lubomira Balazova / Katerina Neumanova / Alzbeta Havrancikova / Iveta Zelingerova	1:01:37.4
7	SWE	Carina Gorlin / Magdalena Wallin / Karin Saterkvist / Marie-Helene Westin	1:01:54.5
8	GER	Heike Wezel / Gabriele Hess / Simone Opitz / Ina Kummel	1:02:22.6
13	USA	Nancy Fiddler / Ingrid Butts / Leslie Thompson / Elizabeth Youngman	1:04:48.5

SKI JUMPING
90 METERS (NORMAL HILL) / February 9

RANK	CTRY	ATHLETE	POINTS
1	AUT	Ernst Vettori	222.8
2	AUT	Martin Hollwarth	218.1
3	FIN	Toni Nieminen	217.0
4	AUT	Heinz Kuttin	214.4
5	FIN	Mika Laitinen	213.6
6	AUT	Andreas Felder	213.5
7	GER	Heiko Hunger	211.6
8	FRA	Didier Mollard	209.7
13	USA	James Holland	201.1
28	USA	John Langlois	188.8
38	USA	Bryan Sanders	184.8
51	USA	Robert Holme	171.3

120 METERS (LARGE HILL) / February 16

RANK	CTRY	ATHLETE	POINTS
1	FIN	Toni Nieminen	239.5
2	AUT	Martin Hollwarth	227.3
3	AUT	Heinz Kuttin	214.8
4	JPN	Masahiko Harada	211.3
5	TCH	Jiri Parma	198.0
6	FRA	Steeve Delaup	185.6
7	ITA	Ivan Lunardi	185.2
8	SLO	Franci Petek	177.1
12	USA	James Holland	175.1
36	USA	Bryan Sanders	137.1
36	USA	Robert Holme	137.1
48	USA	John Langlois	118.4

120-METER TEAM / February 14

RANK	CTRY	ATHLETES	POINTS
1	FIN	Ari-Pekka Nikkola / Mika Laitinen / Risto Laakkonen / Toni Nieminen	644.4
2	AUT	Heinz Kuttin / Ernst Vettori / Martin Hollwarth / Andreas Felder	642.9
3	TCH	Tomas Goder / Frantisek Jez / Jaroslav Sakala / Jiri Parma	620.1
4	JPN	Jiro Kamiharako / Masahiko Harada / Noriaki Kasai / Kenji Suda	571.0
5	GER	Heiko Hunger / Dieter Thoma / Christof Duffner / Jens Weissflog	544.6
6	SLO	Primoz Kopac / Matiaz Zupan / Franci Petek / Samo Gostisa	543.3
7	NOR	Rune Olijnyk / Magne Johansen / Lasse Ottesen / Espen Bredesen	538.0
8	SUI	Markus Gahler / Martin Trunz / Sylvain Freiholz / Stefan Zuend	537.9
12	USA	Robert Holme / John Langlois / Bryan Sanders / James Holland	482.4

NORDIC COMBINED
INDIVIDUAL / February 12

RANK	CTRY	ATHLETE	TIME BEHIND
1	FRA	Fabrice Guy	
2	FRA	Sylvain Guillaume	-48.4
3	AUT	Klaus Sulzenbacher	-1:06.3
4	NOR	Fred Lundberg	-1:26.7
5	AUT	Klaus Ofner	-1:29.8
6	EST	Allar Levandi	-1:34.1
7	JPN	Kenji Ogiwara	-1:57.4
8	POL	Stanislaw Ustupski	-2:28.1
37	USA	Ryan Heckman	-9:13.8
39	USA	Todd Wilson	-9:54.0
40	USA	Timothy Tetreault	-10.21.5
—	USA	Joseph Holland	DNF

TEAM / February 18

RANK	CTRY	ATHLETES	TIME BEHIND
1	JPN	Reiichi Mikata / Takanori Kono / Kenji Ogiwara	
2	NOR	Knut Apeland / Fred Lundberg / Trond Elden	-1:26.4
3	AUT	Klaus Ofner / Stefan Kreiner / Klaus Sulzenbacher	-1:40.1
4	FRA	Francis Repellin / Sylvain Guillaume / Fabrice Guy	-2:15.5
5	GER	Hans / Peter Pohl / Jens Deimel / Thomas Dufter	-4:45.4
6	TCH	Josef Kovarik / Milan Kucera / Frantisek Maka	-9:04.7
7	FIN	Pasi Saapunki / Jari Mantila / Teemu Summanen	-9:06.8
8	USA	Joseph Holland / Timothy Tetreault / Ryan Heckman	-9:08.3

SPEED SKATING
MEN'S 500 METERS / February 15

RANK	CTRY	ATHLETE	TIME
1	GER	Uwe-Jens Mey	37.14
2	JPN	Toshiyuki Kuroiwa	37.18
3	JPN	Junichi Inoue	37.26
4	USA	Dan Jansen	37.46
5	NED	Gerard Van Velde	37.49
5	JPN	Yasunori Miyabe	37.49
7	EUN	Alexandre Goloubev	37.51
8	EUN	Igor Jelezovski	37.57
13	USA	Nick Thometz	37.83
19	USA	Martin Pierce	38.15
22	USA	David Cruikshank	38.28

MEN'S 1000 METERS / February 18

RANK	CTRY	ATHLETE	TIME
1	GER	Olaf Zinke	1:14.85
2	KOR	Kim Yoon-Man	1:14.86
3	JPN	Yukinori Miyabe	1:14.92
4	NED	Gerard Van Valde	1:14.93
5	GER	Peter Adeberg	1:15.04
6	EUN	Igor Jelezovski	1:15.05
7	FRA	Guy Thibault	1:15.36
8	EUN	Nikolai Gouliaev	1:15.46
15	USA	Nick Thometz	1:16.19
16	USA	Eric Flaim	1:16.47
20	USA	Dave Besteman	1:16.57
26	USA	Dan Jansen	1:17.34

MEN'S 1500 METERS / February 16

RANK	CTRY	ATHLETE	TIME
1	NOR	Johann Koss	1:54.81
2	NOR	Adne Sondral	1:54.85
3	NED	Leo Visser	1:54.90
4	NED	Rintje Ritsma	1:55.70
5	NED	Bart Veldkamp	1:56.33
6	GER	Olaf Zinke	1:56.74
7	NED	Falco Zandstra	1:56.96
8	NOR	Geir Karlstad	1:56.98
19	USA	Brian Wanek	1:58.50
24	USA	Eric Flaim	1:59.60
32	USA	Chris Shelley	2:01.11
35	USA	Nathaniel Mills	2:01.54

MEN'S 5000 METERS / February 13

RANK	CTRY	ATHLETE	TIME
1	NOR	Geir Karlstad	6:59.97
2	NED	Falco Zandstra	7:02.28
3	NED	Leo Visser	7:04.96
4	GER	FPlace Dittrich	7:06.33
5	NED	Bart Veldkamp	7:08.00
6	USA	Eric Flaim	7:11.15
7	NOR	Johann Koss	7:11.32
8	EUN	Eugeni Sanarov	7:11.38
12	USA	Brian Wanek	7:13.35
19	USA	Mark Greenwald	7:21.19

MEN'S 10,000 METERS / February 20

RANK	CTRY	ATHLETE	TIME
1	NED	Bart Veldkamp	14:12.12
2	NOR	Johann Koss	14:14.58
3	NOR	Geir Karlstad	14:18.13
4	NED	Robert Vunderink	14:22.92
5	JPN	Kazuhiro Sato	14:28.30
6	AUT	Michael Hadschieff	14:28.80
7	SWE	Per Bengtsson	14:35.58
8	NOR	Steinar Johansen	14:36.09
22	USA	Brian Wanek	14:51.34
24	USA	Mark Greenwald	15:03.02
27	USA	Jeff Klaiber	15:13.65

WOMEN'S 500 METERS / February 10

RANK	CTRY	ATHLETE	TIME
1	USA	Bonnie Blair	40.33
2	CHN	Ye Qiaobo	40.51
3	GER	Christa Luding	40.57
4	GER	Monique Garbrecht	40.63
5	NED	Christine Aaftink	40.66
6	CAN	Susan Auch	40.83
7	JPN	Kyoko Shimazaki	40.98
8	GER	Angela Hauck	41.10
17	USA	Kristen Talbot	41.77
22	USA	Peggy Clasen	41.95
26	USA	Michelle Kline	42.41

WOMEN'S 1000 METERS / February 14

RANK	CTRY	ATHLETE	TIME
1	USA	Bonnie Blair	1:21.90
2	CHN	Ye Qiaobo	1:21.92
3	GER	Monique Garbrecht	1:22.10
4	NED	Christine Aaftink	1:22.60
5	JPN	Seiko Hashimoto	1:22.63
6	ROM	Mihaela Dascalu	1:22.85
7	EUN	Elena Tiouchniakova	1:22.97
8	GER	Christa Luding	1:23.06
29	USA	Peggy Clasen	1:25.31
32	USA	Moira D'Andrea	1:26.13

WOMEN'S 1500 METERS / February 12

RANK	CTRY	ATHLETE	TIME
1	GER	Jacqueline Boerner	2:05.87
2	GER	Gunda Niemann	2:05.92
3	JPN	Seiko Hashimoto	2:06.88
4	EUN	Natalia Polozkova	2:07.12
5	GER	Monique Garbrecht	2:07.24
6	EUN	Svetlana Bajanova	2:07.81
7	AUT	Emese Hunyady	2:08.29
8	GER	Heike Warnicke	2:08.52
15	USA	Mary Docter	2:09.66
21	USA	Bonnie Blair	2:10.89
26	USA	Angela Zuckerman	2:13.21
27	USA	Tara Laszlo	2:13.35

WOMEN'S 3000 METERS / February 9

RANK	CTRY	ATHLETE	TIME
1	GER	Gunda Niemann	4:19.90
2	GER	Heike Warnicke	4:22.88
3	AUT	Emese Hunyady	4:24.64
4	NED	Carla Zijlstra	4:27.18
5	EUN	Svetlana Boiko	4:28.00
6	NED	Yvonne Van Gennip	4:28.10
7	EUN	Svetlana Bajanova	4:28.19
8	GER	Jacqueline Boerner	4:28.52
15	USA	Mary Docter	4:34.51
22	USA	Angela Zuckerman	4:41.88
25	USA	Michelle Kline	4:45.65

WOMEN'S 5000 METERS / February 17

RANK	CTRY	ATHLETE	TIME
1	GER	Gunda Niemann	7:31.57
2	GER	Heike Warnicke	7:37.59
3	GER	Claudia Pechstein	7:39.80
4	NED	Carla Zijlstra	7:41.10
5	EUN	Liudmila Prokacheva	7:41.65
6	EUN	Svetlana Boiko	7:44.19
7	EUN	Svetlana Bajanova	7:45.55
8	NED	Lia Van Schie	7:46.94
17	USA	Mary Docter	8:04.42
23	USA	Tara Laszlo	8:15.00
24	USA	Michelle Kline	8:20.88

SHORT TRACK SPEED SKATING
MEN'S 1000 METERS / February 20

RANK	CTRY	ATHLETE	TIME
1	KOR	Kim Ki-Hoon	1:30.76
2	CAN	Frederic Blackburn	1:31.11
3	KOR	Lee Joon-Ho	1:31.16
4	NZL	Mike McMillen	1:31.32
5	GBR	Willy O'Reilly	1:36.24
6	BEL	Geert Blanchart	1:36.28
7	CAN	Mark Lackie	1:36.28
8	CAN	Michel Daignault	1:37.10
—	USA	Andy Gabel	DQ

MEN'S 5000-METER RELAY / February 22

RANK	CTRY
1	KOR
2	CAN
3	JPN
4	NZL
5	FRA
6	GBR
7	AUS
8	ITA

NOTE: USA did not qualify for Olympic field

WOMEN'S 500 METERS / February 22

RANK	CTRY	ATHLETE	TIME
1	USA	Cathy Turner	47.04
2	CHN	Li Yan	47.08
3	PRK	Hwang Ok Sil	
4	NED	Monique Velzeboer	
5	EUN	Marina Pylaeva	
6	CAN	Nathalie Lambert	
7	EUN	Ioulia Vlasova	
8	CHN	Xiulan Wang	
—	USA	Amy Peterson	elim.

WOMEN'S 3000-METER RELAY / February 20

RANK	CTRY	ATHLETES	TIME
1	CAN		4:36.62
2	USA	Amy Peterson / Darcie Dohnal / Nikki Ziegelmeyer / Cathy Turner	4:37.85
3	EUN		4:42.69
4	JPN		4:44.50

DEMONSTRATION SPORTS

FREESTYLE SKIING

MEN'S BALLET / February 10

RANK	CTRY	ATHLETE	POINTS
1	FRA	Fabrice Becker	28.15
2	NOR	Rune Kristiansen	28.00
3	USA	Lane Spina	27.40
4	CAN	Richard Peirce	27.30
5	SUI	Heini Baumgartner	25.85
6	GER	Armin Weiss	25.65
7	ITA	Roberto Franco	25.50
8	USA	Jeffrey Wintersteen	24.80
11	USA	Trace Worthington	22.35

WOMEN'S BALLET / February 10

RANK	CTRY	ATHLETE	POINTS
1	SUI	Conny Kissling	25.30
2	FRA	Cathy Fechoz	25.20
3	USA	Sharon Petzold	24.10
4	GBR	Julia Snell	22.85
5	SWE	Annika Johansson	22.80
6	USA	Ellen Breen	22.30
7	SUI	Maja Schmid	21.60
8	ESP	Raquel Gutierrez	21.50

MEN'S AERIALS / February 16

RANK	CTRY	ATHLETE	POINTS
1	CAN	Philippe Laroche	237.47
2	CAN	Nicolas Fontaine	228.88
3	FRA	Didier Meda	219.44
4	FRA	Jean-Marc Bacquin	206.71
5	USA	Kris Feddersen	201.74
6	AUT	Hugo Bonatti	198.15
7	USA	Trace Worthington	192.16
8	AUT	Alexander Stoegner	187.67

WOMEN'S AERIALS / February 16

RANK	CTRY	ATHLETE	POINTS
1	SUI	Colette Brand	157.51
2	SWE	Marie Lindgren	155.10
3	GER	Elfie Simchen	153.94
4	GBR	Jilly Curry	151.13
5	EUN	Lina Tcheriazova	150.01
6	NOR	Hilde Lid	144.65
7	AUS	Kirstie Marshall	139.55
8	SUI	Maja Schmid	129.47
—	USA	Sue Michalski	elim.

SPEED SKIING

MEN / February 22

RANK	CTRY	ATHLETE	SPEED	
1	FRA	Michael Prufer	229.299	WR
2	FRA	Philippe Goitschel	228.717	
3	USA	Jeffrey Hamilton	226.700	
4	FRA	Laurent Sistach	225.000	
5	FRA	Claude Basile	223.464	
6	TCH	Petr Kakes	223.325	
7	USA	James Morgan	222.910	
8	AUT	Franz Weber	222.222	
10	USA	John Mueller	221.811	
17	USA	Dale Womack	213.270	

WOMEN / February 22

RANK	CTRY	ATHLETE	SPEED	
1	FIN	Tarja Mulari	219.245	WR
2	NOR	Liss Pettersen	212.892	
3	SUI	Renata Kolarova	210.526	
4	SWE	Anna Morin	209.79Q	
5	USA	Melissa Dimino-Simons	203.620	
6	CAN	Lark Frolek	195.865	
7	FRA	Francoise Beguin	195.972	
8	FRA	Jacqueline Blanc	199.115	
10	USA	Kirsten Culver	193.548	
14	USA	Amy Guras	192.616	
18	USA	Richelle Reichsfeld	187.500	

CURLING

MEN / February 22

RANK	CTRY	RECORD	USA GAME SCORES
1	SUI	4-1	USA vs. CAN 3-7
2	NOR	4-1	USA vs. FRA 6-4
3	USA	3-2	USA vs. SWE 8-4
4	CAN	3-2	USA vs. NOR 3-8
5	GBR	2-2	USA vs. CAN 9-2
6	FRA	1-3	
7	AUS	1-3	
8	SWE	0-4	

WOMEN / February 22

RANK	CTRY	RECORD
1	GER	4-1
2	NOR	3-2
3	CAN	4-1
4	DEN	2-3
5	SWE	2-2
6	GBR	2-2
7	FRA	1-3
8	JPN	0-4
—	USA	DNQ

GAMES OF THE XXVth OLYMPIAD
Barcelona, Spain
July 25 - August 9, 1992

ARCHERY

MEN'S INDIVIDUAL / August 3

RANK	CTRY	ATHLETE
1	FRA	Sebastien Flute
2	KOR	Chung Jae-Hun
3	GBR	Simon Terry
4	NOR	Bertil Martinus Grov
5	USA	Jay Barrs
6	INA	H. Setijawan
7	EUN	Vadim Chikarev
8	FIN	Jari Lipponen
18	USA	Richard "Butch" Johnson
—	USA	Rick McKinney

MEN'S TEAM / August 4

RANK	CTRY	ATHLETES
1	ESP	Juan Holgado / Antonio Vazquez / A. Menendez
2	FIN	Ismo Falck / Jari Lipponen / T. Poikolainen
3	GBR	R. Priestman / Steven Hallard / Simon Terry
4	FRA	Bruno Felipe / Michael Taupin / Sebastien Flute
5	KOR	Kim Hee-Sik / Chung Jae-Hun / Han Seung-Hoon
6	USA	Jay Barrs / Richard "Butch" Johnson / Rick McKinney

WOMEN'S INDIVIDUAL / August 2

RANK	CTRY	ATHLETE
1	KOR	Cho Youn-Jeong
2	KOR	Kim Soo-Nyung
3	EUN	Natalia Valeeva
4	CHN	Wang Xiaozhu
5	USA	Denise Parker
6	EUN	K. Kvrivichvili
11	USA	Jennifer O'Donnell
25	USA	Sherry Block

WOMEN'S TEAM / August 4

RANK	CTRY	ATHLETES
1	KOR	Cho Youn-Jeong / Kim Soo-Nyung / Lee Eun-Kyung
2	CHN	Ma Xiangjun / Wang Xiaozhu / Wang Hong
3	EUN	K. Kvrivichvili / L. Arjannikova / Natalia Valeeva
4	FRA	Severine Bonal / Nathalie Hibon / C. Gabillard
5	SWE	Jenny Sjowall / K. Persson / Liselotte Djerf
6	TUR	N. Nasaridze / Elif Eksi / Zehra Oktem
8	USA	Sherry Block / Jennifer O'Donnell / Denise Parker

ATHLETICS

MEN'S 100 METERS / August 1

RANK	CTRY	ATHLETE	TIME
1	GBR	Linford Christie	9.96
2	NAM	Frank Fredericks	10.02
3	USA	Dennis Mitchell	10.04
4	CAN	Bruny Surin	10.09
5	USA	Leroy Burrell	10.10
6	NGR	Olapade Adeniken	10.12
7	JAM	Raymond Douglas Stewart	10.22
8	NGR	Davidson Ezinwa	10.26
—	USA	Mark Witherspoon	DNF semi.

MEN'S 200 METERS / August 6

RANK	CTRY	ATHLETE	TIME
1	USA	Mike Marsh	20.01
2	NAM	Frank Fredericks	20.13
3	USA	Michael Bates	20.38
4	BRA	Robson Caetano Da Silva	20.45
5	NGR	Olapade Adeniken	20.50
6	GBR	John Paul Lyndon Regis	20.55
7	NGR	Oluyemi Kayode	20.67
8	GBR	Marcus Adam	20.80
—	USA	Michael Johnson	elim. semi.

MEN'S 400 METERS / August 5

RANK	CTRY	ATHLETE	TIME	
1	USA	Quincy Watts	43.50	OR
2	USA	Steve Lewis	44.21	
3	KEN	Samson Kitur	44.24	
4	TRI	Ian Morris	44.25	
5	CUB	Roberto Hernandez Prendes	44.52	
6	GBR	David Grindley	44.75	
7	QAT	Ibrahim Ismail	45.10	
8	JPN	Susumu Takano	45.18	
—	USA	Danny Everett	elim. 2nd rd.	

MEN'S 800 METERS / August 5

RANK	CTRY	ATHLETE	TIME
1	KEN	William Tanui	1:43.66
2	KEN	Nixon Kiprotich	1:43.70
3	USA	Johnny Gray	1:43.97
4	BRA	Jose Luis Barbosa	1:45.06
5	ITA	Andrea Benvenuti	1:45.23
6	GBR	Curtis Robb	1:45.57
7	ALG	Reda Abdenouz	1:48.34
—	USA	Mark Everett	DNF final
—	USA	Jose Parilla	elim. 1st rd.

MEN'S 1,500 METERS / August 8

RANK	CTRY	ATHLETE	TIME
1	ESP	Fermin Cacho Ruiz	3:40.12
2	MAR	Rachid El-Basir	3:40.62
3	QAT	Mohamed Sulaiman	3:40.69
4	KEN	Joseph Chesire	3:41.12
5	KEN	Jonah Birir	3:41.27
6	GER	Jens-Peter Herold	3:41.53
7	ALG	Noureddine Morceli	3:41.70
8	USA	Jim Spivey	3:41.74
—	USA	Steve Holman	elim. semi.
—	USA	Terrance Herrington	elim. 1st rd.

MEN'S 5,000 METERS / August 8

RANK	CTRY	ATHLETE	TIME
1	GER	Dieter Baumann	13:12.52
2	KEN	Paul Bitok	13:12.71
3	ETH	Fita Bayisa	13:13.03
4	MAR	M. Brahim Boutayeb	13:13.27
5	KEN	Yobes Ondieki	13:17.50
6	ETH	Worku Bikila	13:23.52
7	GBR	Rob Denmark	13:27.76
8	ESP	Abel Anton Rodrigo	13:27.80
12	USA	Robert Owen Kennedy, Jr.	13:39.72
—	USA	Ruben Reina	elim. semi.
—	USA	John Trautmann	DNF

MEN'S 10,000 METERS / August 3

RANK	CTRY	ATHLETE	TIME
1	MAR	Khalid Skah	27:46.70
2	KEN	Richard Chelimo	27:47.72
3	ETH	Addis Abebe	28:00.07
4	ITA	Salvatore Antibo	28:11.39
5	MEX	Arturo Barrios Flores	28:17.79
6	MEX	German Silva Martinez	28:20.19
7	KEN	William Koech	28:25.18
8	KEN	Moses Kiptarbet Tanui	28:27.11
10	USA	Todd Williams	28:29.38
—	USA	Steve Plasencia	elim. 1st rd.
—	USA	Aaron Ramirez	elim. 1st rd.

MEN'S 110-METER HURDLES / August 3

RANK	CTRY	ATHLETE	TIME
1	CAN	Mark McKoy	13.12
2	USA	Tony Dees	13.24
3	USA	Jack Pierce	13.26
4	GBR	Tony Jarrett	13.26
5	GER	Florian Schwarthoff	13.29
6	CUB	Emilio Valle	13.41
7	GBR	Colin Jackson	13.46
8	GBR	Hughie Teape	14.00
—	USA	Arthur Blake	DQ semi.

MEN'S 400-METER HURDLES / August 6

RANK	CTRY	ATHLETE	TIME	
1	USA	Kevin Young	46.78	WR
2	JAM	Winthrop Graham	47.66	
3	GBR	Kriss Akabusi	47.82	
4	FRA	Stephane Diagana	48.13	
5	SWE	Niklas Wallenlind	48.63	
6	EUN	Oleg Tverdokhleb	48.63	
7	FRA	Stephane Caristan	48.86	
8	USA	David Patrick	49.26	
—	USA	McClinton Neal	elim. semi.	

3,000-METER STEEPLECHASE / August 7

RANK	CTRY	ATHLETE	TIME
1	KEN	Mathew Birir	8:08.84
2	KEN	Patrick Sang	8:09.55
3	KEN	William Mutwol	8:10.74
4	ITA	Alessandro Lambruschini	8:15.52
5	GER	Steffen Brand	8:16.60
6	GBR	Tom Hanlon	8:18.14
7	USA	Brian Diemer	8:18.77
8	ALG	Azzeddine Brahmi	8:20.71
—	USA	Mark Croghan	elim. semi.
—	USA	Danny Lopez	elim. semi.

MEN'S 20 KM WALK / July 31

RANK	CTRY	ATHLETES	TIME
1	ESP	Daniel Plaza Montero	1:21.45
2	CAN	Guillaume LeBlanc	1:22.25
3	ITA	Giovanni De Benedictis	1:23.11
4	ITA	M. Damilano	1:23.39
5	CHN	Chen Shaoguo	1:24.06
6	IRL	James McDonald	1:25.16
7	MEX	Daniel Garcia	1:25.35
8	HUN	Sandor Urbanik	1:26.08
30	USA	Allen James	1:35.12

MEN'S 50 KM WALK / August 7

RANK	CTRY	ATHLETE	TIME
1	EUN	Andrey Perlov	3:50.13
2	MEX	Carlos Mercenario	3:52.09
3	GER	Ronald Weigel	3:53.45
4	EUN	Valery Spitsyn	3:54.39
5	TCH	Roman Mrazek	3:55.21
6	GER	Hartwig Gauder	3:56.47
7	FIN	V. Kononen	3:57.21
8	MEX	M. Rodriguez	3:58.26
23	USA	Carl Schueler	4:13.38
32	USA	Herm Nelson	4:25.49
—	USA	Marco Evoniuk	DNF

MEN'S 4x100-METER RELAY / August 8

RANK	CTRY	ATHLETE	TIME	
1	USA	Mike Marsh / Leroy Burrell / Dennis Mitchell / Carl Lewis / James Jett (prelims)	37.40	WR
2	NIG	Oluyemi Kayode / Chidi Imoh / Olapade Adeniken / Davidson Ezinwa	37.98	
3	CUB	Andres Simon Gomez / Joel Lamela Loaces / oel Isasi Gonzalez / Jorge Luis Aguilera Ruiz	38.00	
4	GBR	Marcus Adam / Tony Jarrett / John Regis / Linford Christie	38.08	
5	EUN	Pavel Galkin / Edvin Ivanov / Andrey Fedoriv / Vitaly Savin	38.17	
6	JPN	Shinji Aoto / Hisatsugu Suzuki / Satoru Inoue / Tatsuo Sugimoto	38.77	
7	AUS	Christoph Postinger / Thomas Renner / Andreas Berger / Franz Ratzenberger	39.30	
8	CIV	Franck Waotta / Jean Olivier Zirignon / Gilles Bogui / Ouattara Lagazane	39.31	

MEN'S 4x400-METER RELAY / August 8

RANK	CTRY	ATHLETE	TIME	
1	USA	Andrew Valmon / Quincy Watts / Michael Johnson / Steve Lewis / Darnell Hall (prelims) / Chip Jenkins (prelims)	2:55.74	WR
2	CUB	Lazaro Martinez Despaigne / Hector Herrera Ortiz / Norberto Tellez / Roberto Hernandez Prendes	2:59.51	
3	GBR	Roger Black / David Grindley / Kriss Akabusi / John Regis	2:59.73	
4	BRA	Robson Caetano Da Silva / Edielson Rocha Tenorio / Sergio Matias De Menezes / Sidney Telles De Souza	3:01.61	
5	NIG	Udeme Ekpeyong / Emmanuel Okoli / Hassan Bosso / Sunday Bada	3:01.71	
6	ITA	Alessandro Aimar / Marco Vaccari / Fabio Grossi / Andrea Nuti	3:02.18	
7	TRI	Alvin Daniel / Patrick Delice / Neil De Silva / Ian Morris	3:03.31	
8	KEN	Samson Kitur / Agednego Matilu / Simeon Kipkemboi / Simon Kemboi	DNF	

MEN'S MARATHON / August 9

RANK	CTRY	ATHLETE	TIME
1	KOR	Hwang Young-Cho	2:13.23
2	JPN	Koichi Morishita	2:13.45
3	GER	Stephan Timo Freigang	2:14.00
4	JPN	Takeyuki Nakayama	2:14.02
5	ITA	Salvatore Bettiol	2:14.15
6	MAR	Salah Kokaich	2:14.25
7	POL	Jan Huruk	2:14.32
8	JPN	Hiromi Taniguchi	2:14.42
12	USA	Steven Spence	2:15.21
13	USA	Ed Eyestone	2:15.23
17	USA	Robert Kempainen	2:15.53

MEN'S HIGH JUMP / August 2

RANK	CTRY	ATHLETE	METERS	FT/IN
1	CUB	Javier Sotomayor	2.34	7-8 1/4
2	SWE	Patrik Sjoeberg	2.34	7-8 1/4
3	POL	Artur Partyka	2.34	7-8 1/4
3	AUS	Timothy Forsythe	2.34	7-8 1/4
3	USA	Hollis Conway	2.34	7-8 1/4
6	GER	Ralf Sonn	2.31	7-7
7	BAH	Troy Kemp	2.31	7-7
8	CUB	Marino Drake	2.28	7-5 3/4
8	USA	Charles Austin	2.28	7-5 3/4
8	YUG	Dragutin Topic	2.28	7-5 3/4
15	USA	Darrin Plab	2.23	7-3 3/4

MEN'S LONG JUMP / August 6

RANK	CTRY	ATHLETE	METERS	FT/IN
1	USA	Carl Lewis	8.67	28-5 1/2
2	USA	Mike Powell	8.64	28-4 1/4
3	USA	Joe Greene	8.34	27-4 1/2
4	CUB	Ivan Pedroso	8.11	26-7 1/4
5	CUB	J. Jefferson	8.08	26-6
6	GRE	K. Koukodimos	8.04	26-4 1/2
7	EUN	D. Bagrianov	7.98	26-2
8	CHN	Geng Huang	7.87	25-10

MEN'S TRIPLE JUMP / August 3

RANK	CTRY	ATHLETE	METERS	FT/IN
1	USA	Mike Conley	18.17	59-7 1/2
2	USA	Charles Simpkins	17.60	57-9
3	BAH	Frank Rutherford	17.36	56-11 1/2
4	EUN	Leonid Voloshin	17.32	56-10
5	BER	Brian Wellman	17.24	56-6 3/4
6	CUB	Yoelvis Quesada	17.18	56-4 1/2
7	EUN	Aleksandr Kovalenko	17.06	55-11 3/4
8	CHN	Zou Sixin	17.00	55-9 1/4
25	USA	John Tillman	16.22	53-2 3/4

MEN'S POLE VAULT / August 7

RANK	CTRY	ATHLETE	METERS	FT/IN
1	EUN	Maxim Tarassov	5.80	19-0 1/4
2	EUN	Igor Trandenkov	5.80	19-0 1/4
3	ESP	Javier Garcia	5.75	18-10 1/4
4	USA	Kory Tarpenning	5.75	18-10 1/4
5	USA	David Volz	5.65	18-6 1/2
6	FIN	A. Peltoniemi	5.60	18-4 1/2
7	FRA	P. Collet	5.55	18-2 1/2
8	ISR	Evgeny Krasnov	5.40	17-8 1/2
—	USA	Tim Bright	no height	

MEN'S SHOT PUT / July 31

RANK	CTRY	ATHLETE	METERS	FT/IN
1	USA	Michael Stulce	21.70	71-2 1/2
2	USA	James Doehring	20.96	68-9 1/4
3	EUN	Viacheslav Lykho	20.94	68-8 1/4
4	SUI	Werner Gunthor	20.91	68-7 1/4
5	GER	Ulf Timmermann	20.49	67-2 3/4
6	AUT	K. Bodenmuller	20.48	67-2 1/4
7	IOP	Dragan Peric	20.32	66-8
8	EUN	A. Klimenko	20.23	66-4 1/2
10	USA	Ron Backes	19.75	64-9 3/4

MEN'S DISCUS / August 5

RANK	CTRY	ATHLETE	METERS	FT/IN
1	LTU	Romas Ubartas	65.12	213-8
2	GER	Jurgen Schult	64.94	213-1
3	CUB	Roberto Moya	64.12	210-4
4	ROM	Costel Grasu	62.86	206-3
5	HUN	Attila Horvath	62.82	306-1 1/4
6	CUB	J. Martinez	62.64	205-6 1/4
7	EUN	D. Kovtsun	62.04	203-6 1/2
8	EUN	D. Chevchenko	61.78	202-8 1/4
12	USA	Anthony Washington	59.96	196-8 3/4
—	USA	Mike Buncic	elim. qual.	
—	USA	Brian Blutreich	elim. qual.	

MEN'S JAVELIN / August 8

RANK	CTRY	ATHLETE	METERS	FT/IN	
1	TCH	Jan Zelezny	89.66	294-2	OR
2	FIN	Seppo Raty	86.60	284-1	
3	GBR	Steve Backley	83.38	273-7	
4	FIN	Kimmo Kinnunen	82.62	271-1	
5	ISL	S. Einarsson	80.34	263-7	
6	FIN	Juha Laukkanen	79.20	259-10 1/4	
7	USA	Mike Barnett	78.64	258-4	
8	EUN	A. Shevchuk	77.74	255-1	
10	USA	Tom Pukstys	76.72	251-8 1/2	
21	USA	Brian Crouser	74.98	246-0	

MEN'S HAMMER / August 2

RANK	CTRY	ATHLETE	METERS	FT/IN
1	EUN	Andrey Abduvaliyev	82.54	270-9 1/2
2	EUN	Igor Astapkovich	81.96	268-10 3/4
3	EUN	Igor Nikulin	81.38	267-0
4	HUN	Tibor Gecsek	77.78	255-2 1/4
5	EST	Juri Tamm	77.52	254-4
6	GER	Heinrich Weis	76.90	252-3 1/2
7	USA	Lance Deal	76.84	252-1 1/4
8	AUS	Sean Carlin	76.16	249-10 1/2
24	USA	Ken Flax	69.36	227-7
—	USA	Jud Logan	DQ - drug test	

DECATHLON / August 6

RANK	CTRY	ATHLETE	POINTS
1	TCH	Robert Zmelik	8,611
2	ESP	Antonio Penalver	8,412
3	USA	David Johnson	8,309
4	HUN	Dezso Szabo	8,199
5	USA	Robert Muzzio	8,195
6	GER	Paul Meier	8,192
7	FRA	William Motti	8,164
8	EUN	Ramil Ganiev	8,160
—	USA	Aric Long	DNF

WOMEN'S 100 METERS / August 1

RANK	CTRY	ATHLETE	TIME
1	USA	Gail Devers	10.82
2	JAM	Juliet Cuthbert	10.83
3	EUN	Irina Privalova	10.84
4	USA	Gwen Torrence	10.86
5	JAM	Merlene Ottey	10.88
6	BUL	Anelia Dultcheva Nuneva	11.10
7	NGR	Mary Onyali	11.15
8	CUB	Liliana Allen Doll	11.19
—	USA	Evelyn Ashford	elim. semi.

WOMEN'S 200 METERS / August 6

RANK	CTRY	ATHLETE	TIME
1	USA	Gwen Torrence	21.81
2	JAM	Juliet Cuthbert	22.02
3	JAM	Merlene Ottey	22.09
4	EUN	Irina Privalona	22.19
5	USA	Carlette Guidry-White	22.30
6	JAM	Grace Jackson Small	22.58
7	USA	Michelle Finn	22.61
8	EUN	Galina Malchugina	22.63

WOMEN'S 400 METERS / August 5

RANK	CTRY	ATHLETE	TIME
1	FRA	Marie-Jose Perec	48.83
2	EUN	Olga Bryzgina	49.05
3	COL	Ximena Restrepo Gaviria	49.64
4	EUN	Olga Nazarova	49.69
5	CAN	Jill Richardson-Briscoe	49.93
6	USA	Rochelle Stevens	50.11
7	JAM	Sandie Richards	50.19
8	GBR	Phylis Smith	50.87
—	USA	Jearl Miles	elim. semi.
—	USA	Natasha Kaiser	elim. semi.

WOMEN'S 800 METERS / August 3

RANK	CTRY	ATHLETE	TIME
1	NED	Ellen Van Langen	1:55.54
2	EUN	Lilia Nurutdinova	1:55.99
3	CUB	Ana Fidelia Quirot Moret	1:56.80
4	EUN	Inna Yevseyeva	1:57.20
5	MOZ	Maria De Lurdes Mutola	1:57.49
6	ROM	Ella Kovacs	1:57.95
7	USA	Joetta Clark	1:58.06
8	EUN	Lyubov Gurina	1:58.13
—	USA	Julie Jenkins	elim. semi.
—	USA	Meredith Rainey	elim. 1st rd.

WOMEN'S 1,500 METERS / August 8

RANK	CTRY	ATHLETE	TIME
1	ALG	Hassiba Boulmerka	3:55.30
2	EUN	Lyudmila Rogacheva	3:56.91
3	CHN	Qu Yunxia	3:57.08
4	EUN	Tatiana Dorovskikh	3:57.92
5	CHN	Li Liu	4:00.20
6	ESP	Maite Zuniga Dominguez	4:00.59
7	POL	Malgorzata Rydz	4:01.91
8	EUN	Yekaterina Podkopayeva	4:02.03
10	USA	PattiSue Plumer	4:03.42
—	USA	Regina Jacobs	elim. semi.
—	USA	Suzy Hamilton	elim. 1st rd.

WOMEN'S 3,000 METERS / August 2

RANK	CTRY	ATHLETE	TIME
1	EUN	Elena Romanova	8:46.04
2	EUN	Tatiana Dorovskikh	8:46.85
3	CAN	Angela Frances Chalmers	8:47.22
4	IRL	Sonia O'Sullivan	8:47.41
5	USA	PattiSue Plumer	8:48.29
6	EUN	Elena Kopytova	8:49.55
7	USA	Shelly Steely	8:52.67
8	GBR	Yvonne Murray	8:55.85
—	USA	Annette Peters	elim. 1st rd.

WOMEN'S 10,000 METERS / August 7

RANK	CTRY	ATHLETE	TIME
1	ETH	Derartu Tulu	31:06.02
2	RSA	Elana Meyer	31:11.75
3	USA	Lynn Jennings	31:19.89
4	CHN	Huandi Zhong	31:21.08
5	GBR	Liz McColgan	31:26.11
6	CHN	Wang Xiuting	31:28.06
7	GER	Uta Pippig	31:36.45
8	USA	Judi St. Hilaire	31:38.04
—	USA	Gwyn Coogan	elim. 1st rd.

WOMEN'S 100-METER HURDLES / August 6

RANK	CTRY	ATHLETE	TIME
1	GRE	Paraskevi Patoulidou	12.64
2	USA	LaVonna Martin	12.69
3	BUL	Yordanka Donkova	12.70
4	USA	Lynda Tolbert	12.75
5	USA	Gail Devers	12.75
6	CUB	Aliuska Lopez	12.87
7	EUN	Natalia Kolovanova	13.01
8	CUB	Odalys Adams	13.57

WOMEN'S 400-METER HURDLES / August 5

RANK	CTRY	ATHLETE	TIME
1	GBR	Sally Gunnell	53.23
2	USA	Sandra Farmer-Patrick	53.69
3	USA	Janeene Vickers	54.31
4	EUN	Tatyana Ledovskaya	54.31
5	EUN	Vera Ordina	54.83
6	EUN	Margarita Ponomareva	54.83
7	JAM	Deon Hemmings	55.58
8	RSA	Myrtle Bothma	AB
—	USA	Tonja Buford	elim. semi.

WOMEN'S 10 KM WALK / August 3

RANK	CTRY	ATHLETE	TIME
1	CHN	Chen Yueling	44:32
2	EUN	Elena Nikolaeva	44:33
3	CHN	Li Chunxiu	44:41
4	FIN	Sari Miriam Essayah	45:08
5	CHN	Cui Yingzi	45:15
6	SWE	Madelein Svensson	45:17
7	ITA	Anna Rita Sidoti	45:23
8	EUN	Elena Saiko	45:23
20	USA	Michelle Rohl	46:45
26	USA	Debbi A. Lawrence	48:23
27	USA	Victoria S. Herazo	48:26

WOMEN'S 4x100-METER RELAY / August 8

RANK	CTRY	ATHLETES	TIME
1	USA	Evelyn Ashford / Esther Jones / Carlette Guidry-White / Gwen Torrence / Michelle Finn (prelims)	42.11
2	EUN	Olga Bogoslovskaya / Galina Malchugina / Marina Trandenkova / Irina Privalova	42.16
3	NIG	Beatrice Utondu / Faith Idehen / Christy Opara Thompson / Mary Onyali	42.81
4	FRA	Patricia Girard / Odiah Sidibe / Laurence Bily / Marie-Jose Perec	42.85
5	GER	Andrea Phillipp / Silke Beate Knoll / Andrea Thomas / Sabine Gunther	43.12
6	AUS	Melissa Moore / Melinda Gainsford / Kathy Sambell / Kerry Johnson	43.77
7	JAM	Michele Freeman / Juliet Cuthbert / Dahlia Duhaney / Merlene Ottey	AB
8	CUB	Eusebia Riquelme Terrazon / Aliuska Lopez / Idalmis Bonne Rauseaux / Liliana Allen Doll	AB

WOMEN'S 4x400-METER RELAY / August 8

RANK	CTRY	ATHLETES	TIME
1	EUN	Yelena Ruzina / Lioudmila Dzhigalova / Olga Nazarova / Olga Bryzgina	3:20.20
2	USA	Natasha Kaiser / Gwen Torrence / Jearl Miles / Rochelle Stevens / Denean Hill (prelims) / Dannette Young (prelims)	3:20.92
3	GBR	Phylis Smith / Sandra Douglas / Jennifer Stoute / Sally Gunnell	3:24.23
4	CAN	Rosey Edeh / Charmaine Crooks / Camille Anise Noel / Jill Richardson-Briscoe	3:25.20
5	JAM	Catherine Scott / Cathy Ann Rattray Williams / Juliet Campbell / Sandie Richards	3:25.68
6	GER	Uta Rohlander / Heide Meissner / Linda Kisabaka / Anja Rucker	3:26.37
7	AUS	Cathy Freeman / Susan Andrews / Renee Poetschka / Michelle Lock	3:26.42
8	POR	Marta Moreira / Lucrecia Jardim / Elsa Amaral / Eduarda Coelho	3:36.85

WOMEN'S MARATHON / August 1

RANK	CTRY	ATHLETE	TIME
1	EUN	Valentina Yegorova	2:32.41
2	JPN	Yuko Arimori	2:32.49
3	NZL	Lorraine Mary Moller	2:33.59
4	JPN	S. Yamashita	2:36.26
5	GER	Katrin Doerre	2:36.48
6	PRK	Mun Gyong-Ae	2:37.03
7	POR	M. Machado	2:38.22
8	EUN	R. Burangulova	2:38.46
10	USA	Cathy O'Brien	2:39.42
12	USA	Francie Larrieu Smith	2:41.09
21	USA	Janis Klecker	2:47.17

WOMEN'S HIGH JUMP / August 8

RANK	CTRY	ATHLETE	METERS	FT/IN
1	GER	Heike Henkel	2.02	6-7 1/2
2	ROM	Galina Astafei	2.00	6-6 3/4
3	CUB	Ioanat Quintero	1.97	6-5 1/2
4	BUL	S. Kostadinova	1.94	6-4 1/4
5	AUT	S. Kirchmann	1.94	6-4 1/4
6	CUB	Silvia Costa	1.94	6-4 1/4
7	JPN	Megumi Sato	1.91	6-3
8	AUS	A. Inverarity	1.91	6-3
11T	USA	Tanya Hughes	1.88	6-2
17T	USA	Sue Rembao	1.90	6-2 3/4
23T	USA	Amber Welty	1.88	6-2

WOMEN'S LONG JUMP / August 7

RANK	CTRY	ATHLETE	METERS	FT/IN
1	GER	Heike Drechsler	7.14	23-5 1/4
2	EUN	Inessa Kravets	7.12	23-4 1/2
3	USA	Jackie Joyner-Kersee	7.07	23-2 1/2
4	LTU	N. Medvedeva	6.76	22-2
5	ROM	M. Dulgheru	6.71	22-0
6	EUN	I. Muchailova	6.68	21-11
7	USA	Sharon Couch	6.66	21-10 1/4
8	USA	Sheila Echols	6.62	21-8 3/4

WOMEN'S SHOT PUT / August 7

RANK	CTRY	ATHLETE	METERS	FT/IN
1	EUN	Svetlana Krivaleva	21.06	69-1 1/4
2	CHN	Huang Zhihong	20.47	67-2
3	GER	Kathrin Neimke	19.78	64-10 3/4
4	CUB	Belsy Laza	19.70	64-7 1/2
5	CHN	Zhou Tianhua	19.26	63-2 1/4
6	BUL	Svetla Mitkova	19.23	63-1
7	GER	S. Storp	19.10	62-8
8	EUN	Vita Pavlych	18.69	61-3 3/4
11	USA	Ramona Pagel	18.24	59-10 1/4
16	USA	Pam Dukes	16.46	54-0
—	USA	Bonnie Dasse	DQ-drug test	

WOMEN'S DISCUS / August 3

RANK	CTRY	ATHLETE	METERS	FT/IN
1	CUB	Maritza Marten	70.06	229-10
2	BUL	Tsvetanka Khristova	67.78	222-4
3	AUS	Daniela Costian	66.24	217-4
4	EUN	L. Korotkevich	65.52	214-11 1/2
5	EUN	Olga Burova	64.02	210-6
6	CUB	Hilda Ramos	63.80	209-3 3/4
7	EUN	I. Yatchenko	63.74	209-1 1/2
8	BUL	S. Simova	63.42	208-1
20	USA	Connie Price-Smith	58.66	192-5
22	USA	Carla Garrett	58.06	190-6
24	USA	Penny Neer	55.44	181-11

WOMEN'S JAVELIN / August 1

RANK	CTRY	ATHLETE	METERS	FT/IN
1	GER	Silke Renk	68.34	224
2	EUN	Natalia Shikolenko	68.26	223-11
3	GER	Karen Forkel	66.86	219-4
4	GBR	Tessa Sanderson	63.58	208-7 1/4
5	NOR	Elsa Hattestad	63.54	208-5 1/2
6	FIN	Heli Rantanen	62.34	204-6 1/2
7	GER	Petra Meier	59.02	193-7 3/4
8	CUB	Dulce Garcia	58.26	191-1 3/4
12	USA	Donna Mayhew	55.68	182-8
23	USA	Paula Berry	49.00	160-9
—	USA	Karin Smith	DNC-injury	

HEPTATHLON / August 2

RANK	CTRY	ATHLETE	POINTS
1	USA	Jackie Joyner-Kersee	7,044
2	EUN	Irina Belova	6,845
3	GER	Sabine Braun	6,649
4	ROM	Liliana Nastase	6,619
5	BUL	Svetla Dimitrova	6,464
6	GER	Peggy Beer	6,434
7	GER	Birgit Clarius	6,388
8	POL	Urszula Wlodarczyk	6,333
9	USA	Cindy Greiner	6,300
11	USA	Kym Carter	6,256

BADMINTON

MEN'S SINGLES / August 4

RANK	CTRY	ATHLETE	
1	INA	Alan Budi Kusuma	
2	INA	Ardy Bernardus Wiranata	
3	INA	Hermawan Susanto	
3	DEN	Thomas Stuer-Lauridsen	
—	USA	Chris Jogis	elim. 2nd rd.
—	USA	Benny Lee	elim. 1st rd.
—	USA	Thomas Reidy	elim. 1st rd.

MEN'S DOUBLES / August 4

RANK	CTRY	ATHLETES	
1	KOR	Kim Moon-Soo / Park Joo-Bong	
2	INA	Eddy Hartono / Gudy Gunawan	
3	CHN	Li Yongbo / Tian Binghi	
3	MAS	Razif Sidek / Jalani Dato Haji Sidek	
—	USA	Benny Lee / Thomas Reidy	elim. 2nd rd.

WOMEN'S SINGLES / August 4

RANK	CTRY	ATHLETE	
1	INA	Susi Susanti	
2	KOR	Bang Soo-Hyun	
3	CHN	Tang Jiuhong	
3	CHN	Huang Hua	
—	USA	Linda French	elim. 1st rd.
—	USA	Erika von Heiland	elim. 1st rd.
—	USA	Joy Kitzmiller	

WOMEN'S DOUBLES / August 4

RANK	CTRY	ATHLETES	
1	KOR	Hwang Hye Young / Chung So-Young	
2	CHN	Guan Weizhen / Nong Qunhua	
3	CHN	Lin Yanfen / Yao Fen	
3	KOR	Gil Young-Ah / Shim Eun-Jung	
—	USA	Linda French / Joy Kitzmiller	elim. 1st rd.

BASEBALL

FINAL STANDINGS / July 26 - August 5

RANK	CTRY	RECORD	SCORE	USA GAME SCORES	
1	CUB	9-0	11-1	USA vs. ESP	6-1
2	TPE	6-3	(Final)	USA vs. TPE	10-9
3	JPN	6-3	8-3	USA vs. ITA	10-0
4	USA	5-4	(3rd-4th)	USA vs. CUB	6-9
5	PUR	2-5	—	USA vs. PUR	8-2
6	DOM	2-5	—	USA vs. DOM	10-0
7	ITA	1-6	—	USA vs. JPN	1-7
8	ESP	1-6	—	USA vs. CUB	1-6
				USA vs. JPN	3-8

USA TEAM: William Adams / Jeff Alkire / Darren Dreifort / Nomar Garciaparra / Jason Giambi / Rick Greene / Jeffrey Hammonds / Rick Helling / Charles Johnson / Daron Kirkreit / Chad McConnell / Jason Moler / Calvin Murray / Phil Nevin / Chris Roberts / Michael Tucker / Jason Varitek / Ron Villone / B.J. Wallace / Craig Wilson / Chris Wimmer

BASKETBALL

MEN / July 26-August 8

RANK	CTRY	RECORD	SCORE	USA GAME SCORES	
1	USA	8-0	117-85	USA vs. CRO	103-70
2	CRO	6-2	(Final)	USA vs. BRA	127-83
3	LTU	6-2	82-78	USA vs. GER	111-68
4	EUN	5-3	(3rd-4th)	USA vs. ANG	116-48
5	BRA	4-4	90-80	USA vs. ESP	122-81
6	AUS	4-4	(5th-6th)	USA vs. PUR	115-77
7	GER	3-5	—	USA vs. LTU	127-76
8	PUR	3-5	—	USA vs. CRO	117-85

USA TEAM: Charles Barkley / Larry Bird / Clyde Drexler / Patrick Ewing / Earvin Johnson / Michael Jordan / Christian Laettner / Karl Malone / Chris Mullin / Scottie Pippen / David Robinson / John Stockton

WOMEN / July 30 - August 7

RANK	CTRY	RECORD	SCORE	USA GAME	SCORES
1	EUN	4-1	76-66	USA vs. CHN	93-67
2	CHN	3-2	(Final)	USA vs. ESP	114-59
3	USA	4-1	88-74	USA vs. TCH	111-55
4	CUB	3-2	(3rd-4th)	USA vs. EUN	73-79
5	ESP	3-2	—	USA vs. CUB	88-74
6	TCH	1-4			
7	BRA	2-3			
8	ITA	0-5			

USA TEAM: Vicky Bullet / Daedra Charles / Cynthia Cooper / Clarissa Davis / Medina Dixon / Teresa Edwards / Tammy Jackson / Carolyn Jones / Katrina McClain / Suzie McConnell / Vickie Orr / Teresa Weatherspoon

BOXING

LIGHT FLYWEIGHT — (46 KG/101 LBS) / August 8

RANK	CTRY	ATHLETE	DECISION
1	CUB	Rogelio Marcelo	24-10
2	BUL	Daniel Bojinov	
3	PHI	Roel Velasco	
3	GER	Jan Quast	
—	USA	Eric Griffin	elim. 2nd rd.

FLYWEIGHT — (51 KG/112 LBS) / August 9

RANK	CTRY	ATHLETE	DECISION
1	PRK	Choi Choi	12-2
2	MEX	Raul Gonzalez	
3	USA	Timothy Austin	
3	HUN	Istvan Kovacs	

BANTAMWEIGHT — (54 KG/119 LBS) / August 8

RANK	CTRY	ATHLETE	DECISION
1	CUB	Joel Casamayor	14-8
2	IRL	Wayne McCullough	
3	MAR	Mohamed Achik	
3	PRK	Gwang Li	
—	USA	Sergio Reyes	elim. 2nd rd.

FEATHERWEIGHT — (57 KG/125 LBS) / August 9

RANK	CTRY	ATHLETE	DECISION
1	GER	Andreas Tews	16-7
2	ESP	Faustino Reyes	
3	EUN	Ramazi Paliani	
3	ALG	Hocine Soltani	
—	USA	Julian Wheeler	elim. 1st rd.

LIGHTWEIGHT — (60 KG/132 LBS) / August 8

RANK	CTRY	ATHLETE	DECISION
1	USA	Oscar de la Hoya	7-2
2	GER	Marco Rudolph	
3	MGL	Namjil Bayarsaikhan	
3	KOR	Sung Hong	

LIGHT WELTERWEIGHT — (63.5 KG / 140 LBS) / August 9

RANK	CTRY	ATHLETE	DECISION
1	CUB	Hector Vinent	11-1
2	CAN	Mark Leduc	
3	ROM	Leonard Doroftei	
3	FIN	Jyri Kjall	
—	USA	Vernon Forrest	elim. 1st rd.

WELTERWEIGHT — (67 KG/147 LBS) / August 8

RANK	CTRY	ATHLETE	DECISION
1	IRL	Michael Carruth	13-10
2	CUB	Juan Hernandez	
3	THA	Arkom Chenglai	
3	PUR	Anibal Acevedo	
—	USA	Pepe Reilly	elim. 2nd rd.

LIGHT MIDDLEWEIGHT — (71 KG/156 LBS) / August 9

RANK	CTRY	ATHLETE	DECISION
1	CUB	Juan Lemus	6-1
2	NED	Orhan Delibas	
3	HUN	Gyorgy Mizsei	
3	GBR	Robin Reed	
—	USA	Raul Marquez	elim. qtr.

MIDDLEWEIGHT — (75 KG/165 LBS) / August 8

RANK	CTRY	ATHLETE	DECISION
1	CUB	Ariel Hernandez	12-7
2	USA	Chris Byrd	
3	CAN	Chris Johnson	
3	KOR	Seung Lee	

LIGHT HEAVYWEIGHT — (81 KG/178 LBS) / August 9

RANK	CTRY	ATHLETE	DECISION
1	GER	Torsten May	8-3
2	EUN	Rostislav Zaoulitchnyi	
3	HUN	Zoltan Beres	
3	POL	Wojciech Bartnik	
—	USA	Montell Griffin	elim. qtr.

HEAVYWEIGHT — (91 KG/200 LBS) / August 8

RANK	CTRY	ATHLETE	DECISION
1	CUB	Felix Savon	14-1
2	NGR	David Izonritei	
3	NED	Van Der Lijde	
3	NZL	David Tua	
—	USA	Danell Nicholson	elim. qtr.

SUPER HEAVYWEIGHT — (+91 KG/+200 LBS) / August 9

RANK	CTRY	ATHLETE	DECISION
1	CUB	Roberto Balado	13-2
2	NGR	Richard Igbineghu	
3	DEN	Brian Nielsen	
3	BUL	Svilen Roussinov	
—	USA	Larry Donald	elim. qtr.

CANOE · KAYAK

MEN'S C-1 FLATWATER 500 METERS / August 7

RANK	CTRY	ATHLETE	TIME
1	BUL	Nikolai Boukhalov	1:51.15
2	EUN	Mikhail Slivinski	1:51.40
3	GER	Olaf Heukrodt	1:53.00
4	TCH	Slavomir Knazovicky	1:54.51
5	HUN	Imre Pulai	1:54.86
6	CAN	Stephen Cory Giles	1:55.80
7	FRA	Pascal Sylvoz	1:55.96
8	ROM	Victor Partnoi	1:57.34
—	USA	Fred Spaulding	elim. semi.

MEN'S C-1 FLATWATER 1,000 METERS / August 8

RANK	CTRY	ATHLETE	TIME
1	BUL	Nikolai Boukhalov	4:05.92
2	LAT	Ivans Klementjevs	4:06.60
3	HUN	Gyorgy Zala	4:07.35
4	GER	Matthias Roeder	4:08.96
5	FRA	Pascal Sylvoz	4:09.82
6	GBR	Andrew John Train	4:12.58
7	ROM	Victor Partnoi	4:14.27
8	TCH	Jan Bartunek	4:15.25
—	USA	Fred Spaulding	elim. semi.

MEN'S C-2 FLATWATER 500 METERS / August 7

RANK	CTRY	ATHLETE	TIME
1	EUN	Alexandre Masseikov / Dmitri Dovgalenok	1:41.54
2	GER	Ulrich Papke / Ingo Spelly	1:41.68
3	BUL	Martin Marinov / Blagovest Stoyanov	1:41.94
4	ROM	Gheorghe Andriev / Nicolae Juravschi	1:42.84
5	DEN	Arne Nielsson / Christian Frederiksen	1:42.92
6	FRA	Didier Hoyer / Olivier Boivin	1:43.04
7	HUN	Attila Palizs / Gyorgy Kolonics	1:43.27
8	TCH	Jan Bartunek / Waldemar Fibigr	1:44.70
—	USA	Jim Terrell / Stewart Carr	elim. semi.

MEN'S C-2 FLATWATER 1,000 METERS / August 8

RANK	CTRY	ATHLETE	TIME
1	GER	Ulrich Papke / Ingo Spelly	3:37.42
2	DEN	Arne Nielsson / Christian Frederiksen	3:39.26
3	FRA	Didier Hoyer / Olivier Boivin	3:39.51
4	ROM	Gheorghe Andriev / Nicolae Juravschi	3:39.88
5	HUN	Attila Palizs / Gyorgy Kolonics	3:42.86
6	BUL	Martin G. Marinov / Blagovest Stoyanov	3:43.97
7	CAN	Larry Cain / David Frost	3:46.21
8	EUN	Alexei Igraev / Alexandre Gromovitch	3:53.90
—	USA	Greg Steward / Wyatt Jones	elim. semi.

MEN'S C-1 WHITEWATER SLALOM / August 1

RANK	CTRY	ATHLETE	POINTS
1	TCH	Lukas Pollert	113.69
2	GBR	Gareth John Marriott	116.48
3	FRA	Jacky Avril	117.18
4	USA	Jon Lugbill	118.62
5	ITA	Renato De Monti	119.02
6	GER	Martin Lang	119.19
7	FRA	Emmanuel Brugvin	119.19
8	TCH	Juraj Ontko	120.23
11	USA	David Hearn	121.57
21	USA	Adam Clawson	129.23

MEN'S C-2 WHITEWATER SLALOM / August 2

RANK	CTRY	ATHLETE	POINTS
1	USA	Scott Strausbaugh / Joe Jacobi	122.41
2	TCH	Miroslav Simek / Jiri Rohan	124.25
3	FRA	Franck Adisson / Wilfrid Forgues	124.38
4	USA	Jamie McEwan / Lecky Haller	128.05
5	SUI	Ueli Matti / Peter Matti	128.55
6	TCH	Pavel Stercl / Petr Stercl	130.42
7	TCH	Jan Petricek / Tomas Petricek	131.68
8	FRA	Thierry Saidi / Emmanuel Del Rey	132.29
15	USA	Elliot Weintrob / Martin McCormick	150.59

MEN'S K-1 FLATWATER 500 METERS / August 7

RANK	CTRY	ATHLETE	TIME
1	FIN	Mikko Kolehmainen	1:40.34
2	HUN	Zsolt Gyulay	1:40.64
3	NOR	Knut Holmann	1:40.71
4	USA	Norman Bellingham	1:40.84
5	EUN	Sergei Kalesnik	1:40.90
6	SUI	Roberto Liberato	1:41.98
7	ITA	Daniele Scarpa	1:42.00
8	ROM	Marin Gigi Popescu	1:42.24

MEN'S K-1 FLATWATER 1,000 METERS / August 8

RANK	CTRY	ATHLETE	TIME
1	AUS	Clint Robinson	3:37.26
2	NOR	Knut Holmann	3:37.50
3	USA	Greg Barton	3:37.93
4	ROM	Marin Gigi Popescu	3:38.37
5	ITA	Beniamino Bonomi	3:41.12
6	POR	Jose Garcia	3:41.60
7	DEN	Thor Nielsen	3:41.70
8	CAN	Renn J. Crichlow	3:43.46

MEN'S K-2 FLATWATER 500 METERS / August 7

RANK	CTRY	ATHLETE	TIME
1	GER	Kay Bluhm / Torsten Gutsche	1:28.27
2	POL	Maciej Freimut / Wojciech Kurpiewski	1:29.84
3	ITA	Antonio Rossi / Bruno Dreossi	1:30.00
4	ESP	Juan Roman Mangas / J Sanchez De Castro	1:30.93
5	SWE	Karl Sundqvist / Gunnar Olsson	1:31.48
6	DEN	Jesper M. Staal / Thor Nielsen	1:31.84
7	HUN	Ferenc Csipes / Zsolt Gyulay	1:32.34
8	USA	Michael Harbold / Peter Newton	1:33.02

MEN'S K-2 FLATWATER 1,000 METERS / August 8

RANK	CTRY	ATHLETE	TIME
1	GER	Kay Bluhm / Torsten Gutsche	3:16.10
2	SWE	Gunnar Olsson / Karl Sundqvist	3:17.70
3	POL	Grzegorz Kotowicz / Dariusz Bialkowski	3:18.86
4	USA	Greg Barton / Norman Bellingham	3:19.26
5	ITA	Paolo Luschi / Daniele Scarpa	3:20.34
6	HUN	Krisztian Bartfai / Andras Rajna	3:20.71
7	TCH	Rene Kucera / Petr Hruska	3:23.12
8	NZL	Ian Gordon Ferguson / Christopher MacDonald	3:26.84

MEN'S K-4 FLATWATER 1,000 METERS / August 8

RANK	CTRY	ATHLETES	TIME
1	GER	Mario Von Appen / Oliver M. Kegel / Thomas Reineck / Andre G. Wohllebe	2:54.18
2	HUN	Ferenc Csipes / Zsolt Gyulay / Laszlo Fidel / Attila Abraham	2:54.82
3	AUS	Kelvin John Graham / Ian Mark Rowling / Steven Michael Wood / Ramon D. Andersson	2:56.97
4	TCH	Jozef Turza / Juraj Kadnar / Robert Erban / Attila Szabo	2:57.06
5	ROM	Daniel Stoian / Sorin Petcu / Geza Magyar / Romica Serban	3:00.11
6	POL	Maciej Freimut / Wojciech Kurpiewski / Grzegorz Kaleta / Grzegorz Krawcow	3:01.43
7	SWE	Pablo Grate / Jonas Fager / Anders Ohlsson / Hans Olsson	3:01.46
8	BUL	Milko G. Kazanov / Petar Ivanov / Godev E. Yordanov Nikolai / Nikolai Gueorguiev	3:02.08
9	USA	Chris Barlow / Michael A. Herbert / Terry Kent / Mark David Hamilton	3:04.30

MEN'S K-1 WHITEWATER SLALOM / August 2

RANK	CTRY	ATHLETE	POINTS
1	ITA	Pierpaolo Ferrazzi	106.89
2	FRA	Sylvain Curinier	107.06
3	GER	Jochen Lettmann	108.52
4	GBR	Richard Fox	108.85
5	FRA	Laurent Brissaud	109.37
6	SLO	Marjan Strukelj	110.11
7	GBR	Melvyn Jones	110.40
8	IRL	Ian Wiley	110.45
13	USA	Eric Jackson	112.59
16	USA	Richard Weiss	113.12
27	USA	Scott Shipley	119.64

WOMEN'S K-1 FLATWATER 500 METERS / August 7

RANK	CTRY	ATHLETE	TIME
1	GER	Birgit Schmidt	1:51.60
2	HUN	Rita Koban	1:51.96
3	POL	Izabella Dylewska	1:52.36
4	ITA	Josefa Idem	1:52.78
5	AUT	Ursula Profanter	1:53.17
6	FRA	Sabine Goetschy	1:53.53
7	CAN	Caroline Brunet	1:54.82
8	ROM	Sanda Toma	1:54.84
—	USA	Sheila Conover	elim. semi.

WOMEN'S K-2 FLATWATER 500 METERS / August 7

RANK	CTRY	ATHLETE	TIME
1	GER	Ramona Portwich / Anke Von Seck	1:40.29
2	SWE	Susanne Gunnarsson / Agneta Andersson	1:40.41
3	HUN	Rita Koban / Eva Donusz	1:40.81
4	ROM	Sanda Toma / Carmen Simion	1:42.12
5	CAN	Alison Herst / Klara Macaskill	1:42.14
6	POL	Izabella Dylewska / Elzbieta Urbanczyk	1:42.44
7	CHN	Zhao Xiaoli / Ning Menghua	1:42.46
8	DEN	Jeanette B. Knudsen / Yvonne B. Knudsen	1:43.98
—	USA	Traci Phillips / Cathy Marino	elim. semi.

WOMEN'S K-4 FLATWATER 500 METERS / August 8

RANK	CTRY	ATHLETES	TIME
1	HUN	Eva Donusz / Kinga Czigany / Erika Meszaros / Rita Koban	1:38.32
2	GER	Katrin Borchert / Birgit Schmidt / Anke Von Seck / Ramona Portwich	1:38.47
3	SWE	Anna Olsson / Maria Haglund / Susanne Rosenqvist / Agneta Andersson	1:39.79
4	ROM	Sanda Toma / Claudia Nicula / Carmen Simion / Viorica Iordache	1:41.02
5	CHN	Yanfang Wen / Xiaoli Zhao / Menghua Ning / Jing Wang	1:41.12
6	CAN	Caroline Brunet / Alison Herst / Klara Macaskill / Kevyn M. Stafford	1:42.28
7	USA	Traci Phillips / Sheila Conover / Cathy Marino / Alexandra B. Harbold	1:43.00
8	AUS	Anna Maria Wood / Denise E. Cooper / Lynda C. Lehumann / Gayle Joy Mayes	1:43.88

WOMEN'S K-1 WHITEWATER SLALOM / August 1

RANK	CTRY	ATHLETE	POINTS
1	GER	Elisabeth Micheler	126.41
2	AUS	Danielle Woodward	128.27
3	USA	Dana Chladek	131.75
4	GER	Eva Roth	132.29
5	FRA	Marianne Agulhon	132.89
6	GER	Kordula Striepecke	134.49
7	TCH	Zdenka Grossmannova	135.79
8	CAN	Joanne Woods	138.06
9	USA	Cathy Hearn	139.51
25	USA	Maylon Hanold	193.80

CYCLING

MEN'S ONE KM TIME TRIAL / July 27

RANK	CTRY	ATHLETE	TIME
1	ESP	Jose Moreno	1:03.342
2	AUS	Shane Kelly	1:04.288
3	USA	Erin Hartwell	1:04.753
4	GER	Jens Gluecklich	1:04.798
5	ITA	Adler Capelli	1:05.065
6	FRA	F. Lancien	1:05.157
7	NZL	J. Andrews	1:05.240
8	TRI	Gene Samuel	1:05.485

MEN'S MATCH SPRINT / July 31

RANK	CTRY	ATHLETE
1	GER	Jens Fiedler
2	AUS	Gary Neiwand
3	CAN	Curtis Harnett
4	ITA	Roberto Chiappa
5	USA	Ken Carpenter
6	ARG	J. Lovito
7	EUN	Nikolai Kovch
8	ESP	Jose Moreno

MEN'S 4,000-METER INDIVIDUAL PURSUIT / July 29

RANK	CTRY	ATHLETE	TIME
1	GBR	Chris Boardman	3:21.649
2	GER	Jens Lehmann	3:27.357
3	NZL	Gary Anderson	4:31.061
4	AUS	M. Kingsland	4:32.716
5	FRA	P. Ermenault	4:28.838
6	BEL	Cedric Mathy	4:33.942
7	ESP	Adolfo Alperi	4:34.760
8	ITA	Ivan Beltrami	4:36.150
12	USA	Carl Sundquist	

MEN'S 4,000-METER TEAM PURSUIT / July 31

RANK	CTRY	ATHLETES	TIME
1	GER	M. Gloeckner / Jens Lehmann / Stefan Steinweg / Guido Fulst	4:08.791
2	AUS	Brett Aitken / S. McGlede / S. O'Brien / S. O'Grady	4:10.218
3	DEN	Ken Frost / Jimmi Madsen / Jan Petersen / Klaus Kynde	4:15.860
4	ITA	Ivan Beltrami / Rossano Brasi / Ivan Cerioli / Fabrizio Trezzi	4:18.291
5	GBR	Chris Boardman / Paul Jennings / Bryan Steel / Glen Sword	4:14.350
6	EUN	Valeri Batouro / A. Gontchenkov / D. Nelioubine / Roman Saprykine	4:16.685
7	NZL	G. Anderson / N. Donnelly / Carlos Marryatt / Stuart Williams	Overtaken
8	TCH	S. Buchta / Rudolf Juricky / Jan Panacek / Pavel Tesar	Overtaken
9	USA	Dirk Copeland / Matt Hamon / Jim Pollak / Chris Coletta	

MEN'S 50 KM POINTS RACE / July 31

RANK	CTRY	ATHLETE	POINTS
1	ITA	Giovanni Lombardi	44
2	NED	Leon Van Bon	43
3	BEL	Cedric Mathy	41
4	NZL	Glenn McLeay	30
5	TCH	Lubor Tesar	30
6	FRA	Eric Magnin	24
7	GER	Guido Fulst	24
8	SUI	A. Aeschbach	23
—	USA	James Carney	DNA

MEN'S 100 KM TEAM TIME TRIAL / July 26

RANK	CTRY	ATHLETES	TIME
1	GER	Bernd Dittert / Christian Meyer / Uwe Peschel / Michael Rich	2:01.39
2	ITA	F. Anastasia / Luca Colombo / G. Contri / Andrea Peron	2:02.39
3	FRA	Herve Boussard / Faivre-Pierret / P. Gaumont / J. Harel	2:05.25
4	EUN	Igor Dziouba / Oleg Galkin / Pastoukhovitch / Igor Patenko	2:05.34
5	ESP	M. Fernandez / Gonzalez / E. Mancebo / David Plaza	2:06.11
6	POL	G. Piwowarski / A. Sypykowski / D. Baranowski / M. Lesniewski	2:06.34
7	SUI	T. Boutellier / Roland Meier / Beat Meister / T. Rinderknecht	2:06.35
8	TCH	Jaroslav Bilek / Miroslav Liptak / Pavel Padrnos / Frantisek Trkal	2:06.44
16	USA	George Hincapie / Nathan Sheafor / Scott Mercier / John Stenner / Dave Nicholson (INJ)	2:13.35

MEN'S 194-KM ROAD RACE / August 2

RANK	CTRY	ATHLETE	TIME
1	ITA	Fabio Casatelli	4:35.21
2	NED	Hendrik Dekker	4:35.22
3	LAT	Dainis Ozols	4:35.24
4	GER	Erik Zabel	4:35.56
5	EST	Lauri Aus	4:35.56
6	POL	Andrzej Sypykowski	4:35.56
7	FRA	Sylvain Bolay	4:35.56
8	LAT	Arvis Piziks	4:35.56
14	USA	Lance Armstrong	4:35.56
37	USA	Timothy Peddie	4:35.56
75	USA	Bob Mionske	4:42.31

WOMEN'S MATCH SPRINT / July 31

RANK	CTRY	ATHLETE	
1	EST	Erika Salumae	
2	GER	Annette Neumann	
3	NED	Ingrid Haringa	
4	FRA	F. Ballanger	
5	EUN	Galina Enukhina	
6	CAN	Tayna Dubnicoff	
7	JPN	Mika Kuroki	
—	USA	Connie Paraskevin-Young	elim. repechage

WOMEN'S 3,000-METER INDIVIDUAL PURSUIT / July 31

RANK	CTRY	ATHLETE	TIME
1	GER	Petra Rossner	3:41.753
2	AUS	Kathryn Watt	3:43.438
3	USA	Rebecca Twigg	3:52.429
4	DEN	Hanne Malmberg	3:53.516
5	FRA	Jeanne Longo-Ciprelli	3:46.547
6	EUN	S. Samochvalova	3:47.444
7	FIN	Vikstedt-Nyman	3:48.918
8	NED	L. Van Moorsel	3:49.795

WOMEN'S 81-KM ROAD RACE / July 26

RANK	CTRY	ATHLETE	TIME
1	AUS	Kathryn Watt	2:04.42
2	FRA	Jeannie Longo-Ciprelli	2:05.02
3	NED	Monique Knol	2:05.03
4	EUN	N. Kistchuk	2:05.03
5	NOR	Monica Valvik	2:05.03
6	USA	Jeanne Golay	2:05.03
7	AUS	K. Shannon	2:05.03
8	SUI	Luzia Zberg	2:05.03
10	USA	Sally Zack	2:05.03
26	USA	Inga Thompson	2:05.03

DIVING

MEN'S PLATFORM

RANK	CTRY	ATHLETE	TOTAL
1	CHN	Sun Shuwei	677.31
2	USA	Scott Donie	633.63
3	CHN	Xiong Ni	600.15
4	GER	Jan Hempel	574.17
5	GBR	Bob Morgan	568.59
6	EUN	Dmitri Saoutine	565.95
7	GER	M. Kuhne	558.54
8	JPN	Keita Kaneto	529.14
10	USA	Matt Scoggin	492.60

MEN'S SPRINGBOARD

RANK	CTRY	ATHLETE	TOTAL
1	USA	Mark Lenzi	676.53
2	CHN	Tan Liangde	645.57
3	EUN	Dmitri Saoutine	627.78
4	AUS	Michael Andrew Murphy	611.78
5	USA	Kent Ferguson	609.12
6	MEX	J. Mondragon Vazquez	604.14
7	NED	Edwin Jongejans	581.40
8	EUN	Valeri Statsenko	577.92

WOMEN'S PLATFORM

RANK	CTRY	ATHLETE	TOTAL
1	CHN	Fu Mingxia	461.43
2	EUN	Elena Mirochina	411.63
3	USA	Mary Ellen Clark	401.91
4	CHN	Jinhong Zhu	400.56
5	EUN	Inga Afonina	398.43
6	MEX	M.J. Alcala Izguerra	394.35
7	USA	Ellen Owen	392.10
8	ARG	Veronica Ribot DeCanales	384.03

WOMEN'S SPRINGBOARD / August 3

RANK	CTRY	ATHLETE	TOTAL
1	CHN	Gao Min	572.40
2	EUN	Irina Lachko	514.14
3	GER	Brita Pia Baldus	503.07
4	TCH	Heidermarie Bartova	491.49
5	USA	Julie Ovenhouse	477.84
6	EUN	Vera Ilina	470.67
7	GER	Simona Koch	468.96
8	CAN	Mary Kathelene Depiero	449.49
9	USA	Karen LaFace	447.75
10	ARG	Veronica Ribot De Canales	447.42

EQUESTRIAN

INDIVIDUAL JUMPING / August 9

RANK	CTRY	ATHLETE/HORSE	TOTAL
1	GER	Ludger Beerbaum / Classic Touch	0.00
2	NED	Piet Raymakers / Ratina Z	0.25
3	USA	Norman Dello Joio / Irish	4.75
4	FRA	Herve Godignon / Quidam De Revel	6.25
5	NED	Jan Tops / Top Gun	8.25
6	SWE	Maria Gretzer / Marcoville	10.25
7	BEL	L. Philippaerts / Darco	12.25
8	DEN	Merethe Jensen / Maxime	12.75
10	USA	Michael Matz / Heisman	16.25
17	USA	Lisa Jacquin / For The Moment	21.25

TEAM JUMPING / August 4

RANK	CTRY	ATHLETE/HORSE	TOTAL
1	NED	Piet Raymakers / Ratina Z Bert Romp / Waldo E Jan Tops / Top Gun Jos Lansink / Egano	12.00
2	AUT	Boris Boor / Love Me Tender Joerg Muntzner / Graf Grande Hugo Simon / Apricot D Thomas Fruhmann / Genius	16.75
3	FRA	Herve Godignon / Quidam De Revel Hubert Bourdy / Razzia Du P. Michel Robert / Nonix Eric Navet / Quito De Baussy	24.75
4	ESP	Irujo Martinez / Palestro II E. Sarasola / Minstrel Louis A. Cervera / Let's Go B'92 Luis Astolfi / Fino B'92	25.50
5	USA	Anne Kursinski / Cannonball Norman Dello Joio / Irish Lisa Jacquin / For The Moment Michael Matz / Heisman	28.00
6	SUI	W. Melliger / Quinta C Markus Fuchs / Shandor II McNaught-Mandli / Pirol B Thomas Fuchs / Dylano	28.00
7	GBR	Nick Skelton / Dollar Girl Tim Grubb / Denizen M. Whitaker / Monsanta John Whitaker / Milton	28.75
8	SWE	Peter Eriksson / Moritz Henrik Lanner / Cantadou Ulrika Hedin / Lipton Maria Gretzer / Marcoville	37.00

INDIVIDUAL DRESSAGE / August 5

RANK	CTRY	ATHLETE/HORSE	TOTAL
1	GER	Nicole Uphoff / Rembrandt	1626
2	GER	Isabelle Werth / Gigolo	1551
3	GER	Klaus Balkenhol / Goldstern	1515
4	NED	A. VanGrunsven / Olympic Bonfire	1447
5	FIN	Kyra Kyrklund / Edinburg	1428
6	USA	Carol Lavell / Gifted	1408
7	ITA	Pia Laus / Adrett	1389
8	AUT	E. Max-Theurer / Liechtenstein	1380
22	USA	Charlotte Bredahl / Monsieur	elim.
22	USA	Robert Dover / Lectron	elim.
27	USA	Michael Poulin / Graf George	elim.

TEAM DRESSAGE / August 3

RANK	CTRY	ATHLETE/HORSE	TOTAL
1	GER	Nicole Uphoff / Rembrandt Monica Susanne Theodorescu / Grunox Isabelle Regina Werth / Gigolo Klaus Balkenhol / Goldstern	5224
2	NED	Anky Van Grunsven / Olympic Bonfire Annemarie Sanders / Olympic Montreux Tineke Bartels / Olympic Courage Ellen Bontje / Olympic Larius	4742
3	USA	Charlotte Bredahl / Monsieur Michael Poulin / Graf George Robert Dover / Lectron Carol Lavell / Gifted	4643
4	SWE	A. Westerberg / Taktik Ann Behrenfors / Leroy Oscarsson-Goeth / Lille Claus T. Wilhelmson / Caprice	4537
5	DEN	Bent Jensen / Ariston Anne Tornblad / Ravel Lene Hoberg / Bayard Ann Van Olst / Chevalier	4533
6	SUI	Ruth Hunkeler / Afchadi Doris Ramseier / Renatus Otto Hofer / Renzo	4524
7	GBR	Emile Faurie / Virtu Carl Hester / Giorgione Laura Fry / Quarryman Carol Parsons / Vashkar	4522
8	ITA	Conz Dall'Ora / Lahti Paolo Giani / Destino Di Acci D. C. Fantoni / Sonny Boy Pia Laus / Adrett	4491

INDIVIDUAL THREE-DAY EVENT / July 30

RANK	CTRY	ATHLETE/HORSE	TOTAL
1	AUS	Matthew Ryan / Kibah Tic Toc	70.00
2	GER	Herman Blocker / Feine Dame	81.30
3	NZL	Blyth Tait / Messiah	87.60
4	NZL	V. Latta / Chief	87.80
5	AUS	Andrew Hoy / Kiwi	89.40
6	GBR	Karen Dixon / Get Smart	92.60
7	ESP	Luis Alvarez / Mr. Chrisalis	102.20
8	BEL	Karin Donckers / Britt	104.40
17	USA	Jil Walton / Patrona	116.80
48	USA	J. Michael Plumb / Adonis	195.20
52	USA	Stephen Bradley / Sassy Realm	203.20
—	USA	Todd Trewin / Sandscript	elim.

TEAM THREE-DAY EVENT / July 30

RANK	CTRY	ATHLETE/HORSE	TOTAL
1	AUS	David Green / Duncan II	288.60
		Gillian Rolton / Peppermint Grove	
		Andrew Hoy / Kiwi	
		Matthew Ryan / Kibah Tic Toc	
2	NZL	A. Nicholson / Spinning Rhombu	290.80
		V. Latta / Chief	
		Blyth Tait / Messiah	
		Mark Todd / Welton Greylag	
3	GER	M. Baumann / Alabaster	300.30
		C. Mysegaes / Ricardo	
		Ralf Ehrenbrink / Kildare	
		Herbert Blocker / Feine Dame	
4	BEL	Jef Desmedt / Dolleman	333.30
		D. Van Der Elst / Fatal Love	
		Karin Donckers / Britt	
		Willy Sneyers / Drum	
5	ESP	Luis Alvarez / Mr. Chrisalis	388.80
		F. Villalon / Clever Night	
		S. De La Rocha / Kinvarra	
		S. Centenera / Just Dixon	
6	GBR	Richard Walker / Jacana	406.60
		Karen Dixon / Get Smart	
		M. Thomson / King William	
		Ian Stark / Murphy Himself	
7	JPN	K. Iwatani / Lord Waterford	434.80
		Eiki Miyazaki / Mystery Cargo	
		Kojiro Goto / Retalic	
		Y. Kowata / Hellatdawn	
8	IRL	Olivia Holohan / Rusticus	445.80
		Mairead Curran / Watercolour	
		Melanie Duff / Rathlin Roe	
		Eric Smiley / Enterprise	
10	USA	**Jil Walton / Patrona**	515.20
		J. Michael Plumb / Adonis	
		Stephen Bradley / Sassy Reason	
		Todd Trewin / Sandscript	

FENCING

MEN'S INDIVIDUAL FOIL / July 31

RANK	CTRY	ATHLETE
1	FRA	Philippe Omnes
2	EUN	Serguei Goloubitski
3	CUB	Elvis Gregory Gil
4	GER	Udo Wagner
5	ITA	Andrea Borella
6	POL	Marian Sypniewski
7	CUB	Guillermo Betancourt Scull
8	AUT	Joachim Wendt
36	USA	**Michael Marx**
39	USA	**Nick Bravin**
45	USA	**Zaddick Longenbach**

MEN'S TEAM FOIL / August 4

RANK	CTRY	ATHLETES
1	GER	Udo Wagner / Ulrich Rainer Schreck / Thorsten Weidner / Alexander Koch / Ingo Weissenborn
2	CUB	Elvis Gregory Gil / Guillermo Betancourt Scull / Oscar Garcia Perez / Tulio Diaz Babier / Hermenegildo Garcia Marturell
3	POL	Marian Sypniewski / Piotr Kielpikowski / Adam Krzesinski / Cezary Siess / Ryszard Sobczak
4	HUN	Zsolt Ersek / Istvan Busa / Robert Kiss / Robert Gatai / Zsolt Nemeth
5	EUN	Serguei Goloubitski / Dmitri Chevtchenko / Viatcheslav Grigoriev / Anvar Ibraguimov / Ilgar Mamedov
6	ITA	Andrea Borella / Mauro Numa / Stefano Cerioni / Marco Arpino / Alessandro Puccini
7	FRA	Philippe Omnes / Patrick Groc / Patrice Lhotellier / Youssef Hocine / Olivier Lambert
8	KOR	Bong Hyung You / Young Ho Kim / Seung Pyo Kim / Ho-Sung Lee / Seung Yong Lee
—	USA	**DNQ**

MEN'S INDIVIDUAL SABRE / August 2

RANK	CTRY	ATHLETE
1	HUN	Bence Szabo
2	ITA	Marco Marin
3	FRA	Jean-Francois Lamour
4	ITA	Giovanni Scalzo
5	ESP	Antonio Garcia Hernandez
6	ITA	Ferdinando Meglio
7	POL	Robert Koscielniakowski
8	GER	Jurgen Nolte
21	USA	**Michael R. Lofton**
24	USA	**Robert Cottingham**
34	USA	**Steve Mormando**

MEN'S TEAM SABRE / August 7

RANK	CTRY	ATHLETES
1	EUN	Grigorij Kirienko / Alexandre Chirchov / Gueorgui Pogossov / Vadim Gouttsait / Stanislav Pozdniakov
2	HUN	Bence Szabo / Csaba Koves / Gyorgy Nebald / Peter Abay / Imre Bujdoso
3	FRA	Jean-Francois Lamour / Jean-Philippe Daurelle / Franck Ducheix / Herve Granger-Veyron / Pierre Guichot
4	ROM	Daniel Grigore / Vilmos Szabo / Alexandru Chiculita / Victor Dan Gaureanu / Florin Alin Lupeica
5	GER	Jurgen Nolte / Felix Becker / Joerg Kempenich / Jacek Heinrich Huchwajda / Steffen Wiesinger
6	POL	Robert T. Koscielniakowski / Janusz Olech / Marek Gniewkowski / Norbert Jaskot / Jaroslaw Kisiel
7	CHN	Zhaokang Zheng / Zhen Yang / Guihua Jia / Yefei Jiang / Xiankui Ning
8	ITA	Marco Marin / Giovanni Scalzo / Ferdinando Meglio / Giovanni Sirovich / Tonhi Terenzi
9	USA	**Robert Cottingham / John Friedberg / Michael Lofton / Steve Mormando / Peter Westbrook**

MEN'S INDIVIDUAL EPEE / August 1

RANK	CTRY	ATHLETE
1	FRA	Eric Srecki
2	EUN	Pavel Kolobkov
3	FRA	Jean-Michel Henry
4	EST	Kaido Kaaberma
5	GER	Elmar Borrmann
6	ITA	Angelo Mazzoni
7	COL	Mauricio Rivas Nieto
8	HUN	Ivan Kovacs
24	USA	**Robert Marx**
43	USA	**Jon Normile**
55	USA	**Chris O'Loughlin**

MEN'S TEAM EPEE / August 6

RANK	CTRY	ATHLETES
1	GER	Elmar Borrmann / Robert Felisiak / Arnd Rudiger Schmitt / Uwe Gerhard Proske / Vladimir Reznitchenko
2	HUN	Ivan Kovacs / Krisztian Kulcsar / Ferenc Hegedus / Erno Kolczonay / Gabor Totola
3	EUN	Pavel Kolobkov / Andrei Chouvalov / Serguei Kravtchouk / Serguei Kostarev / Valeri Zakharevitch
4	FRA	Eric Srecki / Jean-Michel Henry / Olivier Lenglet / Jean-Francois Di Martino / Robert Leroux
5	ITA	Angelo Mazzoni / Maurizio Randazzo / Sandro Cuomo / Stefano Pantano / Sandro Resegotti
6	ESP	Fernando M. De La Pena Olivas / Raul Lorenzo Maroto Lopez / Manuel Pereira Senabre / Angel Fernandez Garcia / Cesar G. Llorens
7	CAN	Laurie Shong / Bogdan Edmund Nowosielski / Jean-Marc Chouinard / Alain Cote / Allan Francis
8	SWE	Peter Vanky / Tomas Lundblad / Ulf Sandegren / Jerri Bergstrom / Mats Ahlgren
—	USA	**DNQ**

WOMEN'S INDIVIDUAL FOIL / July 30

RANK	CTRY	ATHLETE
1	ITA	Giovanna Trillini
2	CHN	Wang Huifeng
3	EUN	Tatiana Sadovskaia
4	FRA	Laurence Modaine
5	ITA	Margherita Zalaffi
6	ROM	Reka Zsofia Szabo
7	GER	Sabine Christiane Bau
8	GBR	Fiona Jane McIntosh
29	USA	**Caitlin Bildeaux-Banos**
36	USA	**Mary Jane O'Neill**
39	USA	**Molly Sullivan**

WOMEN'S TEAM FOIL / August 4

RANK	CTRY	ATHLETES
1	ITA	Giovanna Trillini / Margherita Zalaffi / Francesca Bortolozzi / Diana Bianchedi / Dorina Vaccaroni
2	GER	Sabine Christiane Bau / Zita-Eva Funkenhauser / Annette Dobmeier / Anja Fichtel-Mauritz / Monika Weber-Koszto
3	ROM	Reka Zsofia Szabo / Claudia Laura Grigorescu / Elisabeta Tufan / Laura Gabriela Badea / Roxana Daniela Dumitrescu
4	EUN	Tatiana Sadovskaia / Olga Velitchko / Elena Glikina / Elena Grichina / Olga Vochtchakina
5	FRA	Laurence Modaine / Isabelle Spennato / Gisele Meygret / Camille Couzi / Julie-Anne Gross
6	CHN	Wang Huifeng / Xiao Aihua / Jie E/ Liang Jun / Ye Lin
7	HUN	Zsuzsa Nemethne-Janosi / Gertrud Stefanek / Ildiko Mincza / Gabriella Lantos / Ildiko Pusztai
8	POL	Anna Sobczak / Barbara Szewczyk / Monika Maciejewska / Kataryna Felusiak / Agnieszka Szuchnicka
9	USA	**Caitlin Bildeaux-Banos / Ann Marsh / Sharon Monplaisir / Mary Jane O'Neill / Molly Sullivan**

FIELD HOCKEY

MEN / July 26 - August 8

RANK	CTRY	SCORE		
1	GER	GER vs. AUS	2-1	(Final)
2	AUS	PAK vs. NED	4-3	(3rd-4th)
3	PAK	ESP vs. GBR	2-1	(5th-6th)
4	NED	IND vs. NZL	3-2	(7th-8th)
5	ESP	MAS vs. EUN	4-3	(9th-10th)
6	GBR	ARG vs. EGY	7-3	(11th-12th)
7	IND			
8	NZL			
9	MAS			
10	EUN			
11	ARG			
12	EGY			
—	USA	DNQ		

WOMEN / July 27 - August 8

RANK	CTRY	SCORE		
1	ESP	ESP vs. GER	2-1 a.e.t.	(Final)
2	GER	GBR vs. KOR	4-3 a.e.t.	(3rd-4th)
3	GBR	AUS vs. NED	2-0	(5th-6th)
4	KOR	CAN vs. NZL	2-0	(7th-8th)
5	AUS			
6	NED			
7	CAN			
8	NZL			
—	USA	DNQ		

a.e.t. — after extra time

GYMNASTICS

MEN'S TEAM COMPETITION / July 29

RANK	CTRY	ATHLETES	TOTAL
1	EUN	Valeri Belenki / R. Charipov / V. Scherbo / Korobtchinski / G. Misioutine / A. Voropaev	585.450
2	CHN	Guo Linyao / Li Chunyang / Li Dashuang / Li Ge / Li Jing / Li Xiaosahuang	580.375
3	JPN	Yutaka Aihara / Takashi Chinen / Y. Hatakeda / Yukio Iketani / M. Matsunaga / D. Nishikawa	578.250
4	GER	Ralf Buchner / Mario Franke / Sylvio Kroll / Sven Tippelt / Oliver Walther / Andreas Wecker	575.575
5	ITA	Paolo Bucci / G. Centazzo / Boris Preti / Ruggero Rossato / Gabriele Sala / A. Viligiardi	571.750
6	USA	**Trent Dimas / Scott Keswick / Jair Lynch / Dominick Minicucci / John Roethlisberger / Chris Waller**	**571.725**
7	ROM	N. Bejenaru / A. Gal / Marius Gherman / Marian Rizan / Adrian Sandu / Nicu Stroia	571.150
8	KOR	Kwang Han / Yoon Han / Jin Jung / Joo Lee / Hong-Chul Yeo	570.850

MEN'S INDIVIDUAL ALL-AROUND / July 31

RANK	CTRY	ATHLETE	TOTAL
1	EUN	Vitali Scherbo	59.025
2	EUN	Grigori Misioutine	58.925
3	EUN	Valeri Belenki	58.625
4	GER	Andreas Wecker	58.450
5	CHN	Li Xiaosahuang	58.150
6	CHN	Guo Linyao	57.925
7	ROM	Marius Gherman	57.700
8	KOR	Joo Lee	57.675
19	USA	**Scott Keswick**	**57.100**
34	USA	**John Roethlisberger**	**56.100**
35	USA	**Chris Waller**	**55.800**

MEN'S FLOOR EXERCISE / August 2

RANK	CTRY	ATHLETE	TOTAL
1	CHN	Li Xiaosahuang	9.925
2	EUN	Grigori Misutin	9.787
2	JPN	Yukio Iketani	9.787
4	KOR	Ryul Yoo Ok	9.775
5	JPN	Yutaka Aihara	9.737
6	EUN	Vitali Scherbo	9.712
7	GER	Andreas Wecker	9.687
8	CHN	Li Chunyang	9.387

MEN'S HORIZONTAL BAR / August 2

RANK	CTRY	ATHLETE	TOTAL
1	USA	**Trent Dimas**	**9.875**
2	EUN	Grigori Misioutine	9.837
2	GER	Andreas Wecker	9.837
4	CHN	Guo Linyao	9.812
5	EUN	Valeri Belenki	9.787
5	JPN	Yoshiaki Hatakeda	9.787
5	JPN	Daisuke Nishikawa	9.787
8	CHN	Li Jing	6.425

MEN'S VAULT / August 2

RANK	CTRY	ATHLETE	TOTAL
1	EUN	Vitali Scherbo	9.856
2	EUN	Grigori Misioutine	9.781
3	KOR	Ryul Yoo Ok	9.762
4	CHN	Li Xiaosahuang	9.731
5	HUN	Zoltan Supola	9.674
6	GER	Sylvio Kroll	9.662
7	HUN	Szilveszter Csollany	9.524
8	JPN	Yutaka Aihara	9.450

MEN'S PARALLEL BARS / August 2

RANK	CTRY	ATHLETE	TOTAL
1	EUN	Vitali Scherbo	9.900
2	CHN	Li Jing	9.812
3	CHN	Guo Linyao	9.800
3	EUN	Igor Korobtchinski	9.800
3	JPN	Masayuki Matsunaga	9.800
6	USA	Jair Lynch	9.712
7	GER	Andreas Wecker	9.612
8	JPN	Daisuke Nishikawa	9.575

MEN'S POMMEL HORSE / August 2

RANK	CTRY	ATHLETE	TOTAL
1	EUN	Vitali Scherbo	9.925
1	PRK	Pae Gil-Su	9.925
3	GER	Andreas Wecker	9.887
4	CHN	Guo Linyao	9.875
5	USA	Chris Waller	9.825
6	JPN	Yoshiaki Hatakeda	9.775
7	CHN	Li Jing	9.250
7	EUN	Valeri Belenki	9.250

MEN'S RINGS / August 2

RANK	CTRY	ATHLETE	TOTAL
1	EUN	Vitali Scherbo	9.937
2	CHN	Li Jing	9.875
3	CHN	Li Xiaosahuang	9.862
3	GER	Andreas Wecker	9.862
5	EUN	Valeri Belenki	9.825
6	HUN	Szilveszter Csollany	9.800
7	JPN	Yukio Iketani	9.762
8	BUL	Kalofer Petrov Khristozov	9.750

WOMEN'S TEAM COMPETITION / July 26

RANK	CTRY	ATHLETES	TOTAL
1	EUN	S. Boguinskaia / Roza Galieva / Tatiana Goutsou / E. Groudneva / T. Lyssenko / Tchoussovitina	395.666
2	ROM	Cristina Bontas / Gina Gogean / Vanda Hadarean / L. Milosovici / Maria Neculita / Mirela Pasca	395.079
3	USA	Wendy Bruce / Dominique Dawes / Shannon Miller / Betty Okino / Kerri Strug / Kim Zmeskal	394.704
4	CHN	He Xuemei / Li Li / Li Yifang / Lu Li / Yang Bo / Zhang Xia	392.941
5	ESP	A. Fernandez / C. Fraguas / Sonia Fraguas / Silvia Martinez / Ruth Rollan / Eva Rueda	391.428
6	HUN	B. Balazs / Ildiko Balog / Kinga Horvath / Andrea Molnar / K. Molnar / Henrietta Onodi	388.602
7	AUS	Monique Allen / Brooke Gysen / J. Monico / Lisa Read / Kylie Shadbolt / Jane Warrilow	387.502
8	FRA	Karine Boucher / M. Colson / Carine Charlier / V. Machado / Chloe Maigre Jenny Rolland	386.052

WOMEN'S INDIVIDUAL ALL-AROUND / July 30

RANK	CTRY	ATHLETE	TOTAL
1	EUN	Tatiana Goutsou	39.737
2	USA	Shannon Miller	39.725
3	ROM	Lavinia Milosovici	39.687
4	ROM	Cristina Bontas	39.674
5	EUN	Svetlana Boguinskaia	39.673
6	ROM	Gina Gogean	39.624
7	EUN	Tatiana Lyssenko	39.537
8	HUN	Henrietta Onodi	39.449
10	USA	Kim Zmeskal	39.412
12	USA	Elizabeth Okino	39.387

WOMEN'S BALANCE BEAM / August 1

RANK	CTRY	ATHLETE	TOTAL
1	EUN	Tatiana Lyssenko	9.975
2	CHN	Li Lu	9.912
2	USA	Shannon Miller	9.912
4	ROM	Cristina Bontas	9.875
5	EUN	Svetlana Boguinskaia	9.862
6	USA	Elizabeth Okino	9.837
7	CHN	Yang Bo	9.300
8	ROM	Lavinia Corina Milosovici	9.262

WOMEN'S FLOOR EXERCISE / August 1

RANK	CTRY	ATHLETE	TOTAL
1	ROM	Lavinia Corina Milosovici	10.00
2	HUN	Henrietta Onodi	9.950
3	EUN	Tatiana Goutsou	9.912
3	ROM	Cristina Bontas	9.912
3	USA	Shannon Miller	9.912
6	USA	Kim Zmeskal	9.900
7	EUN	Oxana Tchoussovitina	9.812
8	BUL	Sylvia Zarkova Mitova	9.400

WOMEN'S UNEVEN BARS / August 1

RANK	CTRY	ATHLETE	TOTAL
1	CHN	Li Lu	10.00
2	EUN	Tatiana Goutsou	9.975
3	USA	Shannon Miller	9.962
4	PRK	Kim Gwang-Suk	9.912
4	ROM	Lavinia Corina Milosovici	9.912
4	ROM	Mirela Ana Pasca	9.912
7	ESP	Cristina Fraguas Sanchez	9.900
8	CHN	Li Li	9.887

WOMEN'S VAULT / August 1

RANK	CTRY	ATHLETE	TOTAL
1	HUN	Henrietta Onodi	9.925
1	ROM	Lavinia Milosovici	9.925
3	EUN	Tatiana Lyssenko	9.912
4	EUN	Svetlana Boguinskaia	9.899
5	ROM	Gina Gogean	9.893
6	USA	Shannon Miller	9.837
7	ESP	Eva Maria Rueda Bravo	9.787
8	USA	Kim Zmeskal	9.593

RHYTHMIC ALL-AROUND / August 8

RANK	CTRY	ATHLETE	TOTAL
1	EUN	Alexandra Timoshenko	59.037
2	ESP	Carolina Pascual	58.100
3	EUN	Oksan Skaldina	57.912
4	ESP	C. Acedo	57.225
5	BUL	M. Petrova	57.087
6	ROM	I. Deleanu	56.612
7	POL	J. Bodak	56.475
8	TCH	L. Oulehlova	56.137
23	USA	Jenifer Lovell	18.062
40	USA	Tamara Levinson	17.237

JUDO

MEN'S EXTRA LIGHTWEIGHT (60 KG/132 LBS) / August 2

RANK	CTRY	ATHLETE	
1	EUN	Nazim Gousseinov	
2	KOR	Hyun Yoon	
3	JPN	Tadanori Koshino	
3	GER	Richard Trautmann	
5	HUN	Jozsef Wagner	
5	FRA	Philippe Pradayrol	
7	VEN	Willis Bernardo Garcia Garcia	
7	MGL	Dashgombo Battulga	
—	USA	Tony Okada	elim.

MEN'S HALF LIGHTWEIGHT (65 KG/143 LBS) / August 1

RANK	CTRY	ATHLETE	
1	BRA	Rogerio Sampaio Cardoso	
2	HUN	Jozsef Csak	
3	GER	Udo Gunter Quellmalz	
3	CUB	Israel Hernandez Planas	
5	BEL	Philip Laats	
5	ESP	Francisco Lorenzo Aparicio	
7	JPN	Kenji Maruyama	
7	KOR	Sang-Moon Kim	
—	USA	James Pedro	elim.

MEN'S LIGHTWEIGHT (71 KG/156 LBS) / July 31

RANK	CTRY	ATHLETE	
1	JPN	Toshihiko Koga	
2	HUN	Bertalan Hajtos	
3	ISR	Shay Oren Smadga	
3	KOR	Hoon Chung	
5	FRA	Bruno Carabetta	
5	GER	Stefan Dott	
7	POL	Wieslaw Blach	
7	MGL	Khaliun Boldbaatar	
—	USA	Mike Swain	elim.

MEN'S HALF MIDDLEWEIGHT (78 KG/172 LBS) / July 30

RANK	CTRY	ATHLETE	
1	JPN	Hidehiko Yoshida	
2	USA	Jason Morris	
3	FRA	Bertrand Damaisin	
3	KOR	Kim Byung-Joo	
5	BEL	Johan Laats	
5	SWE	Lars Adolfsson	
7	ROM	Alexandru Remus Ciupe	
7	EUN	Charip Varaev	

MEN'S MIDDLEWEIGHT (86 KG/189 LBS) / July 29

RANK	CTRY	ATHLETE	
1	POL	Waldemar Legien	
2	FRA	Pascal Tayot	
3	JPN	Hirotaka Okada	
3	CAN	Nicolas Gill	
5	GER	Axel Lobenstein	
5	ROM	Adrian Croitoru	
7	KOR	Yang Jong-Ock	
7	SUI	Daniel Kistler	
—	USA	Joey Wanag	elim.

MEN'S HALF HEAVYWEIGHT (95 KG/209 LBS) / July 28

RANK	CTRY	ATHLETE	
1	HUN	Antal Kovacs	
2	GBR	Raymond Stevens	
3	EUN	Dmitri Sergeev	
3	NED	Theo Meijer	
5	EST	Indrek Pertelson	
5	POL	Pawel Nastula	
7	JPN	Yasuhiro Kai	
7	BEL	Robert Van de Walle	
—	USA	Leo White	elim.

MEN'S HEAVYWEIGHT (+95 KG/+209 LBS) / July 27

RANK	CTRY	ATHLETE	
1	EUN	David Khakhaleichvili	
2	JPN	Naoya Ogawa	
3	FRA	David Douillet	
3	HUN	Imre Csosz	
5	BEL	Harry Van Barneveld	
5	CUB	Frank Esteban Moreno Garcia	
7	ESP	Ernesto Perez Lobo	
7	USA	Damon Keeve	

WOMEN'S EXTRA LIGHTWEIGHT (48 KG/106 LBS) / August 2

RANK	CTRY	ATHLETE	
1	FRA	Cecile Nowak	
2	JPN	Ryoko Tamura	
3	TUR	Hulya Senyurt	
3	CUB	Amarilis Savon Carmenaty	
5	GBR	Karen Valerie Briggs	
5	ALG	Salima Souakri	
7	ESP	Yolanda Soler Grajera	
7	VEN	Maria Elena Villapol Blanco	

WOMEN'S HALF LIGHTWEIGHT (52 KG/114 LBS) / August 1

RANK	CTRY	ATHLETE	
1	ESP	Almudena Munoz Martinez	
2	JPN	Noriko Mizoguchi	
3	CHN	Zhongyun Li	
3	GBR	Sharon Rendle	
5	ITA	Alessandra Giungi	
5	NED	Jessica Gal	
7	ARG	Claudia C. Mariani Ambrueso	
7	POR	Paula Saldanha	
—	USA	Jo Quiring	

WOMEN'S LIGHTWEIGHT (56 KG/123 LBS) / July 31

RANK	CTRY	ATHLETE	
1	ESP	Miriam Blasco Soto	
2	GBR	Nicola Kim Fairbrother	
3	JPN	Chiyori Tateno	
3	CUB	Driulis Gonzalez Morales	
5	USA	Kate Marie Donahoo	
5	BEL	Nicole Flagothier	
7	FRA	Catherine Arnaud	
7	POL	Maria Gontowicz Szalas	

WOMEN'S HALF MIDDLEWEIGHT (61 KG/134 LBS) / July 30

RANK	CTRY	ATHLETE	
1	FRA	Catherine Fleury	
2	ISR	Yael Arad	
3	CHN	Di Zhang	
3	EUN	Elena Petrova	
5	GER	Frauke-Imke Eickoff	
5	KOR	Koo Hyun-Sook	
7	VEN	Xiomara Y. Griffith Mahon	
7	ESP	Begona Gomez Martin	
—	USA	Lynn Roethke	elim.

WOMEN'S MIDDLEWEIGHT (66 KG/145 LBS) / July 29

RANK	CTRY	ATHLETE	
1	CUB	Odalis Reve Jimenez	
2	ITA	Emanuela Pierantozzi	
3	BEL	Heidi Rakels	
3	GBR	Kate Howey	
5	GER	Alexandra Schreiber	
5	FRA	Claire Lecat	
7	USA	Grace L. Jividen	
7	ARG	Laura A. Martinel Acuna	

WOMEN'S HALF HEAVYWEIGHT (72 KG/158 LBS) / July 28

RANK	CTRY	ATHLETE	
1	KOR	Kim Mi-Jung	
2	JPN	Yoko Tanabe	
3	NED	Irene de Kok	
3	FRA	Laetitia Meignan	
5	GER	Regina Felicitas Schuttenhelm	
5	GBR	Josie Horton	
7	POL	Katarzyna Juszczak	
5	SWE	Katarina Hakansson	
—	USA	Sandra Bacher	elim.

WOMEN'S HEAVYWEIGHT (+72 KG/158 LBS) / July 27

RANK	CTRY	ATHLETE	
1	CHN	Xiaoyan Zhuang	
2	CUB	Este Rodriguez	
3	FRA	Natalia Lupino	
3	JPN	Yoko Sakaue	
5	GER	Claudia Edeltraud Weber	
5	POL	Beata Maksymow	
7	EUN	Svetlana Goundarenko	
7	HUN	Eva Granicz	
—	USA	Colleen Rosensteel	elim.

MODERN PENTATHLON
INDIVIDUAL / July 26

RANK	CTRY	ATHLETE	FENCE	SWIM	SHOOT	RUN	RIDE	TOTAL
1	POL	Arkadiusz Skrzypaszek	1,000	1,252	1,120	1,147	1,040	5,559
2	HUN	Attila Mizser	898	1,208	1,135	1,213	992	5,446
3	EUN	Edouard Zenovka	830	1,300	1,240	1,255	736	5,361
4	EUN	Anatoli Starostine	864	1,236	1,120	1,117	1,010	5,347
5	ITA	Roberto Bomprezzi	847	1,148	1,105	1,216	1,010	5,326
6	SWE	Hakan Norebrink	847	1,272	1,030	1,072	1,100	5,321
7	ROM	Marian Gheorghe 8	78	1,252	955	1,108	1,100	5,293
8	GBR	Graham Brookhouse	762	1,304	1,015	1,141	1,070	5,292
9	USA	J. Mike Gostigian	728	1,324	1,105	1,138	980	5,275
20	USA	Rob Stull	983	1,232	1,000	1,114	875	5,204
25	USA	Jim Haley	796	1,256	1,090	988	1,040	5,170

TEAM / July 29

RANK	CTRY	ATHLETES	POINTS
1	POL	Maciej Czyzowicz / Arkadiusz Skrzypaszek / Dariusz Gozdziak	16,018
2	EUN	Anatoli Starostine / Dmitri Svatkovski / Edouard Zenovka	15,924
3	ITA	Gianluca Tiberti / Carlo Massullo / Roberto Bomprezzi	15,760
4	USA	Mike Gostigian / Jim Haley / Rob Stull	15,649
5	HUN	Laszlo Fabian / Attila Kalnoki-Kis / Attila Mizser	15,571
6	GBR	Graham Raymond Brookhouse / Richard Phelps / Dominic J. Mahony	15,571
7	FRA	Joel Bouzou / Christophe Ruer / Sebastien Deleigne	15,441
8	SWE	Per Olov Danielsson / Hakan Norebrink / Per Nyqvist	15,428

ROWING
MEN'S SINGLE SCULLS / August 1

RANK	CTRY	ATHLETE	TIME
1	GER	Thomas Lange	6:51.40
2	TCH	Vaclav Chalupa	6:52.93
3	POL	Kajetan Broniewski	6:56.82
4	NZL	Eric Franciscus Verdonk	6:57.45
5	EST	Juri Jaanson	7:12.92
6	ARG	Sergi Fernandez Gonzalez	7:15.53
19	USA	Greg Walker	7:12.32

MEN'S DOUBLE SCULLS / August 1

RANK	CTRY	ATHLETES	TIME
1	AUS	Stephen Mark Hawkins / Peter Antonie	6:17.32
2	AUT	Arnold Jonke / Christoph Zerbst	6:18.42
3	NED	Henk-Jan Zwolle / Nico Rienks	6:22.82
4	EST	Priit Tasane / Roman Lutoskin	6:23.34
5	POL	Andrzej Marszalek / Andrzej Krzepinski	6:24.32
6	ESP	Miguel Alvarez Villar / Jose Antonio Merin Hierro	6:26.96
9	USA	Greg Springer / Jonathan Smith	6:26.67

MEN'S QUADRUPLE SCULLS / August 2

RANK	CTRY	ATHLETE	TIME
1	GER	Andre Willms / Andreas Hajek / Stephan Volkert / Michael Steinbach	5:45.17
2	NOR	Lars Bjonness / Rolf Thorsen / Kjetil Undset / Per Albert Saetersdal	5:47.09
3	ITA	Gianluca Farina / Rossano Galtarossa / Alessandro Corona / Filippo Soffici	5:47.33
4	SUI	Ueli Bodenmann / Alexander Ruckstuhl / Beat Schwerzmann / Marc-Sven Nater	5:47.39
5	NED	Hans Kelderman / Ronald Florijn / Koos Maasdijk / Rutger Arisz	5:48.92
6	FRA	Fiorenzo Di Giovanni / Fabrice Leclerc / Yves Lamarque / Samuel Barathay	5:54.80
8	USA	Chip McKibben / Robert Kaehler / John Riley / Keir Pearson	5:52.48

MEN'S PAIRS W/O COXSWAIN / August 1

RANK	CTRY	ATHLETE	TIME
1	GBR	Steven Redgrave / Matthew Clive Pinsent	6:27.72
2	GER	Peter J. Hoeltzenbein / Colin Von Ettingshausen	6:32.68
3	SLO	Iztok Cop / Denis Zvegelj	6:33.43
4	FRA	Michel Andrieux / Jean Christophe Rolland	6:36.34
5	BEL	Jaak Van Driessche / Luc Goiris	6:38.20
6	USA	Peter Sharis / John Pescatore	6:39.23

MEN'S PAIRS W/COXSWAIN / August 2

RANK	CTRY	ATHLETE	TIME
1	GBR	Jonathan Searle / Greg Searle / Garry Herbert	6:49.83
2	ITA	Carmine Abbagnale / Giuseppe Abbagnale / Giuseppe Di Capua	6:50.98
3	ROM	Dimitrie Popescu / Nicolaie Taga / Dumitru Raducanu	6:51.58
4	GER	Thomas Woddow / Michael Peters / Peter Thiede	6:56.98
5	CUB	Ismael Carbonell Same / Arnaldo Rodriguez Silva / Roberto Ojeda Gonzalez	6:58.26
6	FRA	Patrick Berthou / Laurent Lacasa / Emmanuel Bunoz	7:03.01
8	USA	John Moore / Aaron Pollock / Stephen Shellans	6:54.78

MEN'S FOUR OARS W/COXSWAIN / August 1

RANK	CTRY	ATHLETES	TIME
1	ROM	Viorel Talapan / Iulica Ruican / Dimitrie Popescu / Nicolaie Taga / Dumitru Raducanu	5:59.37
2	GER	Uwe Jorg Kellner / Ralf Brudel / Thoralf Peters / Karsten Finger / Hendrik Reiher	6:00.34
3	POL	Jacek Streich / Wojciech Jankowski / Tomasz Tomiak / Maciej Lasicki / Michal Cieslak	6:03.27
4	USA	James Neil / Teo Bielefeld / Sean Hall / Jack Rusher / Tim Evans	6:06.03
5	FRA	Yannick Schulte / Philippe Lot / Daniel Fauche / Jean Paul Vergnes / Jean-Pierre Huguet-Balent	6:06.82
6	EUN	Veniamine Bout / Igor Bortnitski / Vladimir Romanichine / Guennadi Krioutchkine / Petr Petrinitch	6:12.13

MEN'S FOUR OARS W/O COXSWAIN / August 2

RANK	CTRY	ATHLETE	TIME
1	AUS	Andrew Cooper / Michael McKay / Nicholas Green / James Tomkins	5:55.04
2	USA	Doug Burden / Jeff McLaughlin / Thomas Bohrer / Patrick Manning	5:56.68
3	SLO	Janez Klemencic / Saso Mirjanic / Milan Jansa / Sadik Mujkic	5:58.24
4	GER	Armin Weyrauch / Matthias Ungemach / Dirk Peter Balster / Markus Vogt	5:58.39
5	NED	Bart Peters / Niels Van Der Zwan / Jaap Krijtenburg / Sven Schwarz	5:59.14
6	NZL	Scott Alexander Brownlee / Christopher S. White / Patrick Edward Peoples / Campbell Clayton-Greene	6:02.13

MEN'S EIGHT OARS W/COXSWAIN / August 2

RANK	CTRY	ATHLETES	TIME
1	CAN	John William Wallace / Bruce Robertson / Michael Joseph Forgeron / Darren Barber / Robert Davies Marland / Michael G. Rascher / Andrew Crosby / Derek Porter / Terrence Michael Paul	5:29.53
2	ROM	Ioan Iulian Vizitiu / Danut Dobre / Claudiu Gabriel Marin / Iulica Ruican / Viorel Talapan / Vasile Dorel Nastase / Valentin Robu / Vasile Ionel Mastacan / Marin Gheorghe	5:29.67
3	GER	Frank Joerg Richter / Thorsten Streppelhoff / Detlef Kirchloff / Armin Eich-holz / Bahne Rabe / Hans Sennewald / Ansgar Wessling / Roland Baar / Manfred Willi Klein	5:31.00
4	USA	Michael Francis Teti / James Scott Munn / Christian Sahs / Jeff Gerard Klepacki / Robert Tharp Shepherd / Malcolm Baker / Richard Kennelly / John MacDougall Parker / Michael James Moore	5:33.18
5	AUS	Simon David Spriggs / Peter James Murphy / Wayne David Diplock / Jaime Fernandez / Ben Philip Dodwell / Sam Patten / Boden Joseph Hanson / Robert Geoffrey Scott / David Edward Garr Colvin	5:33.72
6	GBR	Martin Cross / Tim Foster / Richard Phelps / Jim Walker / Ben Hunt-Davis / Steve Turner / Rupert Obholzer / Jonathan Singfield / Adrian Ellison	5:39.92

WOMEN'S SINGLE SCULLS / August 2

RANK	CTRY	ATHLETE	TIME
1	ROM	Elisabeta Lipa	7:25.54
2	BEL	Annelies Bredael	7:26.64
3	CAN	Silken Suzette Laumann	7:28.85
4	USA	Anne Marden	7:29.84
5	SWE	Maria Brandin	7:37.55
6	FRA	Corinne LeMoal	7:41.85

WOMEN'S DOUBLE SCULLS / August 1

RANK	CTRY	ATHLETE	TIME
1	GER	Kerstin Koeppen / Kathrin Boron	6:49.00
2	ROM	Veronica Cochelea / Elisabeta Lipa	6:51.47
3	CHN	Xiaoli Gu / Huali Lu	6:55.16
4	NZL	Philippa June Baker / Brenda Catherine Lawson	6:56.81
5	GBR	Annabel Juliet Eyres / Alison Jane Gill	7:06.62
6	EUN	Sariia Zakirova / Inna Frolova	7:09.45
11	USA	Cynthia Ryder / Mary Mazzio	7:12.24

WOMEN'S QUADRUPLE SCULLS / August 2

RANK	CTRY	ATHLETE	TIME
1	GER	Kerstin Mueller / Sybille Schmidt / Birgit Peter / Kristina Mundt	6:20.18
2	ROM	Constanta Pipota / Doina Ignat / Veronica Cochelea / Anisoara Dobre	6:24.34
3	EUN	Ekaterina Khodotovitch / Antonina Zelikovitch / Tatiana Oustioujanina / Elena Khloptseva	6:25.07
4	NED	Laurien Vermulst / Marjan Pentenga / Anita Meiland / Harriet Van Ettekoven	6:32.40
5	USA	Kristine Karlson / Alison Townley / Serena Eddy-Moulton / Michelle Knox-Zaloom	6:32.65
6	TCH	Lubica Novotnikova / Michaela Buresova / Hana Kafkova / Irena Soukupova	6:35.99

WOMEN'S PAIRS W/O COXSWAIN / August 1

RANK	CTRY	ATHLETES	TIME
1	CAN	Marnie Elizabeth McBean / Kathleen Heddle	7:06.22
2	GER	Stefani Werremeier / Ingeburg Schwerzmann	7:07.96
3	USA	Stephanie Maxwell-Pierson / Anna B. Seaton	7:08.11
4	FRA	Christine Gosse / Isabelle Danjou	7:08.70
5	GBR	Joanne Sarah Turvey / Miriam Batten	7:17.28
6	BUL	Violeta Ivanova Zareva / Teodora Ivanova Zareva	7:32.67

WOMEN'S FOUR OARS W/O COXSWAIN / August 1

RANK	CTRY	ATHLETES	TIME
1	CAN	Kirsten Barnes / Brenda Susan Taylor / Jessica Monroe / Kay Frances Worthington	6:30.85
2	USA	Shelagh Donohoe / Cindy Eckert / Amy Fuller / Carol Feeney	6:31.86
3	GER	Antje Frank / Gabriele Mehl / Birte Siech / Annette Hohn	6:32.34
4	CHN	Xirong Liu / Yanwen He / Mianying Cao / Shouying Zhou	6:32.50
5	ROM	Victoria Lepadatu / Iulia Bobeica / Adriana Bazon / Maria Padurariu	6:37.24
6	AUS	Jodie Dobson / Emmelia Anne Snook / Megan Leanne Still / Kate Elizabeth Slatter	6:41.72

WOMEN'S EIGHT OARS W/COXSWAIN / August 2

RANK	CTRY	ATHLETES	TIME
1	CAN	Kirsten Barnes / Brenda Taylor / Megan Delehanty / Shannon Crawford / Marnie McBean / Kay Worthington / Jessica Monroe / Kathleen Heddle / Lesley Thompson	6:02.62
2	ROM	Doina Liliana Snep / Doina Robu / Ioana Olteanu / Victoria Lepadatu / Iulia Bobeica / Viorica Neculai / Adriana Bazon / Maria Padurariu / Elena Georgescu	6:06.26
3	GER	Annegret Strauch / Sylvia Doerdelmann / Kathrin Haacker / Dana Pyritz / Cerstin Petersmann / Ute Wagner / Christiane Harzendorf / Judith Zeidler / Daniela Neunast	6:07.80
4	EUN	Svetlana Fil / Marina Znak / Irina Gribko / Sarmite Stone / Marina Souproun / Natalia Stassiouk / Natalia Grigorieva / Ekaterina Kotko / Elena Medvedeva	6:09.68
5	CHN	Lin Zhiai / Ma Lingin / Pei Jiayun / He Yanwen / Liu Xirong / Liang Xiling / Cao Mianying / Zhou Shouying / Li Ronghua	6:12.08
6	USA	Tina Brown / Shannon Day / Betsy McCagg / Mary McCagg / Sarah Gengler / Tracy Rude / Kelley Jones / Diana Olson / Yasmin Farooq	6:12.25

SHOOTING
MEN'S AIR PISTOL / July 28

RANK	CTRY	ATHLETE	SCORE	TOTAL	
1	CHN	Wang Yifu	585	684.8	FOR
2	EUN	Sergei Pyjianov	584	684.1	
3	ROM	Sorin Babii	586	684.1	
4	CHN	Xu Haifeng	583	681.5	
5	FIN	Sakari Paasonen	582	680.1	
6	POL	Jerzy Pietrzak	582	680.1	
7	BUL	Tayno Kiryakov	583	679.7	
8	ITA	R. Di Donna	581	678.5	
14T	USA	Ben Amonette	577		
33T	USA	Darius Young	571		

MEN'S FREE PISTOL / July 26

RANK	CTRY	ATHLETE	SCORE	TOTAL	
1	EUN	K. Loukachik	567	658	
2	CHN	Wang Yifu	565	657	
3	SWE	Ragnar Skanaker	566	657	
4	USA	Darius Young	566	655	
5	ROM	Sorin Babii	561	653	
6	HUN	Istvan Agh	561	652	
7	CHN	Xu Haifeng	565	652	
8	BUL	Tanyo Kiryakov	567	618	AB
19	USA	Ben Amonette	555		

MEN'S RAPID-FIRE PISTOL / July 30

RANK	CTRY	ATHLETE	SCORE	TOTAL	
1	GER	Ralf Schumann	789	885	FOR
2	LAT	A. Kuzmins	785	882	
3	EUN	V. Vokmianine	786	882	
4	POL	D. Kucharczyk	783	880	
5	USA	John McNally	781 semi.		
6	EUN	M. Ignatiouk	779		
9	USA	Roger Mar	586		

MEN'S RUNNING GAME TARGET / August 1

RANK	CTRY	ATHLETE	SCORE	TOTAL	
1	GER	Michael Jakosits	580	673	FOR
2	EUN	Anatolij Asrabaev	579	672	
3	TCH	Lubos Racansky	576	670	
4	EUN	Andrey Vasiliev	576	667	
5	HUN	Jozsef Sike	576	667	
6	GER	Jens Zimmermann	578	667	
11	USA	Rusty Hill	570		
15	USA	Fritz Allen	564		

MEN'S AIR RIFLE / July 27

RANK	CTRY	ATHLETE	SCORE	TOTAL	
1	EUN	Iouri Fedkine	593	695.3	FOR
2	FRA	Franck Badiou	591	691.9	
3	GER	Johann Riederer	590	691.7	
4	FRA	Jean Amat	590	691.6	
5	IOP	G. Maksimovic	592	690.6	
6	AUT	Thomas Farnik	590	690.2	
7	USA	Robert Foth	590	689.4	
8	KOR	Chae Keun-Bae	590	687.8	
11T	USA	David Johnson	589		

MEN'S SMALLBORE RIFLE, THREE POSITIONS / July 31

RANK	CTRY	ATHLETE	SCORE	TOTAL	
1	EUN	Gracha Petikian	1169	1267.4	FOR
2	USA	Robert Foth	1169	1266.6	
3	JPN	Ryohei Koba	1171	1265.9	
4	FIN	Juha Hirvi	1172 OR	1264.8	
5	NOR	Harald Stenvaag	1166	1264.6	
6	SLO	Rajmond Debevec	1167	1262.6	
7	SWE	P. Gabrielsson	1168	1261.1	
8	HUN	Zsolt Vari	1164	1258.6	
21T	USA	David Johnson	1155		

MEN'S SMALLBORE RIFLE, PRONE / July 29

RANK	CTRY	ATHLETE	SCORE	TOTAL	
1	KOR	Lee Eun-Chul	597	702.5	FOR
2	NOR	Harald Stenvaag	597	701.4	
3	IOP	S. Pletikosic	597	701.1	
4	GER	Hubert Bichler	598 NOR	701.1	
5	FRA	Michel Bury	597	700.0	
6	FIN	Juha Hirvi	597	699.5	
7	SWE	P. Gabrielsson	597	699.5	
8	EUN	G. Petikiane	597	699.2	
9	USA	Bill Meek	596		
18	USA	Mike Anti	594		

SKEET MIXED / July 28

RANK	CTRY	ATHLETE	SCORE	TOTAL	
1	CHN	Zhang Shan	200	223	FOR
2	PER	Juan Jorge Giha	198	222	
3	ITA	Bruno Mario Rossetti	198	222	
4	ROM	Ioan Toman	198	222	
5	ESP	Jose Maria Colorado	199	222	
6	USA	Matthew Dryke	198	221	
12	USA	James T. Graves	197		
25T	USA	Connie Fluker	145		

TRAP MIXED / August 2

RANK	CTRY	ATHLETE	SCORE	TOTAL	
1	TCH	Petr Hrdlicka	195	219	FOR
2	JPN	Kazumi Watanabe	195	219	
3	ITA	Marco Venturini	195	218	
4	GER	Joerg Damme	195	218	
5	TCH	Pavel Kubec	196	218	
6	USA	Jay Waldron	195	217	
16T	USA	Bret Erickson	191		
29T	USA	Todd Graves	140		

WOMEN'S AIR PISTOL / August 1

RANK	CTRY	ATHLETE	SCORE	TOTAL	
1	EUN	Marina Logvinenko	387	486.4	FOR
2	IOP	Jasna Sekaric	389	486.4	
3	BUL	Maria Grousdeva	383	481.6	
4	CHN	Lina Wang	381	479.7	
5	SWE	Cris Kajd	381	478.9	
6	ESP	M. Fernandez	382	478.5	
7	ROM	D. Dumitrascu	381	478.1	
8	POL	Miroslawa Sagun	381	477.8	
24T	USA	Connie Petracek	375		
37T	USA	Libby Callahan	372		

WOMEN'S SPORT PISTOL / July 27

RANK	CTRY	ATHLETE	SCORE	TOTAL	
1	EUN	M. Logvinenko	587	684	FOR
2	CHN	Li Duihong	586	680	
3	MGL	D. Munkhbayar	584	679	
4	CRO	Mirela Skoko	578	677	
5	EUN	N. Saloukvadze	583	676	
6	IOP	Jasna Sekaric	583	676	
7	AUS	L. Freh	581	675	
8	POL	Julita Macur	578	674	
24T	USA	Roxane Thompson	572		
29T	USA	Connie Petracek	570		

WOMEN'S AIR RIFLE / July 26

RANK	CTRY	ATHLETE	SCORE	TOTAL	
1	KOR	Yeo Kab-Soon	396	498.2	FOR
2	BUL	Vesela Letcheva	396	495.3	
3	IOP	Aka Binder	393	495.1	
4	TCH	Dagmar Bilkova	393	494.9	
5	EUN	V. Tcherkassova	394	494.6	
6	KOR	Lee Eun-Ju	392	492.6	
7	HUN	Eva Forian	392	492.4	
8	BSH	Mirjana Horvat	393	491.6	
11T	USA	Launi Meili	391		
11T	USA	Debra Sinclair	391		

WOMEN'S SMALLBORE RIFLE, 3-POS. / July 30

RANK	CTRY	ATHLETE	SCORE	TOTAL	
1	USA	Launi Meili	587	684.3	FOR
2	BUL	Nonka Matova	584	682.7	
3	POL	M. Ksiazkiewicz	585	681.5	
4	HUN	Eva Forian	582	679.5	
5	CRO	Suzana Skoko	580	678.7	
6	BUL	Vesela Letcheva	581	678.0	
7	CAN	Sharon Bowes	580	673.6	
8	HUN	Eva Joo	580	673.6	
12	USA	Ann-Marie Pfiffner	578		

SOCCER (FOOTBALL) / July 24 – August 8

RANK	CTRY	SCORE	
1	ESP	3-2	(Final)
2	POL		
3	GHA	1-0	(3rd-4th)
4	AUS		
		ESP vs. GHA	2-0 (semi)
		POL vs. AUS	6-1 (semi)
—	USA	Elim. pool play	

USA TEAM: Yari Allnutt / Dario Brose /Michael Burns / Troy Dayak / Anthony Feuer / Brad Friedel / Rhett Hardy / Chris Henderson / Michael Huwiler / Zak Ibsen / Erik Imler / Cobi Jones / Manuel Lagos / Alexi Lalas / Michael Lapper / Joe Moore / Curtis Onalfo / Cameron Rast / Claudio Reyna / Steve Snow / Dante Washington

SWIMMING

MEN'S 50-METER FREESTYLE / July 30

RANK	CTRY	ATHLETE	TIME	
1	EUN	Alexander Popov	21.91	OR
2	USA	Matt Biondi	22.09	
3	USA	Tom Jager	22.30	
4T	RSA	Peter Rowan Williams	22.50	
4T	FRA	Christophe Kalfayan	22.50	
6	GBR	Mark Foster	22.52	
7	EUN	Guennadi Prigoda	22.54	
8	GER	Nils Rudolph	22.73	

MEN'S 100-METER FREESTYLE / July 28

RANK	CTRY	ATHLETE	TIME
1	EUN	Alexander Popov	49.02
2	BRA	Gustavo Borges	49.43
3	FRA	Stephen Caron	49.50
4	USA	Jon Olsen	49.51
5	USA	Matt Biondi	49.53
6	SWE	Tommy Werner	49.63
7	GER	Christian A. Troeger	49.84
8	EUN	Guennadi Prigoda	50.25

MEN'S 200-METER FREESTYLE / July 26

RANK	CTRY	ATHLETE	TIME	
1	EUN	Evgueni Sadovyi	1:46.70	OR
2	SWE	Anders Holmertz	1:46.86	
3	FIN	Alexander Kasvio	1:47.63	
4	POL	Artur Wojdat	1:48.24	
5	EUN	Vladimir Pychnenko	1:48.32	
6	USA	Joe Hudepohl	1:48.36	
7	GER	Steffen Zesner	1:48.84	
8	USA	Doug Gjertsen	1:50.57	

MEN'S 400-METER FREESTYLE / July 27

RANK	CTRY	ATHLETE	TIME	
1	EUN	Evgueni Sadovyi	3:45.00	WR
2	AUS	Kieren Perkins	3:45.16	
3	SWE	Anders Holmertz	3:46.77	
4	POL	Artur Wojdat	3:48.10	
5	AUS	Ian Robert Brown	3:48.79	
6	GER	Sebastian Wiese	3:49.06	
7	GER	Stefan Pfeiffer	3:49.75	
8	NZL	Danyon Loader	3:49.97	
11	USA	Sean Killion	3:52.76	
—	USA	Dan Jorgensen	scratched finals	

MEN'S 1500-METER FREESTYLE / July 31

RANK	CTRY	ATHLETE	TIME	
1	AUS	Kieren John Perkins	14:43.48	WR
2	AUS	Glen Housman	14:55.29	
3	GER	Joerg Hoffman	15:02.29	
4	GER	Stefan Pfeiffer	15:04.28	
5	GBR	Ian Wilson	15:13.35	
6	SLO	Igor Majcen	15:19.12	
7	USA	Lawrence Frostad	15:19.41	
8	EUN	Viktor Andreev	15:33.94	
12	USA	Sean Killion	15:27.49 #	

prelims.

MEN'S 100-METER BACKSTROKE / July 30

RANK	CTRY	ATHLETE	TIME	
1	CAN	Mark Tewksburg	53.98	OR
2	USA	Jeff Rouse	54.04	
3	USA	David Berkoff	54.78	
4	ESP	Martin Lopez-Zubero	54.96	
5	EUN	Vladimir Selkov	55.49	
6	FRA	Franck Schott	55.72	
7	CUB	Rodolfo Falcon Cabrera	55.76	
8	GER	Dirk Richter	56.26	

MEN'S 200-METER BACKSTROKE / July 28

RANK	CTRY	ATHLETE	TIME	
1	ESP	Martin Lopez-Zubero	1:58.47	OR
2	EUN	Vladimir Selkov	1:58.87	
3	ITA	Stefano Battistelli	1:59.40	
4	JPN	Hajime Itoi	1:59.52	
5	USA	Tripp Schwenk	1:59.73	
6	GER	Tino Weber	1:59.78	
7	HUN	Tamas Deutsch	2:00.06	
8	BEL	Stefaan Maene	2:00.91	
—	USA	Royce Sharp	2:00.97#	

scratched finals, prelim. time

MEN'S 100-METER BREASTSTROKE / July 26

RANK	CTRY	ATHLETE	TIME	
1	USA	Nelson Diebel	1:01.50	OR
2	HUN	Norbert Rozsa	1:01.68	
3	AUS	Philip Rogers	1:01.76	
4	JPN	Akira Hayashi	1:01.86	
5	EUN	Vassili Ivanov	1:01.87	
6	EUN	Dmitri Volkov	1:02.07	
7	GBR	Nick Gillingham	1:02.32	
8	GBR	Adrian David Moorhouse	1:02.33	
10	USA	Hans Dersch	1:02.39 #	

Final B

MEN'S 200-METER BREASTSTROKE / July 28

RANK	CTRY	ATHLETE	TIME	
1	USA	Mike Barrowman	2:10.16	WR
2	HUN	Norbert Rozsa	2:11.23	
3	GBR	Nick Gillingham	2:11.29	
4	ESP	Sergio Lopez Miro	2:13.29	
5	HUN	Karoly Guttler	2:13.32	
6	AUS	Philip John Rogers	2:13.59	
7	JPN	Kenji Watanabe	2:14.70	
8	JPN	Akira Hayashi	2:15.11	
12	USA	Roque Santos	2:15.73	

MEN'S 100-METER BUTTERFLY / July 27

RANK	CTRY	ATHLETE	TIME
1	USA	Pablo Morales	53.32
2	POL	Rafal Szukala	53.35
3	SUR	Anthony Nesty	53.41
4	EUN	Pavel Khnykine	53.81
5	USA	Melvin Stewart	54.04
6	CAN	Marcel Gery	54.18
7	ESP	Martin Lopez-Zubero	54.19
8	EUN	Vladislav Koulikov	54.26

MEN'S 200-METER BUTTERFLY / July 30

RANK	CTRY	ATHLETE	TIME	
1	USA	Melvin Stewart	1:56.26	OR
2	NZL	Danyon Loader	1:57.93	
3	FRA	Franck Esposito	1:58.51	
4	POL	Rafal Szukala	1:58.89	
5	JPN	Keiichi Kawanaka	1:58.97	
6	EUN	Denis Pankratov	1:58.98	
7	ROM	Robert Doru Pinter	1:59.34	
8	AUS	Martin Wade Roberts	1:59.64	
10	USA	David Wharton	2:01.08 #	

Final B

MEN'S 200-METER IND. MEDLEY / July 31

RANK	CTRY	ATHLETE	TIME
1	HUN	Tamas Darnyi	2:00.76
2	USA	Greg Burgess	2:00.97
3	HUN	Attila Czene	2:01.00
4	FIN	Jani Nikanor Sievinen	2:01.28
5	GER	Christian Gessner	2:01.97
6	USA	Ron Karnaugh	2:02.18
7	AUS	Matthew Stephen Dunn	2:02.79
8	CAN	Gary Myers Anderson	2:04.30

MEN'S 400-METER IND. MEDLEY / July 27

RANK	CTRY	ATHLETE	TIME
1	HUN	Tamas Darnyi	4:14.23 OR
2	USA	Eric Namesnik	4:15.57
3	ITA	Luca Sacchi	4:16.34
4	USA	David Wharton	4:17.26
5	GER	Christian Gessner	4:17.88
6	GER	Patrick Kuhl	4:19.66
7	EUN	Serguei Mariniouk	4:22.93
8	JPN	Takahiro Fujimoto	4:23.86

MEN'S 4x100-METER FREESTYLE RELAY / July 29

RANK	CTRY	ATHLETES	TIME
1	USA	Joe Hudepohl / Matt Biondi / Tom Jager / Jon Olsen / Shaun Jordan (prelims)	3:16.74
2	EUN	Pavel Khnykine / Guennadi Prigoda / Iouri Bashkatov / Alexander Popov	3:17.56
3	GER	Christian A. Troeger / Dirk Richter / Steffen Zesner / Mark Pinger	3:17.90
4	FRA	Christophe Kalfayan / Franck Schott / Frederic Lefevre / Stephan Caron	3:19.16
5	SWE	Tommy Werner / Hakan Karlsson / Fredrik Leisler / Anders Holmertz	3:20.10
6	BRA	Jose Carlos Souza-Junior / Gustavo Borges / Emmanuel Fortes Nascimento / Cristano Rosit Michelena	3:20.99
7	GBR	Roland George Lee / Mark Foster / Mike Fibbens / Paul Tony Howe	3:21.75
8	AUS	Christopher John Fydler / Andrew James Baildon / Thomas Stachewicz / Darren Niel Lange	3:22.04

MEN'S 4x200-METER FREESTYLE RELAY / July 27

RANK	CTRY	ATHLETES	TIME
1	EUN	Dmitri Lepikov / Vladimir Pychnenko / Veniamin Taianovitch / Evgueni Sadovyi	7:11.95 WR
2	SWE	Christer Wallin / Anders Holmertz / Tommy Werner / Lars Frolander	7:15.51
3	USA	Joe Hudepohl / Melvin Stewart / Jon Olsen / Doug Gjertsen / Scott Jaffe (prelims) / Dan Jorgensen (prelims)	7:16.23
4	GER	Peter Sitt / Steffen Zesner / Andreas Szigat / Stefan Pfeiffer	7:16.58
5	ITA	Roberto Gleria / Giorgio Lamberti / Massimo Trevisan / Stefano Battistelli	7:18.10
6	GBR	Paul Rory Palmer / Steven John Mellor / Stephen George Akers / Paul Tony Howe	7:22.57
7	BRA	Gustavo Borges / Emmanuel Fortes Nascimento / Teofilo Ferreira Laborne / Christiano Rosit Michelena	7:24.03
8	AUS	Ian Brown / Deane Pieters / Kieren Perkins / Duncan Armstrong	DQ

MEN'S 4x100-METER MEDLEY RELAY / July 31

RANK	CTRY	ATHLETES	TIME
1	USA	Jeff Rouse / Nelson Diebel / Pablo Morales / Jon Olsen / Matt Biondi (prelims) / Hans Dersch (prelims) / Melvin Stewart (prelims) / David Berkoff (prelims)	3:36.93EWR
2	EUN	Vladimir Selkov / Vassili Ivanov / Pavel Khnykine / Alexander Popov	3:38.56
3	CAN	Mark Tewksbury / Jonathan Thomas Cleveland / Marcel Gery / Stephen Clarke	3:39.66
4	GER	Tino Weber / Mark Warnecke / Christian Keller / Mark Pinger	3:40.19
5	FRA	Franck Schott / Stephane Vossart / Bruno Gutzeit / Stephan Caron	3:40.51
6	HUN	Tamas Deutsch / Norbert Rozsa / Peter Horvath / Bela Szabados	3:42.03
7	AUS	Thomas Stachewicz / Philip John Rogers / Jon Sieben / Christopher John Fydler	3:42.65
8	JPN	Hajime Itoi / Akira Hayashi / Keiichi Kawanaka / Tsutomu Nakano	3:43.25

WOMEN'S 50-METER FREESTYLE / July 31

RANK	CTRY	ATHLETE	TIME
1	CHN	Yang Wenyi	24.79 WR
2	CHN	Zhuang Yong	25.08
3	USA	Angel Martino	25.23
4	FRA	Catherine Plewinski	25.36
5	USA	Jenny Thompson	25.37
6	EUN	Natalia Mechtcheriakova	25.47
7	GER	Simone Osygus	25.74
8	NED	Inge De Bruijn	25.84

WOMEN'S 100-METER FREESTYLE / July 26

RANK	CTRY	ATHLETE	TIME
1	CHN	Zhuang Yong	54.65 OR
2	USA	Jenny Thompson	54.84
3	GER	Franziska Van Almsick	54.94
4	USA	Nicole Haislett	55.19
5	FRA	Catherine Plewinski	55.72
6	CHN	Le Jingyi	55.89
7	GER	Simone Osygus	55.93
8	NED	Karin Brienesse	56.59

WOMEN'S 200-METER FREESTYLE /

RANK	CTRY	ATHLETE	TIME
1	USA	Nicole Haislett	1:57.90
2	GER	Franziska Van Almsick	1:58.00
3	GER	Kerstin Kielgass	1:59.67
4	FRA	Catherine Plewinski	1:59.88
5	ROM	Liliana Dobreseu	2:00.48
6	JPN	Suzu Chiba	2:00.64
7	EUN	Olga Kiritchenko	2:00.90
8	CHN	Lu Bin	2:02.10
—	USA	Jenny Thompson	2:01.71 #

scratched finals, prelim. time

WOMEN'S 400-METER FREESTYLE / July 28

RANK	CTRY	ATHLETE	TIME
1	GER	Dagmar Hase	4:07.18
2	USA	Janet Evans	4:07.37
3	AUS	Hayley Jane Lewis	4:11.22
4	USA	Erika M. Hansen	4:11.50
5	GER	Kerstin Kielgass	4:11.52
6	BEL	Isabelle Arnould	4:13.75
7	SWE	Malin Nilsson	4:14.10
8	JPN	Suzu Chiba	4:15.71

WOMEN'S 800-METER FREESTYLE / July 30

RANK	CTRY	ATHLETE	TIME
1	USA	Janet Evans	8:25.52
2	AUS	Hayley Lewis	8:30.34
3	GER	Jana Henke	8:30.99
4	NZL	Philippa Maree Langrell	8:35.57
5	NOR	Irene Dalby	8:37.12
6	TCH	Olga Splichalova	8:37.66
7	USA	Erika Hansen	8:39.25
8	BEL	Isabelle Arnould	8:41.86

WOMEN'S 100-METER BACKSTROKE / July 28

RANK	CTRY	ATHLETE	TIME
1	HUN	Krisztina Egerszegi	1:00.68 OR
2	HUN	Tunde Szabo	1:01.14
3	USA	Lea Loveless	1:01.43
4	AUS	Nicole Dawn Stevenson	1:01.78
5	USA	Janie Wagstaff	1:01.81
6	AUS	Joanne Marie Meehan	1:02.07
7	EUN	Nina Jivanevskaia	1:02.36
8	JPN	Yoko Koikawa	1:03.23

WOMEN'S 200-METER BACKSTROKE / July 31

RANK	CTRY	ATHLETE	TIME
1	HUN	Krisztina Egerszegi	2:07.06 OR
2	GER	Dagmar Hase	2:09.46
3	AUS	Nicole Stevenson	2:10.20
4	USA	Lea Loveless	2:11.54
5	NZL	Anna Katrina Simcic	2:11.99
6	HUN	Tunde Szabo	2:12.94
7	CRC	Sylvia Poll Ahrens	2:12.97
8	AUS	Leigh Christine Habler	2:13.68
9	USA	Janie Wagstaff	2:13.91 #

Final B

WOMEN'S 100-METER BREASTSTROKE / July 29

RANK	CTRY	ATHLETE	TIME
1	EUN	Elena Roudkovskaia	1:08.00
2	USA	Anita Nall	1:08.17
3	AUS	Samantha Riley	1:09.25
4	CAN	Guylaine Cloutier	1:09.71
5	GER	Jana Doerries	1:09.77
6	HUN	Gabriella Csepe	1:10.19
7	ITA	Manuela Dalla Valle	1:10.39
8	GER	Daniela Brendel	1:11.05
12	USA	Megan Kleine	1:11.07 #

Final B

WOMEN'S 200-METER BREASTSTROKE / July 27

RANK	CTRY	ATHLETE	TIME
1	JPN	Kyoko Iwasaki	2:26.65 OR
2	CHN	Lin Li	2:26.85
3	USA	Anita Nall	2:26.88
4	EUN	Elena Roudkovskaia	2:28.47
5	CAN	Guylaine Cloutier	2:29.88
6	CAN	Nathalie Giguere	2:30.11
7	ITA	Manuela Dalla Valle	2:31.21
8	POL	Alicja Peczak	2:31.76
14	USA	Jill Johnson	2:33.89 #

Final B

WOMEN'S 100-METER BUTTERFLY / July 29

RANK	CTRY	ATHLETE	TIME
1	CHN	Hong Qian	58.62 OR
2	USA	Crissy Ahmann-Leighton	58.74
3	FRA	Catherine Plewinski	59.01
4	CHN	Wang Xiashong	59.10
5	AUS	Susan O'Neill	59.69
6	USA	Summer Sanders	59.82
7	GER	Franziska Van Almsick	1:00.70
8	JPN	Rie Shito	1:01.16

WOMEN'S 200-METER BUTTERFLY / July 31

RANK	CTRY	ATHLETE	TIME
1	USA	Summer Sanders	2:08.67
2	CHN	Wang Xiaohang	2:09.01
3	AUS	Susan O'Neill	2:09.03
4	JPN	Mika Haruna	2:09.88
5	JPN	Rie Shito	2:10.24
6	USA	Angie Wester-Krieg	2:11.46
7	DEN	Mette Jacobsen	2:11.87
8	ITA	Ilaria Tocchini	2:13.78

WOMEN'S 200-METER IND. MEDLEY / July 30

RANK	CTRY	ATHLETE	TIME
1	CHN	Li Lin	2:11.65 WR
2	USA	Summer Sanders	2:11.91
3	GER	Daniela Hunger	2:13.92
4	EUN	Elena Dendeberova	2:15.47
5	AUS	Elli Overton	2:15.76
6	CAN	Marianne Luise Limpert	2:17.09
7	CAN	Nancy Sweetnam	2:17.13
8	POL	Ewa Synowska	2:18.85
—	USA	Nicole Haislett	2:17.40 #

scratched finals, prelim time

WOMEN'S 400-METER IND. MEDLEY / July 26

RANK	CTRY	ATHLETE	TIME
1	HUN	Krisztina Egerszegi	4:36.54
2	CHN	LiLin	4:36.73
3	USA	Summer Sanders	4:37.58
4	AUS	Hayley Jane Lewis	4:43.75
5	JPN	Hideko Hiranaka	4:46.24
6	GER	Daniela Hunger	4:47.57
7	JPN	Eri Kimura	4:47.78
8	POL	Ewa Synowska	4:53.32
10	USA	Erika Hansen	4:48.37 #

Final B

WOMEN'S 4x100-METER FREESTYLE RELAY / July 28

RANK	CTRY	ATHLETES	TIME
1	USA	Nicole Haislett / Dara Torres / Angel Martino / Jenny Thompson / Crissy Ahmann-Leighton (prelims) / Ashley Tappin (prelims)	3:39.46 WR
2	CHN	Zhuang Yong / Lu Bin / Yang Wenyi / Le Jingyi	3:40.12
3	GER	Franziska Van Almsick / Simone Osygus / Daniela Hunger / Manuela Stellmach	3:41.60
4	EUN	Natalia Mechtcheriakova / Svetlana Lechoukova / Elena Dendeberova / Elena Choubina	3:43.68
5	NED	Diana Van De Plaats / Mildred Muis / Marianne Muis / Karin Brienesse	3:43.74
6	DEN	Gitta Poulsgaard Jensen / Mette Jacobsen / Berit Raith Puggaard / Mette Norskov Nielsen	3:47.81
7	SWE	Eva Nyberg / Louise Karlsson / Ellenor Svensson / Malin Nilsson	3:48.47
8	CAN	Marianne Luise Limpert / Nicole Dryden / Andrea Nugent / Allison Ann Higson	3:49.37

WOMEN'S 4x100-METER MEDLEY RELAY / July 30

RANK	CTRY	ATHLETES	TIME
1	USA	**Lea Loveless / Anita Nall Crissy Ahmann-Leighton / Jenny Thompson / Nicole Haislett (prelims) / Megan Kleine (prelims) / Summer Sanders (prelims) / Janie Wagstaff (prelims)**	**4:02.54 WR**
2	GER	Dagmar Hase / Jana Doerries / Franziska Van Almsick / Daniela Hunger	4:05.19
3	EUN	Nina Jivanevskaia / Elena Roudkovskaia /Olga Kiritchenko / Natalia Mechtcheriakova	4:06.44
4	CHN	Li Lin / Xia Lou / Hong Qian / Jingyi Le	4:06.78
5	AUS	Nicole Dawn Stevenson / Samantha Linette Riley / Susan O'Neill / Lisa Gaye Curry-Kenny	4:07.01
6	CAN	Nicole Dryden / Guylaine Cloutier / Kristin Louise Topham / Andrea Nugent	4:09.26
7	JPN	Yoko Koikawa / Kyoko Iwasaki / Yoko Kando / Suzu Chiba	4:09.92
8	NED	Ellen Elzerman / Kira Bulten / Inge De Bruijn / Marianne Muis	4:10.87

SYNCHRONIZED SWIMMING

SOLO / August 6

RANK	CTRY	ATHLETE	POINTS
1	**USA**	**Kristen Babb-Sprague**	**191.848**
2	CAN	Sylvie Frechette	191.717
3	JPN	Fumiko Okuno	187.056
4	EUN	Olga Sedakova	185.106
5	FRA	Anne Capron	182.449
6	GRE	Christina Thalassinidov	180.244
7	GBR	Kerry Shacklock	179.839
8	NED	Marjolijn Both	179.354

DUET / August 7

RANK	CTRY	ATHLETES	POINTS
1	**USA**	**Karen Josephson / Sarah Josephson**	**192.175**
2	CAN	Penny Vilagos / Vicky Vilagos	189.394
3	JPN	Fumiko Okuno / Aki Takayama	186.868
4	EUN	Anna Koslova / Olga Sedakova	184.083
5	FRA	Marianne Aeschbacher / Anne Capron	181.795
6	GBR	Kerry Shacklock / Leila Vakil	179.366
7	NED	Marjolijn Both / Tamara Zwart	179.345
8	CHN	Guan Zewen / Wang Xiaojie	177.843

TABLE TENNIS

MEN'S SINGLES / August 6

RANK	CTRY	ATHLETE	RECORD
1	SWD	Jan Ove Waldner	
2	FRA	Jean Philippe Gatien	
3	CHN	Ma Wenge	
3	KOR	Kim Taek Soo	
—	**USA**	**Jim Butler**	**elim. (2-1)**
—	**USA**	**Sean O'Neill**	**elim. (1-1)**

MEN'S DOUBLES / August 4 **RECORD**

RANK	CTRY	ATHLETES
1	CHN	Lu Lin / Wang Tao
2	GER	Steffen Fetzner / Jorg Rosskopf
3	KOR	Kang Hee Chan / Lee Chul Seung
3	KOR	Kim Taek Soo / Yoo Nam Kyu
—	**USA**	**Jim Butler / Sean O'Neill**

WOMEN'S SINGLES / August 5

RANK	CTRY	ATHLETE	RECORD
1	CHN	Deng Yaping	
2	CHN	Qiao Hong	
3	KOR	Hyun Jung Hwa	
3	PRK	Bun Hui Li	
—	**USA**	**Insook Bhushan**	**elim. (2-1)**
—	**USA**	**Diana Gee**	**elim. (1-2)**
—	**USA**	**Lily Hugh**	**elim. (1-2)**

WOMEN'S DOUBLES / August 3

RANK	CTRY	ATHLETES	MATCH SCORE
1	CHN	Deng Yaping / Qiao Hong	
2	CHN	Chen Zihe / Gao Jun	
3	PRK	Li Bun Hui / Yu Sun Bok	
3	KOR	Hong Cha Ok / Hyun Jung Hwa	
—	**USA**	**Diana Gee / Lily Hugh**	**elim.**

TEAM HANDBALL

MEN / July 27 - August 8

RANK	CTRY	SCORE		
1	EUN	EUN vs. SWE	22-20	(Final)
2	SWE	FRA vs. ISL	24-20	(3rd-4th)
3	FRA	SWE vs. FRA	25-23	(semi)
4	ISL	EUN vs. ISL	23-19	(semi)
5	ESP			
6	KOR			
7	HUN			
8	ROM			
—	**USA**	DNQ		

WOMEN / July 30 - August 8

RANK	CTRY	SCORE	USA GAME SCORES
1	KOR	28-21 (Final)	USA vs. EUN 16-23
2	NOR		USA vs. GER 16-32
3	EUN	24-20 (3rd-4th)	USA vs. NIG 23-21
4	GER		USA vs. AUS 17-26
5	AUS		
6	**USA**	NOR vs. EUN 24-23 (semi)	
7	ESP	KOR vs. GER 26-25 (semi)	
8	NIG		

USA TEAM: Sharon Cain / Kim Clarke / Laura Coenen / Laurie Fellner / Tami Jameson / Leora Jones / Portia Lack / Dannette Leininger / Lori Ogren / Pat Neder / Karyn Palgut / Carol Peterka / Angie Raynor / Barb Schaaf / Cindy Stringer / Chryss Watts

TENNIS

MEN'S SINGLES / August 8

RANK	CTRY	ATHLETE	
1	SUI	Marc Rosset	
2	ESP	Jordi Arrese	
3	CRO	Goran Ivanisevic	
3	EUN	Andrei Cherkasov	
—	**USA**	**Pete Sampras**	**elim. 3rd rd.**
—	**USA**	**Jim Courier**	**elim. 3rd rd.**
—	**USA**	**Michael Chang**	**elim. 2nd rd.**

MEN'S DOUBLES / August 7

RANK	CTRY	ATHLETES	
1	GER	Boris Becker / Michael Stich	
2	RSA	Wayne Ferreira / Piet Norval	
3	CRO	Goran Ivanisevic / Goran Prpic	
3	ARG	Javier Frana / Christian Miniussi	
—	**USA**	**Jim Courier / Pete Sampras**	**elim.**

WOMEN'S SINGLES / August 7

RANK	CTRY	ATHLETES	
1	**USA**	**Jennifer Capriati**	
2	GER	Steffi Graf	
3	**USA**	**Mary Joe Fernandez**	
3	ESP	Arantxa Sanchez-Vicario	
—	**USA**	**Zina Garrison**	**elim. 1st rd.**

WOMEN'S DOUBLES / August 8

RANK	CTRY	ATHLETES
1	**USA**	**Gigi Fernandez / Mary Joe Fernandez**
2	ESP	Conchita Martinez / Arantxa Sanchez-Vicario
3	AUS	Rachel McQuillan / Nicole Provis
3	EUN	Leila Meshki / Natalia Zvereva

VOLLEYBALL

MEN / July 26 - August 9

RANK	CTRY	RECORD	USA MATCH SCORES		
1	BRA	8-0	USA vs. JPN	3-2*	15-8, 11-15, 10-15, 17-16, 16-14
2	NED	4-4	USA vs. CAN	3-2	15-12, 15-12, 10-15, 11-15, 16-14
3	**USA**	6-2	USA vs. ESP	3-2	15-6, 14-16, 12-15, 15-10, 15-11
4	CUB	5-3	USA vs. FRA	3-0	15-5, 15-2, 15-8
5	ITA	6-2	USA vs. ITA	3-1	9-15, 16-14, 15-11, 15-13
6	JPN	3-5	USA vs. EUN	3-1	12-15, 15-10, 15-4, 15-11
7	EUN	4-4	USA vs. BRA	1-3	15-12, 8-15, 9-15, 12-15
8	ESP	3-5	USA vs. CUB	3-1	12-15, 15-13, 15-7, 15-11

USA TEAM: Nick Becker / Carlos Briceno / Bob Ctvrtlik / Scott Fortune / Dan Greenbaum / Brent Hilliard / Bryan Ivie / Doug Partie / Bob Samuelson / Eric Sato / Jeff Stork / Steve Timmons
*Result overturned on appeal giving Japan a 3-1 victory.

WOMEN / July 29 - August 7

RANK	CTRY	RECORD	USA MATCH SCORES		
1	CUB	5-0	USA vs. JPN	2-3	15-13, 11-15, 12-15, 15-8, 13-15
2	EUN	3-2	USA vs. EUN	3-2	9-15, 17-15, 15-12, 4-15, 15-11
3	**USA**	4-2	USA vs. ESP	3-0	15-4, 15-5, 15-10
4	BRA	3-3	USA vs. NED	3-1	15-11, 11-15, 15-8, 15-7
5	JPN	3-2	USA vs. CUB	2-3	15-8, 9-15, 15-6, 5-15, 11-15
6	NED	1-4	USA vs. BRA	3-0	15-8, 15-6, 15-13
7	CHN	1-3			
8	ESP	0-4			

USA TEAM: Janet Cobbs / Tara Cross-Battle / Lori Endicott / Caren Kemner / Ruth Lawanson / Tammy Liley / Elaina Oden / Kim Oden / Teee Sanders / Liane Sato / Paula Weishoff / Yoko Zetterlund

WATER POLO August 1-9

RANK	CTRY	RECORD	USA GAME SCORES	
1	ITA	5-0	USA vs. AUS	8-4
2	ESP	5-1	USA vs. TCH	9-3
3	EUN	6-1	USA vs. FRA	11-7
4	**USA**	4-3	USA vs. EUN	5-8
5	AUS	4-2	USA vs. GER	7-2
6	HUN	4-2	USA vs. ESP	4-6
7	GER	2-3-3		
8	CUB	2-6		

USA TEAM: Jeff Campbell / Chris Duplanty / Mike Evans / Kirk Everist / Erich Fischer / Charles Harris / Chris Humbert / Doug Kimbell / Craig Klass / Alex Rousseau / Terry Schroeder / John Vargas / Craig Wilson

WEIGHTLIFTING

52 KG (114 LBS) / July 26

RANK	CTRY	ATHLETE	SNATCH	CLEAN&JERK	TOTAL KG
1	BUL	Ivan Ivanov	115.0	150.0	265.0
2	CHN	Lin Qisheng	115.0	147.5	262.5
3	ROM	Traian Ciharean	112.5	140.0	252.5
4	KOR	Ko Kwang-Ku	112.5	140.0	252.5
5	TUR	Halil Mutlu	112.5	135.0	247.5
6	PRK	Gil Nam Su	100.0	135.0	235.0
7	VEN	Humberto A. Fuentes Rodriguez	100.0	130.0	230.0
8	ESP	Jose Andres Ibanez Puig	100.0	127.5	227.5

56 KG (123 LBS) / July 27

RANK	CTRY	ATHLETE	SNATCH	CLEAN&JERK	TOTAL KG
1	KOR	Chun Byung-Kwan	132.5 NOR	155.0	287.5
2	CHN	Liu Shoubin	130.0	147.5	277.5
3	CHN	Luo Jianming	125.0	152.5	277.5
4	FRA	Laurent Fombertasse	112.5	147.5	260.0
5	JPN	Katsuhiko Sakuma	120.0	135.0	255.0
6	HUN	Tibor Karczag	115.0	140.0	255.0
7	PRK	Yong Chol Kim	110.0	145.0	255.0
8	POL	Marek Gorzelniak	115.0	140.0	255.0

60 KG (132 LBS) / July 28

RANK	CTRY	ATHLETE	SNATCH	CLEAN&JERK	TOTAL KG
1	TUR	Naim Suleymanoglu	142.5	177.5	320.0
2	BUL	Nikolai Peshalov	137.5	167.5	305.0
3	CHN	Yingqiang He	130.0	165.0	295.0
4	BUL	Neno Stoyanov Terziiski	130.0	165.0	295.0
5	GRE	Valerios Leonidis	132.5	162.5	295.0
6	PRK	Hyon Il Ro	127.5	160.0	287.5
7	HUN	Attila Czanka	127.5	157.5	285.0
8	PRK	Jae Son Li	130.0	150.0	280.0
18	**USA**	**Bryan Jacob**	**117.5**	**145.0**	**262.5**

67.5 KG (148.5 LBS) / July 29

RANK	CTRY	ATHLETE	SNATCH	CLEAN&JERK	TOTAL KG
1	EUN	Israel Militossian	155.0	182.5	337.5
2	BUL	Yoto Yotov	150.0	177.5	327.5
3	GER	Andreas Behm	145.0	175.0	320.0
4	ALG	Abdelmanaane Yahiaoui	140.0	175.0	315.0
5	FIN	Jouni Gronman	135.0	170.0	305.0
6	COL	Eyne Acevedo Tabares	130.0	170.0	300.0
7	PRK	Sang Ho Im	135.0	165.0	300.0
8	**USA**	**Tim McRae**	**135.0**	**162.5**	**297.5**
10	**USA**	**Vernon Patao**	**132.5**	**157.5**	**290.0**

75 KG (165 LBS) / July 30

RANK	CTRY	ATHLETE	SNATCH	CLEAN&JERK	TOTAL KG
1	EUN	Fedor Kassapu	155.0	202.5	357.5
2	CUB	Pablo Lara	155.0	202.5	357.5
3	PRK	Myong Nam Kim	162.5	190.0	352.5
4	POL	Andrzej Kozlowski	160.0	192.5	352.5
5	GER	Ingo Steinhofel	155.0	192.5	347.5
6	CUB	Raul Mora Licea	150.0	195.0	345.0
7	POL	Wlodzimierz Chlebosz	155.0	185.0	340.0
8	CHN	Gang Lu	150.0	185.0	335.0

82.5 KG (181.5 LBS) / July 31

RANK	CTRY	ATHLETE	SNATCH	CLEAN&JERK	TOTAL KG
1	GRE	Pyrros Dimas	167.5	202.5	370.0
2	POL	Krzysztof Siemion	165.0	205.0	370.0
3	EUN	Ibragim Samadov	167.5	202.5	370.0
4	PRK	Chol Ho Chon	165.0	200.0	365.0
5	BUL	Plamen Ignatov Bratoitchev	167.5	197.5	365.0
6	CUB	Lino Emerido Elias Ocana	160.0	205.0	365.0
7	GER	Marc Huster	160.0	202.5	362.5
8	CUB	Jose Ernesto Heredia Ledea	165.0	197.5	362.5
17	**USA**	**Roberto "Tony" Urrutia**	**150.0**	**190.0**	**340.0**

90 KG (198 LBS) / August 1

RANK	CTRY	ATHLETE	SNATCH	CLEAN&JERK	TOTAL KG
1	EUN	Kakhi Kakhiachvili	177.5	235.0 EWR	412.5 EOR
2	EUN	Serguei Syrtsov	190.0 OR	222.5	412.5 EOR
3	POL	Sergiusz Wolczaniecki	172.5	220.0	392.5
4	KOR	Kim Byung-Chan	170.0	210.0	380.0
5	BUL	Ivan Khristov Tchakarov	170.0	207.5	377.5
6	CUB	Emilio Lara Rodriguez	165.0	210.0	375.0
7	GBR	Peter May	160.0	195.0	355.0
8	AUS	Harvey John Goodman	157.5	192.5	350.0
13	**USA**	**Bret Brian**	**150.0**	**187.5**	**337.5**

100 KG (200 LBS) / August 2

RANK	CTRY	ATHLETE	SNATCH	CLEAN&JERK	TOTAL KG
1	EUN	Victor Tregoubov	190.0 EOR	220.0	410.0
2	EUN	Timour Taimazov	185.0	217.5	402.5
3	POL	Waldemar Malak	185.0	215.0	400.0
4	FRA	Francis Tournefier	170.0	217.5	387.5
5	BUL	Petar Ivanov Stefanov	170.0	210.0	380.0
6	ISR	Andrey Danisov	175.0	202.5	377.5
7	GER	Udo Guse	167.5	210.0	377.5
8	JPN	Yoshimitsu Nishimoto	165.0	207.5	372.5
15	**USA**	**Wesley Barnett**	**157.5**	**195.0**	**352.5**
—	**USA**	**David Langon**	**elim.**		

110 KG (243 LBS) / August 3

RANK	CTRY	ATHLETE	SNATCH	CLEAN&JERK	TOTAL KG
1	GER	Ronny Weller	192.5	240.0	432.5
2	EUN	Artour Akoev	195.0	235.0	430.0
3	BUL	Stefan Botev	190.0	227.5	417.5
4	ROM	Nicu Vlad	190.0	215.0	405.0
5	POL	Dariusz Osuch	175.0	222.5	397.5
6	GER	Frank Seipelt	170.0	220.0	390.0
7	CUB	Flavio Villavicencia Cabrera	170.0	217.5	387.5
8	GRE	Pavlos Saltsidis	175.0	210.0	385.0
18	USA	Rich Schutz	155.0	192.5	347.5

+110 KG (+ 243 LBS) / August 4

RANK	CTRY	ATHLETE	SNATCH	CLEAN&JERK	TOTAL KG
1	EUN	Alexandre Kourlovitch	205.0	245.0	450.0
2	EUN	Leonid Taranenko	187.5	237.5	425.0
3	GER	Manfred Nerlinger	180.0	232.5	412.5
4	CUB	Ernesto Aguero Shell	182.5	230.0	412.5
5	BUL	Mitko Raikov Mitev	180.0	220.0	400.0
6	TCH	Jiri Zubricky	170.0	222.5	392.5
7	TUR	Erdinc Arslan	170.0	220.0	390.0
8	USA	Mario Martinez	170.0	215.0	385.0
10	USA	Mark Henry	165.0	212.5	377.5

WRESTLING

48 KG (106 LBS) FREESTYLE / August 6

RANK	CTRY	ATHLETE
1	PRK	Il Park
2	KOR	Kim Jong
3	EUN	Vougar Oroudjov
4	ROM	Romica Rasovan
5	USA	Tim Vanni
6	GER	Reiner Heugabel
7	CUB	Aldo Martinez
8	MGL	T. Khosbayar

52 KG (114 LBS) FREESTYLE / August 5

RANK	CTRY	ATHLETE
1	PRK	Li Hak
2	USA	Zeke Jones
3	BUL	V. Jordanov
4	KOR	Kim Sun
5	TUR	Ahmet Orel
6	JPN	Mitsuru Sato
7	IRI	Majid Torkan
8	CAN	C. Woodcroft

57 KG (125 LBS) FREESTYLE / August 7

RANK	CTRY	ATHLETE
1	CUB	Alejandro Puerto
2	EUN	Serquei Smal
3	PRK	Kim Yong Sik
4	TUR	Remzi Musaoglu
5	BUL	Roumen Pavlov
6	USA	Kendall Cross
7	GER	Jurgen Scheibe
8	CAN	Robert Dawson

62 KG (136 LBS) FREESTYLE / August 7

RANK	CTRY	ATHLETE
1	USA	John Smith
2	IRI	Agari Mohammadian
3	CUB	Lazaro Reinoso
4	BUL	Rossen Vassilev
5	EUN	Gazikhan Azizov
6	AUS	Musa Ilhan
7	SUI	Martin Mueller
8	KOR	Sang Shin

68 KG (150 LBS) FREESTYLE / August 5

RANK	CTRY	ATHLETE
1	EUN	Arsen Fadzaev
2	BUL	Valentin Getzov
3	JPN	Kosei Akaishi
4	IRI	Ali Akbarnejad
5	TUR	Fatih Ozbas
6	KOR	Young Ko
7	USA	Townsend Saunders
8	CAN	Chris Wilson

74 KG (163 LBS) FREESTYLE / August 6

RANK	CTRY	ATHLETE
1	KOR	Park Jang
2	USA	Kenny Monday
3	IRI	Amir Khadem
4	EUN	M. Gadjiev
5	POL	K. Walencik
6	CAN	Gary Holmes
7	HUN	Janos Nagy
8	MGL	L. Enkhbayar

82 KG (180 LBS) FREESTYLE / August 7

RANK	CTRY	ATHLETE
1	USA	Kevin Jackson
2	EUN	Elmadi Jabraijlov
3	IRI	Rasul Khadem
4	GER	Hans Gstoettner
5	TCH	Jozef Lohyna
6	TUR	S. Oeztuerk
7	ROM	Nicolae Ghita
8	ESP	F. Iglesias

90 KG (198 LBS) FREESTYLE / August 7

RANK	CTRY	ATHLETE
1	EUN	Makharbek Khadartsev
2	TUR	Kenan Kimsek
3	USA	Chris Campbell
4	MGL	Puntsag Sukhbat
5	IRI	Ayub Bani
6	CUB	Roberto Limonta
7	POL	M. Garmulewicz
8	ITA	Renato Lombardo

100 KG (220 LBS) FREESTYLE / August 5

RANK	CTRY	ATHLETE
1	EUN	Leri Khabelov
2	GER	Heiko Balz
3	TUR	Ali Kayali
4	KOR	Tae Kim
5	POL	A. Radomski
6	IND	Subhash Verma
7	USA	Mark Coleman
8	HUN	Sandor Kiss

130 KG (286 LBS) FREESTYLE / August 6

RANK	CTRY	ATHLETE
1	USA	Bruce Baumgartner
2	CAN	Jeffrey Thue
3	EUN	David Gobedjichvili
4	TUR	Mahmut Demir
5	GER	A. Schroder
6	IRI	Ali Karbalai
7	CHN	Chunguang Wang
8	KOR	Sung Park

48 KG (106 LBS) GRECO-ROMAN / July 29

RANK	CTRY	ATHLETE
1	EUN	Oleg Koutcherenko
2	ITA	Vincenzo Maenza
3	CUB	Wilber Sanchez
4	GER	Fuat Yildiz
5	ROM	I. Dascalescu
6	IRI	Reza Simkhah
7	NOR	Lars Ronningen
8	IND	Pappu Yadav
—	USA	Mark Fuller

52 KG (114 LBS) GRECO-ROMAN / July 28

RANK	CTRY	ATHLETE
1	NOR	Jon Ronningen
2	EUN	Alfred Ter-Mkrttchian
3	KOR	Min Kyung-Kap
4	USA	Shawn Sheldon
5	BUL	Bratan Tzenov
6	ROM	V. Rebegea
7	FIN	Ismo Kamesaki
8	IOP	S. Rizvanovic

57 KG (125 LBS) GRECO-ROMAN / July 30

RANK	CTRY	ATHLETE
1	KOR	An Han-Bong
2	GER	Rifat Yildiz
3	CHN	Zetian Sheng
4	EUN	A. Ignatenko
5	CUB	William Lara
6	ROM	Marian Sandu
7	FIN	Keijo Pehkonen
8	USA	Dennis Hall

62 KG (136 LBS) GRECO-ROMAN / July 30

RANK	CTRY	ATHLETE
1	TUR	Akif Pirim
2	EUN	Serguei Martynov
3	CUB	Juan Luis Maren
4	POL	W. Zawadzki
5	HUN	Jeno Bodi
6	USA	Buddy Lee
7	BUL	S. Grigorov
8	SUI	Hugo Dietsche

68 KG (150 LBS) GRECO-ROMAN / July 28

RANK	CTRY	ATHLETE
1	HUN	Attila Repka
2	EUN	Islam Dougoutchiev
3	USA	Rodney Smith
4	CUB	C. Rodriguez
5	FRA	Ghani Yalouz
6	IRI	A. Chamangoli
7	POL	Ryszard Wolny
8	CAN	Douglas Yeats

74 KG (163 LBS) GRECO-ROMAN / July 29

RANK	CTRY	ATHLETE
1	EUN	Mnatsakan Iskandarian
2	POL	Jozef Tracz
3	SWE	Torgjoern Kornbakk
4	CUB	Nestor Almanza
5	FRA	Yvon Riemer
6	AUT	Anton Marchl
7	TCH	Jaroslav Zeman
8	CAN	Karlo Kasap
—	USA	Travis West

82 KG (180 LBS) GRECO-ROMAN / July 30

RANK	CTRY	ATHLETE
1	HUN	Peter Farkas
2	POL	Piotr Stepien
3	EUN	Daoulet Tourlykhanov
4	SWE	M. Fredriksson
5	FIN	Timo Niemi
6	IOP	Goran Kasum
7	GER	Thomas Zander
8	TCH	Pavel Frinta
10	USA	Dan Henderson

90 KG (198 LBS) GRECO-ROMAN / July 30

RANK	CTRY	ATHLETE
1	GER	Maik Bullmann
2	TUR	Hakki Basar
3	EUN	Gogui Kogouachvili
4	SWE	M. Ljungberg
5	IRI	Hassan Babak
6	USA	Michial Foy
7	CUB	Reynaldo Pena
8	ITA	S. Campanella

100 KG (220 LBS) GRECO-ROMAN / July 28

RANK	CTRY	ATHLETE
1	CUB	Hector Milian
2	USA	Dennis Koslowski
3	EUN	Serguei Demiachkievitch
4	POL	Andrzej Wronski
5	GER	A. Steinbach
6	ROM	Ion Ieremciuc
7	HUN	Norbert Nottny
8	KOR	Sung Song

130 KG (286 LBS) GRECO-ROMAN / July 29

RANK	CTRY	ATHLETE
1	EUN	Alexandre Kareline
2	SWE	Tomas Johansson
3	ROM	Ioan Grigoras
4	HUN	Laszlo Klauz
5	CAN	Andrew Borodow
6	CHN	Lei Tian
7	FIN	Juha Ahokas
8	GRE	P. Pikilidis
—	USA	Matt Ghaffari

YACHTING

MEN'S 470 / August 3

RANK	CTRY	ATHLETES	NEt PTS.
1	ESP	Jordi Calafat / Francisco Sanchez	50.00
2	USA	Morgan Reeser / Kevin Burnham	66.70
3	EST	Tonu Toniste / Toomas Toniste	68.70
4	FIN	Petri Leskinen / Mika Aarnikka	69.70
5	NOR	H. Johannessen / Pal McCarthy	71.70
6	GBR	Paul Brotherton / Andrew Hemmings	76.40
7	NZL	C. Greenwood / Jon Bilger	80.40
8	GER	Wolfgang Hunger / Rolf Schmidt	82.40

MEN'S LECHNER / August 2

RANK	CTRY	ATHLETE	NET PTS.
1	FRA	Franck David	70.70
2	USA	Michael Gebhardt	71.10
3	AUS	Lars Kleppich	98.70
4	NZL	Anthony Bruce Kendall	105.70
5	AUT	Christoph Sieber	110.10
6	ESP	Asier Fernandez	117.00
7	NED	Stephan Van Den Berg	117.70
8	ISR	Amit Inbar	118.10

FINN / August 3

RANK	CTRY	ATHLETE	NET PTS.
1	ESP	Jose Van Der Ploeg	33.40
2	USA	Brian Ledbetter	54.70
3	NZL	Craig Monk	64.70
4	GBR	S. Childerley	68.10
5	SWE	Fredrik Loof	68.70
6	SUI	Othmar Mueller	70.00
7	FRA	Xavier Rohart	75.00
8	AUT	Hans Spitzauer	79.40

FLYING DUTCHMAN / August 2

RANK	CTRY	ATHLETES	NET PTS.
1	ESP	Luis Doreste / Domingo Manrique	29.70
2	USA	Paul Foerster / Stephen Bourdow	32.70
3	DEN	Jorgen Bojsen / Jens Bojsen	37.70
4	NZL	Murray Selwyn Jones / Gregory John Knowles	68.00
5	GER	Albert Batzill / Peter Lang	70.40
6	SWE	Mats Nyberg / Johan Lindell	78.40
7	NOR	Ole Pollen / Knut Frostad	80.70
8	SUI	Jan Eckert / Piet Eckert	81.70

TORNADO / August 2

RANK	CTRY	ATHLETES	NET PTS.
1	FRA	Yves Loday / Nichlas Henard	40.40
2	USA	Randy Smyth / Keith Notary	42.00
3	AUS	Mitch Booth / John Forbes	44.40
4	NZL	Rex Sellers / B. Jones	51.70
5	CAN	David Sweeney / Kevin Smith	62.70
6	NED	Van Teylingen / Paul Manuel	65.00
7	AUT	Andreas Hagara / Roman Hagara	65.40
8	BRA	Lars Schmidt / Clinio Freitas	69.70

STAR / August 1

RANK	CTRY	ATHLETES	NET PTS.
1	USA	Mark Reynolds / Hal Haenel	31.40
2	NZL	Roderick Davis / Donald John Cowie	58.40
3	CAN	D. MacDonald / Eric Jespersen	62.70
4	NED	Mark Neeleman / Johannes Leo Schrier	64.00
5	SWE	Hans Wallen / Bobby Lohse	65.00
6	GER	Hans Vogt / Joerg Fricke	69.70
7	AUS	Colin Beashel / David Giles	71.40
8	GRE	Iakovos Kisseoglou / Dimitris Boukis	84.00

SOLING / August 4

RANK	CTRY	ATHLETES	NET PTS.
1	DEN	Jesper Bank / Steen Secher / Jesper Seier	
2	USA *	Kevin Mahaney / Jim Brady / Doug Kern	
3	GBR	Lawrie Smith / Robert Cruikshank / Ossie Stewart	
4	GER	Jochen Schumann / Thomas Flach / Bernd Jakel	
5	SWE	Magnus Holmberg / Bjoern Alm / Johan Barne	
6	ESP	Fernando Leon / F. De Borbon / Alfredo Vazquez	
7	CAN	Robert Thomson / Robert Flinn / Philip Gow	56.10
8	NZL	Russell Coutts / S. Daubney / G. Fleury	64.70

WOMEN'S 470 / August 3

RANK	CTRY	ATHLETES	NET PTS.
1	ESP	Theresa Zabell / Patricia Guerra	29.70
2	NZL	Leslie Jean Egnot / Janet Shearer	36.70
3	USA	Jennifer Isler / Pamela Healy	40.70
4	EUN	Larissa Moscalenko / Elena Pakholtchik	43.00
5	JPN	Yumiko Shige / Alicia Kinoshita	53.70
6	FRA	Florence Le Brun / Odile Barre	65.70
7	ITA	Maria Quarra / Anna Barabino	68.70
8	GER	Peggy Hardwiger / Christina Pinnow	71.70

WOMEN'S LECHNER / August 2

RANK	CTRY	ATHLETES	NET PTS.
1	NZL	Barbara Anne Kendall	47.80
2	CHN	Xiaodong Zhang	65.80
3	NED	Dorien De Vries	68.70
4	FRA	Maud Herbert	78.00
5	USA	Lanee Butler	95.70
6	GBR	Penny Way	99.40
7	ITA	Alessandra Sensini	101.40
8	NOR	Jorunn Horgen	102.70

WOMEN'S EUROPE / August 3

RANK	CTRY	ATHLETES	NET PTS.
1	NOR	Linda Andersen	48.70
2	ESP	Natalia Via Dufresne	57.40
3	USA	Julia Trotman	62.70
4	NZL	Jennifer Armstrong	65.00
5	DEN	Dorte Jensen	65.70
6	EST	Krista Kruuv	67.10
7	NED	Martine Van Leeuwen	67.70
8	ITA	Arianna Bogatec	69.00

DEMONSTRATION SPORTS

TAEKWONDO

MEN'S FINWEIGHT — 50 KG / August 5

RANK	CTRY	ATHLETE
1	DEN	Gergely Salim
2	USA	Juan Moreno
3	INA	Jefi Tri Aji
3	ESP	Javier Argudo Sesmilo

MEN'S FLYWEIGHT — 54 KG / August 4

RANK	CTRY	ATHLETE
1	VEN	Arlindo Gouveia Colina
2	INA	Dirc Richard Talumewo
3	TPE	Ming-Sung Wang
3	KOR	Sung Kyo Seo
—	USA	no entry

MEN'S BANTAMWEIGHT — 58 KG (128 LBS) / August 3

RANK	CTRY	ATHLETE	
1	MEX	William Cordova Santamaria	
2	CAN	Sayed Youssef Najem	
3	PHI	Stephen Fernandez	
3	ITA	Domenico D'Alise	
—	USA	Han Won Lee	elim. 1st rd.

MEN'S FEATHERWEIGHT — 64 KG / August 5

RANK	CTRY	ATHLETE
1	KOR	Byong Cheol Kim
2	TUR	Ekrem Boyali
3	CAN	Woo Yong Jung
3	ITA	Luca Massaccesi
—	USA	no entry

MEN'S LIGHTWEIGHT — (70.1 KG / 154 LBS) / August 4

RANK	CTRY	ATHLETE	
1	ESP	Jose Santolaria Martos	
2	IRI	Fariborz Askari	
3	TPE	Kuei-Ming Chou	
3	FRA	Djamel Khali	
—	USA	James Villasana	elim. 1st rd.

MEN'S WELTERWEIGHT — (76 KG / 168 LBS) / August 3

RANK	CTRY	ATHLETE
1	KOR	Tae Kyoung Ha
2	CAN	Jae Hun Lee
3	IRI	Reza Mehmandoost Somesarayi
3	KUW	Mohammad Jassem Al Qaimi
—	USA	no entry

MEN'S MIDDLEWEIGHT — (83 KG / 183 LBS) / August 4

RANK	CTRY	ATHLETE
1	USA	Herbert Perez
2	ESP	Juan Solis Godoy
3	EGY	Khaled Ibrahim
3	JOR	Ammar Sbeihi

MEN'S HEAVYWEIGHT — (+83 KG / +183 LBS) / August 3

RANK	CTRY	ATHLETE
1	KOR	Je Kyoung Kim
2	NIG	Emmanuel Oghenejobo
3	EGY	Amr Hassan
3	AUS	Simon Hosking
—	USA	no entry

WOMEN'S FINWEIGHT — (43 KG / 95 LBS) / August 5

RANK	CTRY	ATHLETE
1	TPE	Yueh-Ying Lo
2	INA	Rahmi Kurnia
3	GBR	Amanda Broadbent
3	MEX	Monica Torres
—	USA	no entry

WOMEN'S FLYWEIGHT — (47 KG / 103 LBS) / August 4

RANK	CTRY	ATHLETE
1	ESP	Elisabet Delgado Cazorla
2	ITA	Piera Muggiri
3	USA	Terry Poindexter
3	TUR	Arzu Tan

WOMEN'S BANTAMWEIGHT — (51 KG / 112 LBS) / August 3

RANK	CTRY	ATHLETE
1	KOR	Eun Suk Hwang
2	USA	Diane Murray
3	MAS	King Hung Hi
3	FRA	Catherine Noble

WOMEN'S FEATHERWEIGHT — (55 KG / 121 LBS) / August 5

RANK	CTRY	ATHLETE
1	TPE	Ya-Ling Tung
2	TUR	Aysegul Ergin
3	PHI	Beatriz Lucero
3	MEX	Dolores Knolle Weaver
—	USA	no entry

WOMEN'S LIGHTWEIGHT — (60 KG / 132 LBS) / August 4

RANK	CTRY	ATHLETE
1	TPE	Yi-An Chen
2	INA	Susiliawati
3	KOR	Eun Ok Jeung
3	MAR	Hafida El Ouacef
—	USA	no entry

WOMEN'S WELTERWEIGHT — (65 KG / 143 LBS) / August 3

RANK	CTRY	ATHLETE
1	ESP	Elena Benitez Morales
2	FRA	Brigitte Geffroy
3	CAN	Shelley Vettese-Baert
3	USA	Danielle Laney

WOMEN'S MIDDLEWEIGHT — (70 KG / 154 LBS) / August 4

RANK	CTRY	ATHLETE
1	KOR	Sun Hee Lee
2	CAN	Marcia King
3	GRE	Morfou Drosidou
3	AUS	Denise Parmley
—	USA	no entry

WOMEN'S HEAVYWEIGHT (+70 KG / +154 LBS) / August 3

RANK	CTRY	ATHLETE
1	ESP	Coral Astrid Bistuer Ruiz
2	NZL	Susan Graham
3	USA	Lynette Love
3	VEN	Adriana Carmona

ROLLER HOCKEY July 26 - August 7

RANK	CTRY	RECORD	MATCH SCORE	
1	ARG	7-2-2	USA vs. JPN	10-1
2	ESP	9-1-1	USA vs. ARG	4-4
3	ITA	7-3-1	USA vs. ITA	2-13
4	POR	7-4	USA vs. SUI	5-2
5	BRA	5-4-1	USA vs. POR	3-7
6	NED	2-7-1		
—	USA	2-2-1	elim.	

USA TEAM: Dickie Chado / Brady Donoghue / Jeffrey Gibson / Plim Howard / Karl Huckaby / Keith Huckaby / David Jones / Johnny Raglin / Mike Stevenson / Jimmy Trussell

PELOTA July 25 - August 5

MEN'S PALETTE LEATHER

RANK	CTRY
1	ARG
2	ESP
3	FRA

MEN'S FRONTENIS

RANK	CTRY
1	MEX
2	ESP
3	ARG

MEN'S COSTA PUNTA

RANK	CTRY
1	ESP
2	FRA
3	MEX

MEN'S HAND DOUBLES (TRINQUETTE)

RANK	CTRY
1	MEX
2	ESP
3	FRA

MEN'S PALETTE RUBBER

RANK	CTRY
1	ARG
2	FRA
3	ESP

MEN'S PALETTE

RANK	CTRY
1	ESP
2	MEX
3	ART

MEN'S SHORT PALETTE

RANK	CTRY
1	ESP
2	MEX
3	CUB

MEN'S HAND SINGLES

RANK	CTRY
1	ESP
2	FRA
3	CUB

MEN'S HAND DOUBLES

RANK	CTRY
1	ESP
2	FRA
3	MEX

WOMEN'S FRONTENIS

RANK	CTRY
1	MEX
2	ESP
3	CUB